Being a True VIP

Also by the Author

Encyclopedia of Management Theory (2013)

Management Theory in Action: Real-World Lessons for Walking the Talk (2010)

Cultural Mythology and Global Leadership (2009)

Handbook of Organizational and Managerial Wisdom (2007)

Being a True VIP

Managing Importance in Yourself and Others

Eric H. Kessler

palgrave
macmillan

First published 2016 by
PALGRAVE MACMILLAN

The author has asserted his right to be identified as the author of this work in accordance with the Copyright, Designs and Patents Act 1988.

Palgrave Macmillan in the UK is an imprint of Macmillan Publishers Limited, registered in England, company number 785998, of Houndmills, Basingstoke, Hampshire, RG21 6XS.

Palgrave Macmillan in the US is a division of Nature America, Inc., One New York Plaza, Suite 4500, New York, NY 10004-1562.

Palgrave Macmillan is the global academic imprint of the above companies and has companies and representatives throughout the world.

Hardback ISBN: 978-1-137-44804-0
E-PUB ISBN: 978-1-137-44805-7
E-PDF ISBN: 978-1-137-44806-4
DOI: 10.1057/9781137448064

Distribution in the UK, Europe and the rest of the world is by Palgrave Macmillan®, a division of Macmillan Publishers Limited, registered in England, company number 785998, of Houndmills, Basingstoke, Hampshire RG21 6XS.

Library of Congress Cataloging-in-Publication Data

Kessler, Eric H., author.
  Being a true VIP : managing importance in yourself and others / Eric H. Kessler.
    pages cm
  Includes bibliographical references and index.
  ISBN 978-1-137-44804-0 (alk. paper)
  1. Management—Psychological aspects.   2. Self-perception.   3. Respect.
I. Title.
  HD31.2.K47 2016
  650.1—dc23
                                                        2015033522

A catalogue record for the book is available from the British Library.

With appreciation of all that I am inside and all that is inside me, which synergistically shape the infinite as well as intimate cinema of our significance and value.

And to my father, who passed away during the time that I was writing this book, and without whom it would not have been possible.

Contents

List of Figures

List of Tables

Part I

The Importance of Importance

I

Introduction

Importance is important. It is also complex, but can be understood,
and even managed, using the model described in this book.

Chapter 1 presents the book's central thesis. In this chapter we will discuss why Importance is important. We will also address common, albeit
false, assumptions to first clarify what Importance is *not* and then, from
this, develop both a) a working definition of Importance and b) a general
model for understanding and managing Importance. At the conclusion of
the chapter, we will describe the book's primary vehicles for helping you to
UNDERSTAND (via model building), IDENTIFY (via case illustrations),
PERSONALIZE (via reflective exercises), and APPLY (via guided checklists)
the above.

Importance and Being a True VIP

Are you reading this book from a first-class seat?
Is a velvet rope currently separating you from a crowd?
Do you have a special-access pass hanging from your neck?
Are these the only ways that you can be important?
In other words, a very important person, a VIP?

Psst . . . the answer is no! If you are curious as to why, please read on.

OK, let's change the pace a bit. Here is a trick question: Who is more
important—a movie star, firefighter, stay-at-home parent, Internet mogul,
soup kitchen server, teacher, professional sports all-star, soldier, doctor, lawyer, artist, architect, mechanic, or CEO?

Why is this a trick question? Because it directs your attention away from
the real meaning of Importance. In actuality, it is up to each person to decide
for himself or herself if they are important.

So . . . the only way that you can really be important, a true VIP, is if you
choose to be one.

The desire to become a VIP runs wide and deep in our society. If you look around during the course of a normal day, you will see signs of it—overt and implicit—all around you. Importance distinctions are located in such varied places as airplane cabins and nightclub booths, office layouts and amusement park lines, club rosters and organizational charts, ending credits and opening mastheads, as well as within various other sanctioned pecking orders. We may experience VIP-ness (or not) at work, at home, in school, or in the neighborhood. We may have its symbols flashed on our mobile device and television screens. We may have its emblems engraved on our vehicles and stitched into our attire. Certainly wherever there are hierarchy and status distinctions we will be tempted, even encouraged, to consequently regard some people as relatively more important than others.[1]

However, Importance does not always go hand in hand with higher rank, and it is not always equated with more money or more power. To really understand it, and ultimately to manage it, one has to drill down deeper to examine the three words that comprise the acronym "VIP": Very Important Person.

We know what "very" means: a lot . . . versus a minute or negligible amount. We know what "person" means: a human being . . . versus a mineral, vegetable, or another type of animal. But what does the equally common but much more ambiguous and equivocal word "important" really mean?

Please continue to indulge me by taking a few moments to ask yourself, and honestly reflect on and answer, a few more questions:

- Are you important? Why or why not?
- How do you become important? Is there one best way to do this?
- Do you make others feel important? Is there one best way to do this?
- Under what conditions do you feel most important? Least important?
- Is your sense of Importance exclusively positive or negative? Unwaveringly high or low?
- Is it a good thing to feel important? Should you even care about it?
- Do you use your Importance well? Could you use it better?

Over a span of several years, I have posed versions of these questions many, many times to many, many people. I have probably asked these questions of myself just as often. Concurrently, I have scoured a vast array of literatures and research streams, searching for clues as to possible answers.

One thing that became evident during the process is that, despite the vast range of replies given by all the different and diverse sets of sources, *common patterns* in their answers do, in fact, emerge. Seemingly disparate perspectives do, in fact, converge. Surface irreconcilabilities do, in fact, merge. In short, there are answers to be had! It just takes a lot of digging, a ton of reflecting, a fair amount of theorizing, and a whole bunch of integrating. But if we do it right, the journey can pay off in spades. With systematic model building, we can identify the key factors that influence, configure, mediate and moderate, mobilize and mitigate, and arise from Importance.

In addition, it also became clear from this project that it is perfectly *natural* and *normal* for a person to search for, and even aspire to, their own particular VIP-ness. The Importance journey is core to us—both generally as a collective and specifically as individuals. There is nothing inherently bad, shameful, or egotistical in examining one's Importance. In fact, as long as it is done prudently, clarifying and customizing your Importance is very much worth doing from intellectual, emotional, and behavioral perspectives. It can help us to be better, feel better, and even do better. It can also allow us to help others in these capacities.

More than this, what is perhaps the most meaningful pattern to me (yes, I am going to give this away in the first few pages of the book!) is that the way a person answers the above questions is by and large a matter of *choice*. What I am saying here is that we have a significant degree of control over our sense of Importance—our paths, our filters, our conditions, our standards, as well as how we structure it, use it, and leverage it. In a similar vein, we also have the ability to impact others' Importance. These insights are simultaneously a source of great power and, as the characteristic dialogues of Spiderman tell us (or, if you prefer, the existentialist arguments of philosopher Jean-Paul Sartre[2]), correspondingly great responsibility.

Thus a core tenet of this book is that Importance is ultimately *manageable*. If Importance has predictable patterns, and these patterns emerge naturally as a function of our choices, it stands to reason that we can systematically understand, identify, shape, and even enhance our, as well as others' VIP-ness using the model and guidelines presented in the following pages.

Now I am certainly not the first person to ask these questions about Importance and, even more assuredly, I will not be the last. For instance, psychologists have been looking at Importance-related issues, in some form or another, for pretty much as long as there have been psychologists. So have philosophers, who tend to approach the matter from a loftier bird's-eye, versus data-driven and grassroots, perspective. A person's sense of Importance can also be informed using anthropological and sociological, physical and spiritual, chemical and biological, economic and political, legal and ethical, and a host of similarly related lenses. In my home field of management, it underlies many of our theories and through them can be linked to such bottom-line implications as performance and satisfaction levels. Lamentably, though, with regard to the topic in question, these sweeping streams of thought and their corresponding conclusions are all too often neither well explicated nor well connected.

Yet even if one does not partake in any of these literatures, there is still no escaping the criticality of the subject. One has just to be alive to experience feelings of Importance or lack thereof. Throughout each of our days, we continually receive potential feedback on it from those we encounter . . . our parents and teachers, friends and family, colleagues and clients, leaders and reports, passersby and acquaintances, and all of these are accentuated via the host of technological interfaces that we interact with in the daily praxis of life. However, since they each tend to highlight different aspects of and adopt different perspectives toward Importance, they do not always combine easily and can be difficult to meaningfully digest.

So with so many disparate, disconnected streams of information and feedback, what can we really say about Importance in general, or about our personal Importance in particular, and why should we believe any of it?

In this book I will present an integrated model of Importance derived from a large-scale investigative project and meta-theoretical review of the key conditions, the essential nature, and the critical consequences of how we fundamentally conceptualize our self-subjective significant value.

This is not something that you can just jump into without the proper context. Therefore, before we can even attempt to address these questions about Importance, let us first set our stage, define our terms, and delineate our parameters.

Why Importance[3] Is Important

It has been famously said that the deepest urge in human nature is to be important.[4] To believe that you are significant. To feel valued.

The collective aspiration for Importance has reverberated throughout our history and has infused much of humankind's spiritual, scientific, professional, and societal journeys. It underlies the belief, hope, or desire that life is not trivial; it has significance; it has value; it matters!

The individual quest for Importance is also a central factor in people's personal principles, aspirations, and actions. It underlies the belief, hope, or desire that *my* life is unique; it has significance; it has value; I matter!

The idea of Importance is not only foundational; it is also ubiquitous. We use the term "important" all the time and in a wide variety of venues. Think about it: How many times this day/week/month/year have you uttered the word? Have you referred to an object or subject, an issue or idea, an appointment or engagement, a sports game or work of art, a movie or book, a topic or task by its presence or absence of Importance? Have you ranked yourself, or been ranked, or ranked others by some overt or implied measure of Importance?

Yet despite its profound nature and perennial interest, the key relationships that underlie Importance are not well understood. There have been many musings, for sure, but few focused studies or publications on the topic and a disconcerting deficiency of integrative, synergistic reviews that weave together the existing areas of inquiry. In fact, we have very little direct evidence, cogent arguments, clear models, grounded hypotheses, or authoritative theses of what Importance really means, what fundamentally determines Importance, if there are different types of Importance, and if and when Importance is even a good thing.

Thus we will proceed with the following understandings. The topic of Importance is *important* because there is a gap between (a) what we need to know about it and (b) what we actually know about it. That is to say, our requisite understanding and proper management of Importance is simultaneously in high, and growing, demand as well as in relatively short, and shrinking, supply.

High, Growing Demand

The need for Importance is *central*. People want to feel important. As suggested by the preceding discussion, this need is persistent, and it is at our core.

The need for Importance is also *broad* and *impactful*. In a word, Importance has important implications; it has the potential to affect our performance, engagement, and satisfaction levels across nearly every tier and sphere of our lives. Our macro sense of Importance can impact our global production and satisfaction capacities, promote more engaged societies and citizenries, and facilitate a happier humanity. Our meso sense of Importance can impact our organizational production and satisfaction capacities, promote more engaged firms and movements, and facilitate a happier workforce. Our micro sense of Importance can impact our personal production and satisfaction capacities, promote more engaged individuals and families, and facilitate a happier experience.

The need for Importance is also *growing*. In the modern world, Importance matters more than ever—changes in technology, societal mores, and communication networks have increased people's drive to become, feel, be seen as, and dynamically manage their Importance. For example, social media trends (e.g., Facebook friends, Twitter followers, Instagram likes, LinkedIn connections) have dramatically extended the arenas, and subsequently pressures, on our quests for Importance. No longer are there any time-outs or times-offs. We are constantly faced with image- and brand-management demands and all the investments and anxieties that go along with them.[5] In addition, the modern media climate and other interactive real-time technologies have combined to magnify fluctuations in prevailing tastes, preferences, and opinions as well as accelerate their endemic changes. No longer are there safe, stable havens of unchanging winds. We are witnessing seismic shifts in popularities, fashions, styles, and trends like never before.[6] Thus, for many, and not just teenagers or public figures, managing perceived Importance has become a near 24/7 phenomenon.

In sum, the need for knowledge on Importance is in high demand, and this demand is increasing exponentially in terms of its content and pace.

Short, Shrinking Supply

The direct body of knowledge on Importance is *lacking*. Though it relates to many topics and issues, there is remarkably little written specifically about this topic. Go ahead—do a Google search on the term "importance." Wading through the initially impressive 477 million-plus hits that a searcher encounters,[7] they will be faced with a loosely connected and often superficially relevant hodgepodge of vague, conflicting definitions and waves of subjective pontifications proclaiming or even advertising the relative Importance of this or that while casually, almost haphazardly, throwing the term around without ever really defining it. There is functionally next to nothing out there that crystalizes or ties together the different ideas on Importance and works toward a substantiated, common conceptualization. And more than this, there is also a noticeable absence of systematic model building and, as such, a clear way to capture the differentially grounded, particularly codified sets of direct and indirect, moderated and mediated, antecedent and resulting, and deep-seated and discernable relationships.

The indirect body of knowledge on Importance is also, at best, *confusing*. As evidenced by the above, there is an incredibly large collection of research from proximal domains that relates in one way or another to this simple yet penetrating question of Importance. Unfortunately, the proverbial forests are almost impenetrable in their trees' semantic discrepancies, nuanced manipulations, divergences of methodology and approach, and as a result, linguistic, substantial, and connective confusion. And more than this, the muddling is getting worse, not better. Proponents appear increasingly calcified in their approaches and myopic in their focus, in a preponderate sense focused more on building protective walls that isolate rather than interactive bridges that unite. They wind up more often than not talking past as opposed to talking with each other, pitting thesis against antithesis and thereby impeding rather than accelerating the quest for synthesis. As such, there exists a palpable need to compile, integrate, and reconcile what is out there and push this knowledge to a point where it can illuminate the process whereby we seek, create, and utilize Importance.

In sum, the supply of integrated knowledge on Importance is in relatively short demand, and this supply is severely, increasingly constrained.

So to get to the bottom of this, we must first clear away some of the brush, or if you prefer, tune out some of the static that impedes a deep and sharp understanding of the concept. We will thereby start by surfacing and then removing some of its most pesky barriers—that is, by first addressing what Importance is *not*.

What Importance Is NOT

It is absolutely critical to note that when we speak about one's sense of Importance, we are *not* simply talking about "ego" in the common use of the term. Importance should not be equated with being "full of oneself," having a "big head," and possessing an overinflated sense of self-worth.[8] In fact, it is something entirely different that, lamentably, might be eventually mismanaged into ego but can also be properly channeled into something much, much better.

Said plainly, Importance might sadly devolve into the negative when it becomes an exaggerated, isolated, and superficial image that is selfishly pursued and defensively, actively manipulated for its own aggrandizement.

However—and this is key—Importance is not inherently, and does not have to become, any of these things. Let us take the misconstruals one by one to show how this is so.

Is Importance necessarily an exaggerated phenomenon?

No. Certainly a person could think too much, or too little, of their value and their significance. That is to say, Importance can be inflated, but it might just as well be underappreciated. In general, one should advocate neither an "I am everything" nor an "I am nothing" approach to Importance. Each of these can be equally dysfunctional and, as such, present substantial problems to both the subject and those they interact with. Moreover, we will show that a person's sense of Importance can also be too stable (never changing and evolving) or too fickle (always in flux and hyper-sensitive from one situation to another). Again, each of these extremes presents unique challenges. Message: There are different fundamental natures (i.e., levels and types) of Importance. So please accept the notion that being a VIP does not necessarily mean the same thing or look the same way to everyone.

Is Importance necessarily an isolated and superficial phenomenon?

No. Certainly a person could be more internally or externally focused in how they approach Importance. That is to say, our Importance can be tied exclusively to personal characteristics and qualities . . . or it can be looked at in terms of how we act, what we produce, where we are positioned, whom we help, and to what greater causes or larger organizations we advance. Moreover, a person could be more generic, or reflective, in how they approach Importance. That is to say, our Importance can follow a cookie-cutter template that may or may not gel with our strengths and values . . . or it can be thoughtfully customized to resonate with our unique profile. Message: There are different paths and filters to Importance. So please accept the notion that people can strive to be VIPs in different ways.

Is Importance necessarily a selfish phenomenon?

No. Certainly a person could be more myopic, or broad-minded, in how they approach Importance. That is to say, our Importance can be a purely personal, self-oriented motivation . . . or it can be gauged by the service that we perform, the contribution that we make, the ideas that we create, and the good that we do. In fact, depending on whether it is seen as more of an individualistic or collectivistic phenomenon, it might run counter to prevailing norms and be differentially sanctioned in various societies, organizations, groups, and families. Message: There are different contexts and criteria for Importance. So please accept the notion that you can be a VIP in one situation and not in another; it is inexorably intertwined with one's external context and internal scale.

Is Importance necessarily a defensive and actively manipulated phenomenon?

No. Certainly a person could be more protective, or developmental, in how they approach Importance. That is to say, our Importance can be used to slant the public-relations spin and guard against threats to our image . . . or as a catalyst to learn, to grow, and to increase our literal as well as figurative worth. Moreover, a person could be more genuine, or calculating, in how they approach Importance. That is to say, our Importance can be an actively distorted product of how we want to be . . . or it can be a deep-seated, natural, honest background reflection and continuous check on the value that we add. Message: There are different uses for Importance. So please accept the notion that becoming a VIP is located more in the beginning of your story and in how it is told, not something found only at the end of it.

Taking these together, we can say that at its worst, Importance can deteriorate into the most negative conceptions of ego. However, at its best, it can also enlighten our self-conception and how we think about ourselves, enhance our emotional well-being and how we feel about ourselves, and impel our performance and how we behave in personal as well as professional settings. Message: There are different outcomes of Importance. So achieving a sense of VIP-ness can be good or bad. To reiterate a point made earlier, there is nothing wrong with seeking to comprehend and enhance Importance as long as it is done reflectively and sensibly.

Therefore, before reading any further, I ask that you please move any "egotistical," "surface," "selfish," and "defensive" labels or other personal misconceptions to the side as you think about the topic of our book. Do not equate VIP with being a conceited elitist. Instead, be open-minded to the notion that there are more and less healthy, productive, sincere, and justifiable ways of feeling that one is valuable and significant.

To extend this point, let us move to formally state our definition and delineate our terms.

A Working Definition of Importance

What is the definition of Importance?[9] Origins of the term can be traced back to medieval Latin *importare* and *importantia*, and through to the modern "important"—being of weight or consequence. From this, the term has been defined fairly consistently by print dictionaries such as *Merriam-Webster's*: "Meaningfully impacts, or rates highly on a scale measuring, something that is cared about. Consequential relevance." Web-based definitions are similar, for example Google offers definitions of the adjective "important" as "being of great significance or value; likely to have a profound effect on success, survival, or well-being" and the noun "importance" as "the state or fact of being of great significance or value."

In this book we attempt to capture these core elements to establish the following working definition of Importance: *The attribution to oneself of significant value.*

Breaking these components down as an equation, or forming a function, it would look like this:

$$I = f(V * S)$$

Where: I = Importance, V = Value, and S = Significance

Value

"Value" can be defined[10] as the return that something can be exchanged for, or more generally, as the worth or regard that something is deemed to deserve. Its approximating synonyms include "usefulness," "advantage," "benefit," "gain," "profit," "merit," "helpfulness," and "avail."

It is in essence a measure of *direction* and *relevance*—in other words, a question of *what* is good and why. Value relates to the things that you care about; that is, your beliefs and priorities. Your meaning.[11] But more than this, it also relates to the impact something can have on these desired outcomes. In this sense, its approximation represents a calibration or facilitation of success[12]— your happiness, your goals and objectives, your contribution. From a personal perspective, value can also be associated with "making a difference" and "leaving one's mark."

Value asks the question "Is something *good*?" Personal value asks the related question "Am I good?" Thus a VIP sees, or seeks, in the self the manifestation of some value.

The "goodness" of something, or of someone, relative to one's priorities, beliefs, and goals, is reflected in the following colloquial observations. Warren Buffett:[13] "Price is what you pay. Value is what you get." Albert Einstein:[14] "Try not to become a man of [conventional] success, but rather try to become a man of value."

Value is influenced by many factors, including one's culture (anthropology, history), one's substance (physiology), one's context (sociology, management, institutional theory), one's belief system (philosophy, religion), and one's attitudes and motives (psychology). We will address these in Chapter 2 and then integrate them into our model of Importance in the subsequent chapters.

Significance

"Significance" can be defined[15] as the quality of having notable worth or influence. Deserving of attention. Its approximating synonyms include "seriousness," "gravity," "weight," "degree," and "momentousness."

It is in essence a measure of *magnitude* and *consequence*—in other words, a question of "how much" value is substantial or enough. In this vein, significance is attached to the things that you deem non-trivial, consequential, unique. From a personal perspective, significance is calculated—as regards to one's judgment and enacted decision-making models—as per the quantification of value beyond some defined threshold. Making a "real" difference.

Significance asks the question "Is something good *enough*?" Personal significance asks the related question "Am I good enough?" Thus a VIP sees, or seeks, significance in their value.

The degree or magnitude of something's, or someone's, value is reflected in the following observations. Soren Kierkegaard:[16] "It seems essential, in relationships and all tasks, that we concentrate only on what is most significant and important." Aristotle:[17] "The aim of art is to represent not the outward appearance of things, but their inward significance."

Significance is influenced by many factors, including internally and externally determined status, via the relative social, professional, or other standing that we attribute to someone or something. We will also address these ideas in Chapter 2 and integrate them into our model of Importance in the subsequent chapters.

Self-Subjective Significant Value

In the book, we focus on an individual's perceived personal sense of his or her own significant value. In short: self-subjective Importance.

We do *not* seek in any way to advance, advocate, or endorse a singular or objective assessment of the Importance of one person versus another. Contrary to universal, linear modeling, such as that found in Maslow's popularized hierarchy of human needs,[18] there is no one prepotent path to VIP-ness. Rather, we view Importance from the perspective of a focal individual. Your measure of your Importance. What is in your eyes, your head, your heart. This may or may not correspond to others' "scores," but for our purposes here, the distinction is irrelevant. We treat perceived personal significant value as intertwined with the idea of one's self-image[19] or how a person sees the self as derived from individual, relational, and institutional or social cues. Our sense of Importance comprises a core part of, and actively influences, our self-concept and self-identity. However, and as argued later in the book, it in actuality interacts with and helps produce a person's diverse set of images and identities.

Throughout our discussions we will link Importance with related concepts and research from a host of intellectual pursuits and research domains, such as chemistry, biology, physics, psychology, sociology, management, politics, economics, law, and philosophy. Woven together, they can be integrated to produce an amalgamated conception of a person's sense of their significant value.

A General Model for Understanding and Managing Importance

In this book we will offer you what we believe to be the most focused, grounded, and compelling analysis to date of Importance in order to clarify the above issues and related questions.

We will start by presenting an original, easy-to-understand model and follow this with practical guidelines so that you can come to grips with Importance in an overarching sense as well as relate its generic lessons to managing the particulars in your life.

Constructing the model that you are about to see was no easy task. It is the product of an extraordinarily broad, deep, and time-consuming research project spanning many different disciplinary areas and their relevant

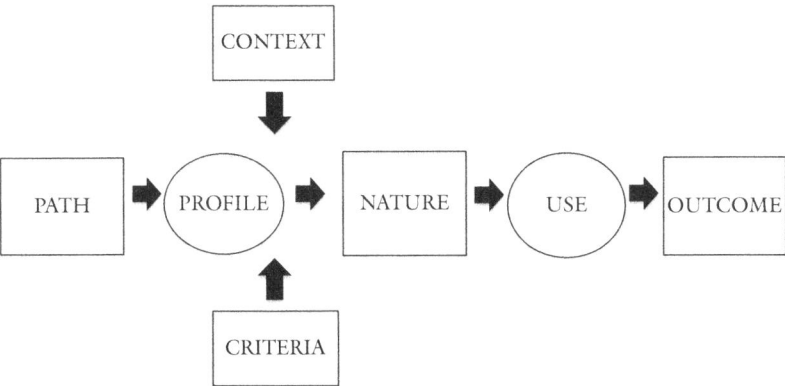

Figure 1.1   Modeling the *Conditions, Nature,* and *Consequences* of Importance.

literatures, integrating many scholarly studies and applied/colloquial stories, translating and reconciling many diverse terminologies and constructs, and organizing them so that one can gain a semblance of clarity, consistency, and thereby approximate a set of its most influential associations and logical interdependencies.

At its essence, the model takes a vast amount of theoretical and empirical evidence and boils it down to reveal the core relationships between the *nature,* the *conditions,* and the *consequences* of Importance.

The first part of the model presents the *conditions* that drive one's sense of significant value. You will see that there are many different *paths* that lead to Importance (Chapter 3), a range of personal *profile* filters that *mediate* their resonance on Importance (Chapter 4), and an assortment of macro/external/ outside *context* (Chapter 5) as well as micro/internal/inside *criteria* (Chapter 6) variables that *moderate* their influence on Importance.

The second part of the model outlines the *nature* that forms one's sense of significant value. You will see that Importance can be described in terms of its various forces and forms (Chapter 7). That is to say, one can experience it in different valences and magnitudes as well as across different levels of analysis and degrees of dynamic stability.

The third and final part of the model presents the *consequences* that emerge from one's sense of significant value. You will see that Importance, depending on the way that you *use* it (Chapter 8), can facilitate varied cognitive, affective, and conative *outcomes* (Chapter 9).

The Vehicles for Managing Importance

First and foremost, the heart of the book focuses on developing and describing the aforementioned relationships to help the reader better UNDERSTAND the nature, conditions, and consequences of Importance. This model building is our primary goal. However, this is not our only goal. Several additional learning tools are also utilized to bring the material, and specifically the model, to life.

Second, we will offer the reader an opportunity to IDENTIFY the unfolding of these ideas and insights within the ebb and flow of the praxis of life. We will start by embedding into this book a fictional unfolding story in which we present a "model" family—parents, children, relatives, neighbors, friends—each illustrating different parts of the theory and arguments: drivers, profile, conditions, criteria, nature, use, and outcomes. As the plot develops, the reader will see these characters vary in the ways they define Importance, seek Importance, customize Importance, contextualize Importance, assess or "score" Importance, achieve Importance, engage Importance, and are impacted by Importance. Our objective here is that you will use this book as both a mirror and a window.

See yourself in the book's observations and, perhaps, embodied in one or more different parts of its characters. In this sense, the book represents a *mirror*. That is to say, a reflective tool for understanding and improving oneself, for determining if and what type of VIP you wish to be, and ultimately as an aid for making better choices.

See your colleagues in the book's observations and, perhaps, embodied in one or more different parts of its characters. In this sense, the book represents a *window*. That is to say, an observational tool for deciphering and helping others, for determining if and what type of VIP you can help them to be, and ultimately as an aid for improving management strategies.

So let us now introduce our model family: The Normans. The Normans are a vibrant, diverse clan with a broad range of activities and an evolving family story. More specifically, through the chapters of their lives, we will visit them in several places and stages: dropping in at their home, at the neighborhood high school, when they go away to college, where they participate in their communities, how they go through different family rites and rituals, during a social night out, and during a typical day at work.

In addition, we will also present a cross-section of organizationally embedded case studies that are essentially amalgams of my interviews with, and observations of, different individuals' experiences with their sense of Importance. Again, the characters can be utilized as either mirrors or as windows. More specifically, through the vignettes, we will be granted "insider access," traveling behind the scenes to visit a varied collection of businesses, associations, and establishments: a restaurant, financial institution and bank, insurance and sales office, medical facility, art gallery, law firm, and auto supplies manufacturing plant.

Together the illustrations will help you see that these characters will vary in the conditions, nature, and consequences of their Importance:

- They seek it from different sources.
- They process it in different ways.
- They experience it in different places.

- They evaluate it through different lenses.
- They realize it in different manners.
- They use it in different capacities.
- They are impacted by it across different dimensions.

Third, after this, we will offer the reader an opportunity to PERSONALIZE the material. Here you will be able to test yourself, to ask some "wicked questions"[20] that are meant not to evaluate your mastery of materials but instead to inspire deep reflection, surface implicit assumptions, challenge paradoxical feelings, explore underlying patterns, and elicit ideas about one's significance and value.

Fourth and finally, we will invite the reader to APPLY the material. Here you will be offered guided checklists for formulating and executing development plans oriented toward (a) making better *personal* choices to optimize your Importance—being a True VIP—and (b) crafting better *professional* strategies to manage others' Importance—helping them to be True VIPs.

So let us now matriculate through the model and take up these important questions.

2

Foundation

*What we know about Importance is based
within and across a broad range of knowledge areas.*

Chapter 2 presents a variety of basic research streams that are related to our central thesis. In this chapter we will discuss the foundations of Importance from several scholarly viewpoints. Specifically we will scour a broad array of disciplines and engage a diverse set of thinkers and researchers to approximate the essence of Importance. We will do this by asking the question "Am I important?" from a (1) physical perspective, as a material entity; (2) psychological perspective, as an individual entity; (3) sociological perspective, as a collective entity; (4) managerial perspective, as a functional or organizational entity; (5) institutional perspective, as a political, economic, and legal entity; and (6) philosophical perspective, as an abstract or spiritual entity. At the conclusion of the chapter, we will coalesce the upshots of the above insofar as they inform the aforementioned integrated model of Importance.

In short, we cannot embark on this journey without considering those who have taken up similar quests, albeit from diverse and differentially related perspectives. Our scope has been defined in the prior chapter. Now in this chapter our foundation needs to be established. The following is an encapsulated review (because a comprehensive history would take many volumes, not to mention many eons) that attempts to capture the core insights from the way that scholars have attempted to answer the question from their discipline-specific viewpoints. It should not be seen, or evaluated, by prejudicial perspectives of what views are right versus wrong, or better versus worse, or more central versus peripheral. Instead, it should be appreciated for its general representation of the diverse history of inquiry that has attempted to delineate, directly and indirectly, the key issues surrounding Importance. It should also be seen as an amalgamated feeder source for the key variables that might be included in a meta-modeling effort.

Am I Important PHYSICALLY . . .
as a Material Entity?

If we are to view our significant value from a physical perspective, there are various lenses from the natural sciences that we might utilize.

In a very general sense, we might address the question "Am I important?" from a physical perspective by looking at some of the ideas endemic in natural sciences (e.g., chemistry and physics), life sciences (e.g., biology and neurology), and earth sciences (e.g., geology, ecology, and meteorology). Within these fields there are complementary sets of principles that can be readily accessed and then integratively considered.

Natural Sciences—Chemistry and Physics

Utilizing the implements of chemistry and physics, we might examine Importance in terms of the structure of the universe and our place in it. Such an inquiry would include both micro/quantum as well as macro/classical considerations.[1]

Briefly, chemistry is the branch of science that deals with the elemental composition, structure, and properties of substances of which matter is composed and the transformations that they undergo. Just as briefly, physics is the branch of science concerned with the nature and properties of matter and energy (e.g., potential, kinetic) and the way that they act on each other within the infinitesimally small as well as across the epically immense.[2] Together they help us understand Importance as it pertains to both (a) the system that we comprise—that is, inside the immediate boundaries of our physical selves—and (b) the system we are comprised within—that is, outside of the immediate boundaries of our physical selves.

In terms of micro, quantum considerations—looking inside ourselves—our Importance might be contextualized in terms of the nature of the substance that comprises our material configuration. Here we would examine our Importance on the basis of our fundamental components and their compounds. We might ask the questions: Do we as a system embody elemental significance and value? Embedded within us do we have molecular significance and value?

Importance might be calibrated here at a microscopic level and with regard to the nature of our genetics, our chemical makeup, our mass, and our energy. Indeed, humankind has been attempting to better understand, influence, or even control some of its elemental, atomic reality, for example, via modern-day advances in nanotechnology where we manipulate molecules at the atomic and subatomic levels to reimagine productive and process functions. To appreciate the level of scale endeavored, consider that one nanometer equals a billionth of a meter. Here we strive to become both the subject that can alter material Importance, such as by decoding the genome and modifying DNA, as well as the object that itself can be altered. Notwithstanding the specific target, the results are similar—expanded understanding of and influence over our relative Importance with regard to the smallest building blocks of what we know as reality.

In terms of macro, classic considerations—looking outside ourselves—our Importance might be contextualized in terms of our role in a larger physical configuration. Here we might ask the questions: Do we, within a system, have cosmic significance and value? Embedded within a superordinate experience, do we have mechanical and/or otherwise contributing significance and value?

Importance might be calibrated here at a celestial level and with regard to our place within a larger universe or multiverse design. Indeed, humankind has been attempting to better understand, influence, or even control some of its cosmic, relativistic reality, for example, via modern-day advances in theoretical physics and space exploration. In the former, we travel figuratively in our minds via our thoughts, reaching for insights a la Einstein-like "gedankenexperiments" and increasingly sophisticated cumulative conceptual extrapolations. This is consistent with Plato-like theoretical, idealized knowledge advancement. In the latter, we travel literally via advanced telescopic observations, satellite communications, and rocket-propelled commutation technologies. This is consistent with Aristotle-like empirical, contextualized knowledge advancement. Notwithstanding the "vehicle," the results are similar—expanded understanding of and influence over our relative Importance with regard to the most expansive synthesis of what we know as reality.

So, the upshot, from a natural science perspective, is this: We simultaneously comprise and are composed of complex, dynamic, interdependent substance configurations of matter and energy. That is to say, we have a material identity and a material reality that might have elementary as well as cosmic significance and value. Through various efforts, we may understand and influence some of our significant value within this reality.

Life Sciences—Biology and Neurology

Briefly, biology is the study of living organisms and their vital processes.[3] It can be divided into many specialized fields that cover their morphology, physiology, anatomy, behavior, origin, and distribution. Utilizing the implements of biology, we might examine Importance in terms of the structure of the classification of species and our place in it. Such an inquiry would include anatomy, physiology, and their evolutionary patterns to deliberate both static snapshot as well as dynamic cinematic consideration.

In terms of relatively static, anatomical considerations, our Importance might be contextualized in terms of us as beings and our bodies as living snapshots. We might ask the question "Do we have physiological, functional significance and value?" Importance might be calibrated here at an organic level and with regard to the dimensions of our physiology. Indeed, humankind has been attempting to better understand, influence, or even control some of its organic reality, for example, via modern-day advances in nutrition, pathology, and medical science. We are at a point in history where agricultural and dietary research has given us unprecedented jurisdiction over what we ingest. This is both for the better, such as in the imagination of healthier alternatives, and for the worse, as evidenced by the proliferation of creatively processed "junk" foods. We can identify, and in some cases treat, ailments that have haunted humans for millennia. We can supplement, complement, and even alter our anatomical functioning in ways never imagined. We can push the boundaries of our athletic achievements to become faster, stronger, and more mobile, agile, and dexterous. Notwithstanding the mechanisms, the results are similar—expanded understanding, and perhaps control, of our relative physical significance and value.

In terms of more dynamic, developmental considerations, our Importance might be contextualized in terms of us as unfolding iterations and our bodies as living cinema. We might ask the question "Do we have emergent, evolutionary significance and value?" In Darwinian terms, do our variations have what it takes to be selected and retained? Importance might be calibrated here at a genus level and with regard to the perpetuation of our species, and also at the family level with the perpetuation of our genes via kin. Indeed, humankind has been attempting to better understand, influence, or even control some of its evolutionary reality, for example, via modern-day advances in cloning and genetics. The genome has been decoded, and even manipulated, via interventions in the laboratory and the ecosphere. It has led some to say that natural selection and evolution has been surpassed, even replaced, by manual selection and evolution.[4] This has expanded our influence of our dynamic physical significance and value.

Of particular interest in this domain of inquiry is the field of neuroscience. This endeavor has as its focus the structure or function of our network of nerve cells and the brain. Neurology is, at its core, the branch of medicine or biology that deals with the anatomy, physiology, and functioning of central and peripheral nervous systems, especially in relation to integrative behavior and learning.[5] Utilizing the implements of neuroscience, we might examine Importance in terms of the structure of the brain, its supportive elements, and their place in empowering (or defining) us. Such an inquiry would include both considerations of the physical location and nature of *thoughts* as well as the physical location and nature of *feelings* and their integration and translation into tangible actions.[6]

As per the above, in terms of cognitive considerations, our neurological Importance might be contextualized in terms of our thought process, of cerebral brain structure and function, of material, neurological explanations for reason and rationality. We might ask the question "Do we have cognitive significance and value?" Importance might be calibrated here at an intellectual level and with regard to our mind. Indeed, humankind has been attempting to better understand, influence, or even control some of its logical reality, for example, via modern-day advances in the sciences (in discovering our intellectually significant value), education and pedagogy (in disseminating our intellectually significant value), and engineering (in enacting and expanding our intellectually significant value).

Also as per the above, in terms of emotional considerations, our neurological Importance might be contextualized in terms of our feeling process, of affective brain structure and function, of material, neurological explanations for happiness and well-being. We might ask the question "Do we have aesthetic significance and value?" Importance might be calibrated here at an affective level and with regard to our emotions and to our spirit. Indeed, humankind has been attempting to better understand, influence, or even control some of its emotional reality, for example, via modern-day advances in therapy (in external enhancement and remedy of our spiritually- and emotionally-anchored significant value) and meditation (in internal enhancement and remedy of our spiritually- and emotionally-anchored significant value).

So the upshot from a life science perspective is this: We comprise and are composed of complex, dynamic, interdependent configurations of body and mind. That is to say, we have an organic identity and an organic reality that might have biological and neurological static as well as dynamic significance and value. Through various efforts we may understand and influence some of our significant value within this reality.

Earth Sciences—Ecology, Geology, and Meteorology

Briefly, ecology is the branch of science that deals with the relationships of organisms to one another and to their physical environments. Geology is the branch of science that deals with the history and structure of the earth's physical substance and its life, especially as recorded in rocks and soil. Meteorology is the branch of science concerned with the processes and phenomena of the atmosphere, especially as a means of understanding and forecasting the weather.[7] Together they form the essential elements of the earth sciences. Utilizing the implements of ecology, geology, and meteorology, we might examine Importance in terms of the structure of the ecosystem and our place in it. Such an inquiry would include both local as well as global environmental considerations.

In terms of local considerations, our Importance might be contextualized in terms of defined physical situations. We might ask the question "Do we have native, location-specific significance and value?" Importance might be calibrated here at a community level and with regard to our societies. Indeed, humankind has been attempting to better understand, influence, or even control some of its localized reality, for example, via modern-day advances in urban planning. By and large, we are no longer hapless observers or helpless pawns seeking favorable contexts in which to live and work. In many ways we can create our context: in the expansion and even reimagination of cities (e.g., the trailblazing initiatives in Curitiba, Brazil, or New York City[8]), in the design improvements of buildings and campuses, in the progression of commutation and power options, in the enhancement of infrastructures, in the development of neighborhoods and districts, and in the integration of domestic and recreational environments. This has expanded understanding, and perhaps increased control, of our community-related significance and value.

In terms of global considerations, our Importance might be contextualized in terms of interdependent, changing configurations. We might ask the question "Do we have global, sustainability-related significance and value?" Importance might be calibrated here at an environmental level and with regard to our shared planet. Indeed, humankind has been attempting to better understand, influence, or even control some of its global reality, for example, via modern-day advances in climatology, oceanography, and sustainability. We can to some degree influence, even control, our weather. We erect climate-controlled edifices. We install HVAC systems. We invent observational and forecasting models. We wear specialized apparel (so effectively that one can be warm when hiking in the Arctic tundra or dry when exploring the deepest reaches of the seas). Moreover, we reengineer buildings, networks, and systems so that they are more self-sustaining and less vulnerable to external shock and internal degradation. This has expanded understanding, and perhaps increased control, of our planetary significance and value.

So the upshot from an earth science perspective is this: We comprise and are composed of complex, dynamic, interdependent configurations of relationships, structures, and environments. That is to say, we have a systemic identity and a systemic reality that might have ecological significance and value. Through various efforts, we may understand and influence some of our significant value within this reality.

Summary

Taken together the bottom line of such an inquiry might be that there are many factors—from the natural, life, and earth sciences—that influence how we see and assess ourselves as an important material, organic, and systemic physical entity and how we form *physical identities*.

Am I Important PSYCHOLOGICALLY…
as an Individual Entity?

Let me now don my psychologist hat.[9] We might address the question "Am I important?" from a psychological perspective by first looking at it in a *descriptive* psychological sense.

According to the American Psychology Association,[10] psychology refers to "the study of the mind and behavior. The discipline embraces all aspects of the human experience—from the functions of the brain to the actions of nations, from child development to care for the aged. In every conceivable setting, from scientific research centers to mental health services, 'the understanding of behavior' is the enterprise of psychologists." Psychologists throughout the ages have worked to identify the human experience, or self, as a totality of conscious and unconscious contents (c.f., Carl Jung), which include collections of characteristics (c.f., Gordon Allport), motives/needs (c.f., Abraham Maslow), and/or attitudes (c.f., Milton Rosenberg) that influence their actions (c.f., Carl Rogers).[11]

One can describe the self along objective, relatively more reliably measurable dimensions or along subjective, more internally interpretable dimensions.

Personality

From an *objective* standpoint we, as persons, are said to have a personality. Your personality is the set of characteristics and patterns of action that make you who you are. It can be categorized and calibrated along a host of dimensions. For example, three of the most prominent macro measures of personality are the Myers-Briggs, Big Five, and HEXACO models.[12]

The Myers-Briggs Personality Type Indicator contains four dimensions that categorize people into one of 16 different personality types according to how they use their perception and make decisions. The dimensions are extroversion versus introversion, sensing versus intuition, thinking versus feeling, and judging versus perception.

The Big Five, or five-factor, model of personality posits several discrete continuums of major facet-rich traits (generalized, characteristic, stable tendencies that explain how people tend to behave across diverse situations):

1. Extraversion: Whether a person is relatively talkative, energetic, and bold versus quiet, shy, and withdrawn
2. Agreeableness: Whether a person is relatively cooperative, sympathetic, and kind versus cold, rude, and unsympathetic
3. Conscientiousness: Whether a person is relatively responsible, efficient, organized, and thorough versus disorganized, careless, sloppy, and inefficient
4. Emotional stability/neuroticism: Whether a person is relatively relaxed and unemotional versus nervous, moody, insecure, and irritable
5. Openness to experience: Whether a person is relatively imaginative, philosophical, creative, and deep versus uninquisitive, unimaginative, unsophisticated, and shallow.

The HEXACO model includes the Big Five but adds a sixth dimension of honesty/humility, which describes whether a person is relatively honest, modest, and sincere versus greedy, boastful, and sly.

So, all things considered, let us say that psychological selves have different predilections and patterned ways of seeing, coalescing, and interacting with their worlds. Depending on a host of moderating and mediating variables, these patterns can have more or less significant value. For example, greater extraversion qualities and behaviors might be more functional in a social situation or position whereas a relatively introverted nature might be preferred in more individualistic and isolated conditions.

Ability

In addition, we can also be said to possess various types and amounts of abilities that can be translated into specific skills. Abilities can be measured in a variety of ways: cognitively, physically, affectively/emotionally, behaviorally, and so on.

From a physical sense, we can be said to possess various physical abilities to various degrees. For example, one organization lists the following dimensions that influence strength, endurance, flexibility, balance, and coordination:[13]

- Dynamic flexibility: The ability to quickly and repeatedly bend, stretch, twist, or reach out with your body, arms, and/or legs
- Dynamic strength: The ability to exert muscle force repeatedly or continuously over time, involving muscular endurance and resistance to muscle fatigue
- Explosive strength: The ability to use short bursts of muscle force to propel oneself (as in jumping or sprinting) or to throw an object
- Extent flexibility: The ability to bend, stretch, twist, or reach with your body, arms, and/or legs
- Gross body coordination: The ability to coordinate the movement of your arms, legs, and torso together when the whole body is in motion
- Gross body equilibrium: The ability to keep or regain your body balance or stay upright when in an unstable position
- Stamina: The ability to exert yourself physically over long periods of time without getting winded or out of breath
- Static strength: The ability to exert maximum muscle force to lift, push, pull, or carry objects
- Trunk strength: The ability to use your abdominal and lower back muscles to support part of the body repeatedly or continuously over time without giving out or fatiguing

From a cognitive and emotional sense, we can also delineate a series of intellectual ability types, including the following:[14]

- General cognitive intelligence: The ability to think or analyze information and situations that leads to or causes effective or superior performance
- Emotional and social intelligence: Composed of two component sets: emotional competency to recognize, understand, and use emotional information about oneself that leads to or causes effective or superior performance, and social competency to recognize, understand, and use emotional information about others that leads to or causes effective or superior performance
- Cultural intelligence: Composed of meta-cognitive and cognitive (thinking, learning, and strategizing), motivational (efficacy and confidence, persistence, value congruence, and affect for the new culture), and behavioral (social mimicry, and behavioral repertoire) competencies

So, all things considered, let us say that psychological selves have different aptitudes for interacting with their worlds. Depending on a host of moderating and mediating variables, these aptitudes can have more or less significant value. For example, gross body coordination might be relatively more functional for a concert pianist and trunk strength for a firefighter; cognitive intelligence might be relatively more functional for a theoretical physicist and social intelligence for a diplomat.

From a *subjective* psychological standpoint we, as persons, are said to have self-awareness and, as such, a self-concept.

Self-Concept

The self-concept[15] is a complex collection of thoughts, feelings, and behaviors that come from people's awareness of themselves as both subject (the experiencing, knowing, and reflective dimensions of selfhood that people associate with their self-awareness) and object (the agentic actor that we experience when we actively engage the world and interact with other people). These construals can be independent, defined in more individualistic terms of the persons and their attributes, and interdependent, defined in more collectivist terms in relation to others. In fact, all of these might very well be operative at once, forming a "self as kaleidoscope" of shifting, varied, and multifaceted constructs coalescing across different experiences and within shared trajectories. This kaleidoscope is constructed and reconstructed in our "self-talk,"[16] or biographical narratives that make sense of how our perceptions and experiences form the system of the self and subsequently enable both appraisal and regulation of the self.

Our self-concept may be more or less complex and dynamic depending on its content and structure.[17] Regarding content, self-perceptions can vary across such dimensions as quantity, quality, valence, and congruence. Regarding structure, people organize their self-perceptions into different collections of relatively interdependent or compartmentalized categories.

Related to the self-concept are ideas of how people can, from a functional perspective, better understand and manage it. A person might have self-awareness insofar as they develop a conscious identification of the self as both a subject and object capable of engaging the world in particular ways. A person might have self-reflection insofar as they can observe their conceptions in the face of experience and better comprehend their future thoughts, feelings, and behaviors. A person might have self-regulation insofar as they can utilize it to further the pursuit of their goals and inhibit counterproductive thoughts and behaviors.

So, all things considered, let us say that we can understand and manage our selves and the various perspectives/aspects of our selves to different degrees. Depending on a host of moderating and mediating variables, these outlooks can have more or less significant value. For example, self-awareness might be key for achieving person–job fit, and self-regulation might be particularly functional for resisting tangential, dysfunctional, or immoral temptations at jobs.

Values and Attitudes

We have values about ourselves and how we interact with our world. Values are the relatively stable guiding principles that underpin the way people think, behave, and are motivated. They serve as standards that guide people's actions, judgments, and choices they make in their arenas of engagement (e.g., societal, organizational, cultural, political, economic, and religious.)[18] Milton Rokeach distinguishes between two interlinked typologies of values: instrumental values, which refer to desirable modes of conduct, and terminal values, which refer to desirable end states of existence. Solomon Schwartz proposes a framework of ten different value types: power, achievement, hedonism, stimulation, self-direction, universalism, benevolence, tradition, conformity, and security.

So, all things considered, let us say that we care about and see different things in different ways, including our selves and aspects of our selves. Depending on a host of moderating and mediating variables, these priorities and worldviews can have more or less significant value. For example, valuing achievement might be a better fit in a highly competitive context, whereas valuing tradition might be a better fit in a more conservative climate.

We also form attitudes about ourselves. Attitudes are summary evaluations of a psychological object (including oneself) to denote a subjective level of valence. We know many things about attitudes.[19] We have found that they emerge from a number of factors, including internal (e.g., personal values) and external (e.g., context, norms) variables, can be influenced by cognitions and feelings, and can be altered by perspective. We also know that attitudes can be stronger or weaker, more or less favorable, unidimensional or multidimensional, and can be directed outward toward a group or object, or inward toward oneself. The outcome of one's attitudes, including self-attitudes, can take the form of cognitive (thoughts), affective (feelings), and conative (behaviors) consequences. The connections between an attitude and these outcomes are most powerful when they are more specific and closer in correspondence.

So, all things considered, let us say that we are more or less positive about different things (including our selves and aspects of our selves) to different degrees. Depending on a host of moderating and mediating variables, these outlooks can have more or less significant value. For example, our attitudes could drive us to pursue more (e.g., pluralistic) versus less (e.g., prejudicial) socially acceptable behaviors, and these can vary widely depending on the different groups, organizations, and societies that we find ourselves in.

In addition to the aforementioned descriptive discussion, we might also address the question "Am I important" from a psychological perspective by looking at it in an *evaluative* sense. This is because the self is not just a vehicle for description but also a mechanism of calibration. That is to say, we can apply our values and attitudes to our self-concept to develop appraisals of ourselves.

Self-Evaluation

More than just understanding the self, self-evaluation processes reflect those factors that influence people's assessments and estimates of themselves.[20] Psychologists have extensively studied self-esteem as one major dimension along which people evaluate themselves. Other related dimensions include self-efficacy and self-worth.

Self-esteem refers to an individual's own overarching evaluation of his or her abilities and subsequent feelings of capability and confidence stemming from those evaluations. Or in other words, it is the level of competence that we feel in ourselves to face the obstacles in life.[21] This is among the most popularly familiar and frequently cited—yet at the same time most complex, confusing, and least understood—concept in psychology used to understand the self. In a word, there are mountains upon mountains written on self-esteem but, taken together, the landscape confuses and confounds just as much if not more so than it elucidates and orients.

To be sure, there is currently no commonly accepted, comprehensive, overall theory of self-esteem. In the research literature, it is simultaneously connected to and distinguished from a host of other phenomena. There is also much contradiction and debate as to the veracity, and relevance, of its "findings" and assertions. However, there are useful pockets of knowledge in this body of work that we might extract to construct a better understanding of how it contributes to a sense of Importance. For example, in the terms of the figurative father of the concept, William James referred to self-esteem as our feelings of competence and "what we back ourselves to be and do." Charles Cooley added to this the notion of a "looking glass," whereby we construct it by considering others' opinions and integrating them with our viewpoints. It might therefore be something that is calibrated statically, in the moment, as well as longitudinally, as a cumulative assessment over time.

Perhaps some of the subsequent confusion can be attributed to the proliferation of diverse definitions of self-esteem that abounded within the academic and popular spheres. As per a number of reviews, such as in the *Encyclopedia of Management Theory*[22] and work by Brockner,[23] esteem has been conceptualized in many different ways, and these ways are both conceptually distinct—they describe different phenomenon—as well as practically distinct—they cannot serve as surrogates for each other.[24] For example, they include: (a) contingent, comparative esteem that is based on mainly extrinsic, relative criteria versus stable and cumulative esteem that is based on mainly intrinsic considerations;[25] (b) generalized or global esteem, encompassing the whole individual across engagements versus state- or domain-specific esteem, referring to and varying between specified aspects and/or a specified instances and/or at specified points in time (e.g., organizationally based self-esteem);[26] and (c) trait-based esteem, where it cannot be taught or altered to a meaningful degree versus malleable esteem, open to interpretations as well as interventions and nontemporary improvements.[27]

Moreover, there is significant confusion as to the dimensions of self-esteem and their relationship, which will be detailed in the following sub-section. Briefly, embedded in the fuzzy construct can be found both (a) competency assessments related to self-efficacy, that is, a measure of what you can do, and (b) regard assessments related to self-worth.[28] It also merits noting that self-esteem might be best incorporated as but one single component dimension within the larger umbrella of core-self evaluation[29] composed of self-esteem, generalized self-efficacy, locus of control, and emotional stability. Notwithstanding the confusions and redundancy within the trait and personality literature, and weary of potential obscurations inherent in mingling already intermingled constructs (e.g., self-esteem itself contains different, often poorly identified dimensions), it is nonetheless telling that some point to a potentially latent or higher-order factor that relates to how one regards or evaluates oneself.

There is also much debate about the outcomes of self-esteem. Some advocate specific interventions to boost self-esteem, and these populate the self-help shelves of bookstores and libraries worldwide. For example, Nathaniel Branden[30] promotes "six pillars" for nurturing self-esteem, although many question their validity and usefulness: (1) living consciously, (2) self-acceptance, (3) self-responsibility, (4) self-assertiveness, (5) living purposefully, and (6) personal integrity. Some advocate a balancing of self-esteem, where too little can lead to dangerous levels of meekness and too much to similarly dangerous levels of vanity. Some advocate realistic construals that accurately reflect one's state, whereas others suggest that one manipulate and manage one's image or brand. Some trumpet its causal functionality in promoting satisfaction, confidence, and a host of other positive outcomes, whereas others question the direction and veracity of causality. Some claim that it boosts performance, whereas others point to weak or moderate statistically justified conclusions. Some say that training can enhance it, whereas others, as mentioned before, have raised vital concerns and meaningful doubt about this agency.

These definitional, dimensional, and functional inconsistencies are further compounded by a variety of methodological issues and the diverse approaches in its measurement.[31] That is to say, there are wide discrepancies in how people assess and calibrate esteem. For example, Rosenberg's widely used Self-Esteem Scale will not necessarily produce results consistent with the Coopersmith Self-Esteem Inventory, the Piers-Harris Scale, the Janis-Field Scale, or numerous other proliferations.

The preceding issues have led some to conclude that after much attention and study, the concept has been "poorly defined" and "badly measured,"[32] with a lack of rigor and proliferation of instruments and measurements,[33] and as such the research to date has produced "a confusion of results that defies interpretation."[34]

Moreover, there are further ambiguities to consider in terms of the use or practical employment of self-esteem. It is useful to point out that one can seek to discover, verify, maintain, enhance, or even distort one's self-esteem.

Discovery embodies thoughts and actions in the service of finding and form-ing one's concept and its sense of Importance. Verification embodies thoughts and actions in the service of categorizing and confirming one's concept and its sense of Importance. Maintenance embodies thoughts and actions in the service of defending and protecting one's concept and its sense of Importance. Enhancement embodies thoughts and actions in the service of improving or emphasizing one's concept and its sense of Importance. Distortion embod-ies thoughts and actions in the service of exaggerating and advertising, often through the strategically managed self-presentation process of "impression managing" one's concept and its sense of Importance.

This latter point suggests that we are not passive with regard to self-concept. In fact, we actively shape our image.[35] On the one hand, when these efforts are focused outward, toward (mis)leading other people, it is called *impression management*. Impression management describes the process where people work to influence the attributes and evaluations that others ascribe to them. People might be motivated to manage their image because of social desirabil-ity (acceptance) and functional reasons (e.g., a way of creating more power and attaining desired outcomes). On the other hand, when these efforts are focused inward, toward (mis)leading the self, it is called *self-deception*. This is a tendency, perhaps borne of disposition and/or circumstance, whereby one selectively, inaccurately sees oneself in a favorably biased light. People might be motivated to engage in such behaviors due to emotional or cognitive dis-sonance between actual and desired self-image. Together the active attention paid to one's image suggests that this energy can attempt to (a) skew—fool yourself or others into seeing a false self, (b) crystalize—help yourself or oth-ers see the self more accurately, or (c) reconcile—resolve differences within and between public and private selves.

In general, notwithstanding the enormous amount of confusion with regard to the fuzzy idea of self-esteem, we might say—depending on previ-ously discussed definitions, dimensions, functions, methods, and measure-ments that one adopts—that people like, or perhaps respect, or perhaps assess, or perhaps present their selves and/or aspects of their selves in different lights and then to different degrees. Given this, it is particularly important to tease out the multiple, often intermingled components both in content and in con-struct embedded in its conceptualization. Thus we focus our remaining atten-tion here on two of the often amalgamated and/or equated but nonetheless critically distinct ideas conveyed within the esteem conversation: self-efficacy and self-worth.

In brief, *self-efficacy* refers to a person's estimate of his or her capacity to mobilize resources and orchestrate performance on a specific task.[36] It is derived from Albert Bandura's Social Cognitive Theory[37] and, although it is frequently confused with esteem, represents not an overall level of affir-mation or self-liking but instead a specific assessment of or confidence in one's fitness to perform a defined act to defined standards. Here one's effi-cacy beliefs are found to derive from and develop in four principle ways: past successes and mastery experiences, social modeling and relatable precedents, social persuasion and feedback, and assessments of prevailing conditions and resource states. These beliefs then influence individuals' expectations and self-enhancing or self-debilitating contruals as well as their resultant choices. As such, efficacy is a core component of many behavioral models including Vrooms' well-regarded Expectancy Theory of motivation, representing an individual's believe that their actions can execute a desired performance.

Alternatively, and also in brief, *self-worth* refers to one's assessment, based on a variety of contingencies, of one's value as a person.[38] Feelings of self-worth are self-evaluations as well as affective feelings toward one's basic merit as a human being. This is probably the closest we have come to the idea of Importance. For example, Crocker and Knight[39] argue that "high self-esteem is often regarded as the holy grail of psychological health—the key to happiness, success . . . however this rosy view of high self-esteem has detractors . . . the importance of self-esteem lies . . . in what people believe they need to be or do to have value and worth as a person."

These studies should be commended for exploring different paths to worth and recognizing that people differ as to what they believe their worth to be contingent upon (for more on this see Chapter 3 in our book). However existing constructs of self-worth are themselves muddy, and their measures are perhaps even muddier. Regarding the former, it is not entirely clear if worth should be conceptualized as a facet, a factor, a manifestation, an alternative, an antecedent, an outcome, a moderator, or simply something altogether different from other self-esteem-like approaches . . . probably because it is used as each of these by different proponents and at different times. Regarding the latter, the core 35-item Contingencies of Self-Worth[40] scale combines several disparate constructs and separate evaluative dimensions into the single measure. For example, the instrument asks respondents to evaluate: their opinion of themselves, reactions to how others see them, how they see themselves, reactions to how others feel about them, how they feel about themselves, how they regard themselves, their sense of self-worth, their sense of self-esteem, and their sense of self-respect. As we know, these are all very different things and do not neatly combine or necessarily co-vary. Notwithstanding, the line of inquiry itself represents a key advance in how we make sense of the "efficacy" and "worthiness" aspects of esteem and leads naturally to the subsequent consideration of self-subjective personal Importance.

Summary

All in all, let us say that we also have different ways of looking at our psychological selves. Depending on a host of moderating and mediating variables, these conceptions can have more or less significant value.

Taken together, the bottom line of such an inquiry might be that there are many objective (personality, ability), subjective (self-concept, values, and attitudes), and evaluative (self-esteem, efficacy, and worth) psychological factors that influence how we see and assess ourselves as an (important) individual entity and how we form *individual (self) identities*.

Am I Important SOCIOLOGICALLY . . .
as a Collective Entity?

Let me now don my sociologist hat.[41] Sociologically speaking, we might focus on a variety of levels of association that impact individuals' significant value. For the purposes of this discussion, we divide them here into micro (group) and macro (society) considerations.

Micro—Groups

We might address the question "Am I important?" from a micro sociological perspective by first looking at it in the context of *groups*.

Groups are collections of two or more people that identify, or are identified, in terms of shared process and/or content dimensions. There are a number of group characteristics that are particularly germane to the topic at hand. First, we must recognize that groups are structured by their *norms* and *roles*. As such, we might then assess our Importance relative to these overall and compartmentalized guideposts.

Norms are group-based standards regarding appropriate social behavior, appearance, and attitudes.[42] They are the unwritten rules about how members think, dress, and act. They define what is deemed *normal*. When people orient their selves in accordance with norms, particularly those that are injunctive in nature, they are endorsed; when they oppose them, they are ostracized. That is, what is considered appropriate, and the degree to which one is aligned with this, are heavy factors in determining a person's assessment of significant value. Of course, some norms are more easily noticed and more central than others. It is these types of salient, fundamental standards that exert a particularly strong force on group members.

Roles are group-based constructions of differentiated social categories and the expectations that are attached to them.[43] Briefly, a role is a differentiated position and accompanying script/task set constructed within a larger and often but not necessarily hierarchical system. Some examples of roles are parent and child, teacher and student, general and sergeant, running back and wide receiver. Members who occupy roles are known as role actors or role occupants. They are expected to conform to their role expectations and, insofar as they do so, gain rewards or incur sanctions. In a group, it is important to "know your role" and operate in a manner that is consistent with it. Thus people will act differently dependent on the roles that they occupy. They will also be assessed as to their significant value based on (a) that endemic in their role—some roles might be more prized or "important" than others; and (b) their execution of that role—some people are a better fit or more productive in their given roles than others. Dysfunctions that might destroy one's perceived value include role conflict (incongruous or misaligned expectations), role overload (unrealistic or miscast expectations), or role ambiguity (unclear or amorphous expectations).

Second, groups are activated by their *status* and *power*. As such, we might assess our Importance relative to these relational dynamics. Status is the comparative standing of one's role in or contribution to the group. It can be gained through formal means (e.g., appointment, election) or informal means (e.g., political maneuvers, contextualized perceptions of one's characteristics, such as age, gender, intelligence, etc.). There are obvious relationships between self-regarded status and self-perceived Importance. This is true in the abstract as well as in the expanded potential and options that status usually affords.

Power is the capacity or potential to influence others and get things done.[44] The most popular theoretical framework for understanding the bases of power emerges from the research of French and Raven in the late 1950s. In brief, people might realize potential influence through personal or positional sources. Personal sources include referent power, which stems from respect, charisma, and identification, and expert power, which stems from knowledge, information, abilities, and skills. Positional sources include legitimate power, which stems from location in an organization's hierarchy, reward power, which stems from the control over desirable resources, and coercive power, which stems from the wielding of real, perceived, or threatened punishments. The relative possession of power as well as its use—either being on the delivery or receiving end of it—can very well impact one's perceived significant value. Acquiring power, its enhancement or erosion, and its dynamic comparisons and conflicts are therefore all relevant variables when considering Importance.

Thus, in general, we might expect significant value to be greater when it is aligned with group norms, prioritized in roles, endemic in status designations, and enhanced with effectively constructed and leveraged power bases.

Macro—Societies

We might also address the question "Am I important?" from a macro sociological perspective by next looking at it in the context of *societies*.

Social structure can be understood in a variety of ways,[45] for example, in the degree to which it is stratified into classes or castes (and the resultant class consciousness), the relative mobility within and between strata, the degree of equity among and across strata, and subsequent social archetypes, stereotypes, and challenges such as prejudice and discrimination. Underlying all of these, however, is the fundamental conception of culture and corresponding cultural values.

The cultural values of a society provide the foundation for and context within which a society's norms are established and justified. As per Kluckhohn and Strodtbeck and others, a culture is a shared set of commonly held general principles and values that influence people's assumptions, perceptions, and behavior.[46] Cultural values, in turn, are "belief(s) pertaining to desirable end states or modes of conduct, that transcends specific situations, guides selection or evaluation of behavior, people, and events, and [are] ordered by importance relative to other values to form a system of value priorities."[47] There is often a hierarchy of cultural values that are more or less core, as well as a scope of values that can be seen as more (etic) or less (emic) universal.[48] There is also a literal and "silent" language in which these values are manifest, for example, not only in the literal but also in the contextualized use of time and space.[49] Some have argued for the application of these ideas to the study of interpersonal, organizational, and leadership effectiveness.[50]

Of course, it is not enough to know *that* societies differ; one must know *how* they differ. In his seminal research, Geert Hofstede has represented societal or cultural values as "software of the mind" and has delineated several of their dimensions:[51]

1. Power distance: The extent to which members of a society's organizations and institutions (e.g., agencies, firms, family) accept and expect that power is distributed unequally
2. Uncertainty avoidance: The extent to which members of a society feel uncomfortable and anxious in unstructured, novel, and unique situations outside the boundaries of existing rules and laws
3. Individualism versus collectivism: The extent to which members of a society have independent versus interdependent construals and are integrated into cohesive groups
4. Masculinity versus femininity: The extent to which members of a society emphasize stereotypically assertive, competitive (masculine) or modest, caring (feminine) values
5. Long- versus short-term orientation (later added based on research by Michael Bond): The extent to which members of a society pursue savings, thrift, and investment or here-and-now living and spending

Thus, in general, we might expect significant value to be greater when its paths are aligned with and endorsed by cultural values. For example, anticipating a greater emphasis on personal achievement in a more individualistic environment, stability in a more uncertainty-avoidance environment, and planning in a more long-term environment.

Summary

Taken together, the bottom line of such an inquiry might be that there are many factors—from micro (groups) to macro (societies)—that influence how we see and assess ourselves as a (important) social entity and how we form *social identities*.

Am I Important MANAGERIALLY . . .
as a Functional / Organizational Entity?

Now let me don my management hat.[52] A review of the relevant literature suggests that functional/organizational Importance can be ascertained at many levels, including the following:

- Micro: Individual-level, re: human resources and human capital
  Do we add significant value alone, as an asset?

- Meso: Interpersonal-level, re: management dynamic
  Do we add significant value together, as part of an interactive process?

- Macro: Structural-level, re: contextual design
  Do we add significant value systemically, as embedded in a structure?

- Strategic: Policy-level, re: engaged advantage
  Do we add significant value competitively, as charged with a mission?

First, we might address the question "Am I important?" from a functional or organizational perspective by first looking at it in the micro individual dynamic. One way that we assess significance and value is with regard to people as "human resources" and, as such, a calibration of their human capital.[53] In essence, this approach suggests that people are as important assets in the essential production processes of goods and services and that "proper investments in human capital," in the forms of employee (general as well as specific) recruitment and selection, training and development, performance appraisal, labor relations, and compensation management programs has the potential to offer organizations high returns. In essence, the idea is that people can add significant current and future value to their organizations through their knowledge, skills, and abilities. In addition, they can also command greater compensation for this value. Recent research has applied these ideas to the fields of human resource management (e.g., harmonizing individual and organizational systems) and talent management (e.g., getting, using, and keeping your highest-value employees). Embedded within these systems are fundamental organizational behavior theories of human perception, motivation, judgment, and interaction.[54] Here we speak of better and worse ways of adding significant value via setting goals, reinforcing behavior, and inspiring intrinsic commitment.[55]

Thus from a micro perspective, we might have more or less significant value depending on our overall knowledge, skills, and abilities (known as KSAs) and our specific application of these to address our tasks, duties, and responsibilities (known as TDRs).

Second, we might also address the question "Am I important?" from a functional or organizational perspective by then looking at it in the meso interpersonal dynamic. One way that we assess significance and value is with regard to people's process management dynamics. There is a rich history of research and model building in this area. For example, Henri Fayol's principles of management[56] describes the basic people-oriented management activities (planning, organizing, coordinating, controlling, and commanding) and principles (e.g., discipline, order, fairness, and spirit) that are oriented toward getting the greatest value from employees. The Hawthorne researchers[57] emphasize the "manager-employee partnership," embraced the "complexity of relationships" that affect people, and promoted processes that "placed a high value on "human growth, potential, and dignity" instead of treating people as "simple extensions of workplace machines." Peter Drucker[58] advocates for an approach to management as a discipline that focused on people, power, values, and responsibilities to further such aims as innovation and entrepreneurship, social impacts and social responsibilities, and the spirit of performance. Henry Mintzberg[59] outlines different roles that managers might play in doing this, for example, as an interpersonal leader or liaison, information disseminator or monitor, and decision-making resource allocator and disturbance handler. More recently, positive organizational scholars[60] add to these notions that management "unlocking the secrets to human resilience, vitality, desire to achieve, creativity and growth can bring an organization to an uncommon level of excellence."

Thus from a meso perspective, we might have more or less significant value depending on our management acumen and how we can get the most out of the management process to enhance others' KSAs and execute TDRs.

Third, we might further address the question "Am I important?" from a functional or organizational perspective by then looking at it in the macro context dynamic. One way that we assess significance and value is with regard to visible, invisible, and dynamic design.

With regard to "visible" structure or design of organizations, a person's Importance is a function of the division of labor and overt technical organizational design.[61] As a horizontally and vertically *differentiated* component, individuals' Importance can be seen to vary. For example, flatter organization structures may increase constituent significant value, whereas within taller organizations significant value (especially if you are at the bottom) may be reduced. With thinner organizations, structures may create more specialized significant value, whereas with wider organizations, more significant value may be more generalized. As an *integrative* mechanism, individuals' Importance can be seen to vary. For example, more intimately and intensively coupled organizations may increase connective significant value, whereas within less connected organizations significant value may be compartmentalized. As a *decision* maker, individuals' Importance can be seen to vary. For example, more decentralized and empowering organizations may increase evaluative significant value, whereas within more centralized organizations significant value may be less if at the node and more if at the hub. Moreover, more informal and mutually adjusting organizations may increase discretionary significant value, whereas within more standardized and formalized organizations significant value may likewise be less if at the node and more if at the hub.

With regard to the "invisible" structure of organizations, a person's Importance is a function of the dominant or prevailing corporate culture.[62] For example, Importance can be seen to vary to the extent that an individual influences, and conforms with, core cultural assumptions, manifest cultural values, and tangible cultural artifacts. This might be magnified by the strength of their role in cultural transfer, particularly its socialization and social learning components. Corporate cultures in general can be seen as more important when they are valuable, rare, and not easily replicated. Corporate cultures can enable greater Importance by their participants when they empower and engage their people (*involvement*), facilitate coordinated actions and promote consistency of behaviors with core business values (*consistency*), translate the demands of the organizational environment into action (*adaptability*), and provide a clear sense of purpose and direction (*mission*).[63]

With regard to the dynamic structure of organizations, a person's Importance is a function of their contribution to creative, choice, and change processes. For example, Importance can be seen to vary to the extent that an individual facilitates or retards the innovation creative destruction process, promotes or inhibits incremental and frame-breaking activity, connects problems and solutions to choice opportunities, and acts as a force for as opposed to barriers against progressive change.[64]

Thus from a macro perspective, we might have more or less significant value depending on our place in the formal/informal/dynamic organizational system.

Fourth, we might further address the question "Am I important?" from a functional or organizational perspective by then looking at it in the *strategic-policy* dynamic. Here conjoined ways that we assess significance and value are with regard to internal orientation and external engagement. Regarding internal processes, we might assess significant value based on (a) strategic resources, (b) strategic action, and (c) strategic competencies.

In terms of strategic resources, Importance is a function of the nature of the resources to be deployed and/or the faculty to deploy said resources more or less ably. To the former, as per the Resource-Based View of the Firm,[65] we comprise heterogeneously amalgamated, distributed, and configured units and bundled capacities for value creation. The better the resource utilization capacity, the greater the Importance. To the latter, as per the Upper-Echelons Theory and Agency Theory,[66] we are the contracted decision makers that are charged to utilize expertise and information for identifying, acquiring, arranging, and utilizing capacity. The better the resource deployment capacity, the greater the Importance.

In terms of strategic action, Importance is a function of the fidelity of proactive planning and the alacrity of reactive adjusting. To the former, as per Business Policy and Corporate Strategy theories,[67] we develop and implement the long-run and short-run goals of overall (corporate) entities and their specific (business) engagements. The better the visions and frameworks, the greater their Importance. To the latter, as per varied, more emergent Models of Strategy,[68] we actively interpret and flexibly adapt to our realities to chart an emergent path. The better the agility, the greater the Importance.

In terms of strategic competencies, Importance is a function of the alignment of core processes within and across boundaries. To the former, as per theories of Core Competence and Value Chain,[69] we construct unique, enduring knowledge bases and dynamic routines/capabilities that can be tailored to produce superior primary and support activities. The better the path-dependent processes, the greater the Importance. To the latter, as per theories of Competitive Advantage and National Platforms,[70] we direct these activities to establish superior differentiated or low-cost positions and catalytic conditions for facilitating marketplace success. The better the focal niches and shared platforms, the greater the Importance.

Regarding external processes, we might assess significant value based on (a) strategic fit and (b) strategic engagement. In terms of strategic fit, it is imperative to note that organizations are embedded in interdependent relationships with forces beyond their boundaries. As per Systems Theory,[71] organizations are composed of, and comprise, interrelated networks of component parts acting jointly on each other where properties and changes in a part of the shared system have complex consequences for its other parts. Systems can be more or less open in nature. Within their parameters they strive for the resolution of inconsistencies and the promotion of fit within social (e.g., Institutional Theory) and technical (e.g., Contingency Theory) dimensions.[72] The more robust the intersections, the greater the Importance.

In terms of strategic engagement, it is imperative to note that organizations are more or less capable of influencing forces beyond their boundaries. As per Game Theory[73] intelligent managers have the ability to confront situations and engage players to select strategies that maximize their and their organizations' payoffs. They can do this through a number of means, including the obtaining of resources and optimization of power-dependence relationships (e.g., Resource Dependence Theory), reducing of costs associated with the processing of inputs into outputs (e.g., Transaction Cost Theory), optimizing of value creation across performance dimensions (e.g., Balanced Scorecard), and sustaining co-determined mutual value between symbiotic parties over time (e.g., Stakeholder Theory, Triple Bottom Line).[74] The more logically and/or ethically effective the interaction, the greater the Importance.

Thus from a strategic perspective, we might have more or less significant value depending on our contribution to the competitive formulation, implementation, and execution process.

Summary

Taken together, the bottom line of such an inquiry might be that there are many general and specific managerial factors that influence how we see and assess ourselves as an (important) functional entity and how we form *organizational identities*.

Am I Important INSTITUTIONALLY . . .
as a Political, Economic, and Legal Entity?

Now let me don my institutional hat.[75] Whereas there are multiple dimensions that can impact a person's significant value, we focus here on three of the most prominent: *political, economic, and legal*.

Political Systems

We might address the question "Am I important?" from an institutional perspective by first looking at it in the political dimension.

Political systems (i.e., governments) refer to the means of exercising direction and control over the actions of the members, citizens, or inhabitants of communities, societies, and states. They include rules by which a state, community, or other such entity is governed. They comprise bodies of peoples that set and administer public policy and exercise executive, political, and sovereign power through customs, institutions, and laws within a state.[76] In essence a political definition of self, and by extension one's significant value, can be found within one's role in their political system as a citizen. Since there are many different types of political systems, it stands to reason that different political systems would view the individual, and as such the significant value of the individual, in different lights. Whereas one might also make the case that different political parties within a given system determine significant value differently, we restrict our attention here to the more pronounced systemic, rather than the nuanced within-system, dynamics.

There are three broad types of political system:[77] democracy, socialism/communism, and totalitarianism.

A democratic political system is based on the belief that citizens should be directly involved in their government's decision making, that government is under the jurisdiction of its free peoples, exercised either directly or through representatives, and that these representatives are elected and can be recalled, impeached, or voted out by their people based on the perceived performance of their jobs. Essential to democracies are safeguards such as constitutionally guaranteed freedoms and bills of rights, as well as regulating/monitoring mechanisms such as a free press and a balance of power. All things being equal, something or someone has greater significant value in a democracy when they are voted to higher and/or more strategic offices. That is to say, Importance is largely dependent on the electorate.

A socialist/communist political system is based on the belief that collectivist goals are preeminent over individualistic goals in government decision making, that the common good is more important than individual freedoms, and that government holds much of the power over its people and their activities. All things being equal, something or someone has greater significant value in a socialist or communist political system when they are deemed to be more important by those in power. That is to say, Importance is largely dependent on the will of the government.

A totalitarian political system is based on the belief that paternal protection is essential for the well-being of society, that a single person or political party exercises absolute control over all spheres of human life and prohibits any real challenge or opposition that might threaten its rule, and that government control is formed on the basis of single political parties, single religious groups or principles, or single tribes or sects. All things being equal, something or someone has greater significant value in a totalitarian political system when they are aligned with the prevailing power holders. That is to say, Importance is largely dependent on the particular leader(s)' discretion.

So, all things considered, let us say that governments can administrate in a way that impacts our sense of selves. From a democratic perspective, our significant value might be seen on the higher side, as *interdependent competitors/partners*. The individual actor is critically important within this context; they actively, directly vote on and run the system. From a socialist perspective, our significant value might be seen in a more moderate manner, as *collectively coordinated members*. The individual actor is somewhat important within this context; they indirectly enable the system. From a totalitarian perspective, our significant value might be seen on the lower side, as *paternalistically overseen pawns*. The individual actor is generally less important within this context; they passively execute the system.

Economic Systems

We might also address the question "Am I important?" from an institutional perspective by next looking at it in the economic dimension.

Economic systems (i.e., economies) refer to the means of production and distribution of goods and services as well as allocation of resources in a society.[78] They comprise economic actors, homo economicus, or persons that desire to maximize their needs and desires.[79] In essence, an economic definition of self, and by extension one's significant value, can be found within one's role in one's production and consumption system. Since there are many different types of economic system, it stands to reason that they would view the individual, and as such the significant value of the individual, in different lights.

There are three broad types of economic systems:[80] capitalistic or market economies, command or central economies, and mixed economies.

Within a capitalistic or market economic system, (a) productive activities are privately owned, (b) production is determined by the interaction of supply and demand, signaled by the (market) price system, and (c) governments facilitate free and fair competition between agents. All things being equal, something or someone has greater significant value when there is increased desirability and decreased availability for that resource. That is to say, Importance is dependent on the "invisible" hand of supply and demand.

Within a command or centralized economic system, (a) productive activities are state owned, (b) production is determined by centralized planners, and (c) governments determine and allocate what is best for the good of society. All things being equal, something or someone has greater significant value when it is deemed as such by those few persons who are charged with its determination. That is to say, Importance is dependent on the "visible" hand of government planning.

Within a mixed economic system, (a) there are both privately and state-held sectors of productive activities, (b) production is determined by both free markets and centralized planners, and (c) governments adopt a strategic portfolio approach to the economy with varying degrees of proactive and reactive stewardship. Thus Importance is dependent on a hybrid of the "visible" and "invisible" hands.

So, all things considered, let us say that economies can be guided in a way that impacts our sense of selves. From a capitalistic perspective, our significant value might be seen on the higher side, as *privately incentivized agents*. The individual actor is critically important within this context; they drive the system. From a mixed perspective, our significant value might be seen as a middle ground within the above, as *strategically deployed but autonomous assets*. The individual actor is moderately important within this context; they contribute to the system. From a command perspective, our significant value might be seen on the lower side, as *publicly controlled instruments*. The individual actor is generally less important within this context; they are largely compliant, acquiescent agents within the system.

Legal Systems

We might further address the question "Am I important?" from an institutional perspective by finally looking at it in the legal dimension.

Legal systems refer to the means of interpreting and enforcing the laws of a society. They are composed of rules or laws that regulate behavior along with the processes by which the laws are enforced and through which redress for grievances is obtained. Legal systems typically include (a) a judicial system (the judiciary) to determine, interpret, apply, and resolve disputes within the law in the name of the state, and (b) a criminal justice system—law enforcement that is directly involved in apprehending, prosecuting, defending, sentencing, and punishing those who are suspected or convicted of criminal offenses.[81] In essence a legal definition of self, and by extension one's significant value, can be found within one's role in their legal system as a (natural) person, in other words, a member of society, or not, and a holder of rank or office with all the rights to which that entitles him or her and the duties on which it imposes.[82] Specifically, legal persons can sue and be sued, own property, and enter into contracts.[83] Since there are many different types of legal systems, it stands to reason that different legal systems would view the individual, and as such the significant value of the individual, in different lights.

There are three broad types of legal systems:[84] common law, civil law, and theocratic law.

Within a common-law system, rules and regulations are based mainly on detailed sets of codes. Here the court system, via judges, oversees and resolves cases based on the interpretation of these characteristics to the particular circumstances. As such, there is a greater degree of flexibility to this system than some others.

Within a civil law system, rules and regulations are based mainly on tradition, precedent, and custom. Here the court system, via judges, oversees and resolves cases based on the application of these instructions to manifest situations. As such, there is less flexibility, and often less adversarial and equivocal argumentation, in this system than some others.

Within a theocratic law system, rules and regulations are based mainly on religious teachings. Here the court system, again via judges, oversees and resolves cases based on the revelation of these canons and teachings to ascribed/proscribed situations. As such, there tends to be more strictness in these systems than in others.

So, all things considered, let us say that legal systems can be adjudicated in a way that impacts our sense of selves. From a common-law perspective, our significant value might be seen as an *interaction of path-dependent actors*. The individual actor is critically important within this context; they interpret the system. From a civil-law perspective, our significant value might be seen as an *aggregation of strictly systematized participants*. The individual actor is moderately important within this context; they cumulatively compose the system. From a theocratic perspective, our significant value might be seen as a *congregate of divinely guided subjects*. The individual actor is generally seen as less important within this context; they tend to be more passive, conforming agents within the system.

Summary

Taken together, the bottom line of such an inquiry might be that there are many factors—from economics, political science, and law—that influence how we see and assess ourselves as an (important) institutional entity and how we form *institutional (economic-political-legal) identities*.

Am I Important PHILOSOPHICALLY...
as an Abstract or Spiritual Entity?

Now let me don my philosopher hat.[85] Philosophy asks the big questions. And "Am I important?" is certainly one of them. Without delving too far into its nuanced, technical, often esoteric, and frequently debated vernacular, let us try to extract some of the key aspects of a *philosophical* approach to Importance. Our goal here is twofold: to consider philosophic insights in the abstract in and of themselves (because it is good to think), and to explore what aspects need to be factored into our model (because it is also good to get things done—to better understand our Importance and manage it well).

From my particular philosophic perspective, one's self-subjective Importance can be seen *descriptively* as an aspect of the self's unique, persisting identity that is accessed through a process of self-knowledge and *evaluatively* to assess and ascribe a degree of respect to it.[86] So the philosophical questions that we need to ask here are, first, "Is there a self? Does it have an identity? And if so, can it be understood?" and second, "Can it be assessed? And if so, is it important?"

Descriptive

We might address the question "Am I important?" from a philosophic perspective by first looking at it in the *descriptive*: the self, identity, and self-knowledge.

There can be no sense of Importance if there is no self (i.e., nothing to talk about) or no way of understanding its identity (i.e., no way of talking about it).

When we consider such matters, we are in essence exploring the process of gaining self-knowledge. More precisely, and in more impressive language, we are considering the *epistemology* (method and nature of understanding) used to access one's *ontology* (reflections about the nature of one's existence). One way that we do this is by shining an introspective light on one's thoughts and feelings, values and motivations, experiences and perceptions, and a host of other dimensions. To consider self-knowledge from a Western perspective is to visit the worlds of Plato and Aristotle as well as Rene Descartes, John Locke, David Hume, Bertrand Russell, and a host of venerated others. There is (surprise, surprise!) no universal agreement to how these questions should be answered but instead a variety of subsequent debates both semantic and substantive.

The following is my take. Let us accept that, depending on your particular predilections and perspective, you may like it or dislike it, more or less. However, what is critical here is not so much the consensus of conclusion but rather having the consensual conversation. Rene Descartes[87] famously posited that we can know that we exist, that we have a nature, and that thinking, and this includes introspecting about one's existence, was proof of this existence and nature. You probably know the argument: *cogito ergo sum.* The thinking about the self is what validates that we have a self. And furthermore this knowledge of the self has been extolled as a hallmark or pinnacle of nature and existence—aka. wisdom (see Plato's *Apology*)—and among the highest achievements of those leading themselves and others toward the good (see Aristotle's *Ethica Nicomachea*). Indeed our extraordinary higher-order consciousness of the systemic, dynamic sense of self has been borne out by recent advances in neuroscience, complexity theory, and increasingly sophisticated models of the mind[88]. So, let us answer the question "Is there a self?" with a somewhat cautious but nevertheless fairly well corroborated *yes*. Whew, this is good news! Otherwise, with no self, we would be forced to end the book here . . . and my publisher would not be very pleased.

Now we move to the question of whether this self can be attributed a distinct nature or "identity." Let us say that the self has an identity—an active, discernable essence derived from synergistic sets of characteristics—to the extent that we can make self-attributions and that these attributions are distinctively cumulative, continuous, and reinforcing.[89] To this, as per Kierkegaard, it is we as "subjective thinkers" who engage our thought in the reflective inner understanding of our own consciousness so as to comprehend what is "true for me" and in this individually constructed reality discover how we are to then exist and live.[90]

Put another way, our subjective self-identity can be interpreted as both subject as well as object. I can be understood by *that I see* and *that I am seen.* If you have seen the wonderful James Cameron movie *Avatar* and recall the key phrase "I see you," this provides a way of making sense of the argument. Traditionally I, as the subject, can see. You, as the object, are seen. It is an external dyadic relationship. But I can also look inward to see myself. Thus I am also an object, and as such I can also be seen. The interesting twist in our book is that we are talking about "I see I." How we see ourselves, subject to the nature and biases endemic in ourselves as simultaneously the perceiver and the perceived.

The short explanation for how we see—this refers to self as subject, the first "I" in "I see I"—is that our perceived world is in essence a unique subjective construction of external reality, if indeed one even exists. It is expressed within an internal sense-making process. What I see is that which I (moderate argument) imperfectly perceive through my various senses, biases, and filters or (extreme argument) as entirely self-constructed.[91] In this view, the phrase "subjective reality" is redundant; our reality, the world that we see, is unavoidably subjective. Just witness the different realities that are voiced when different people watch the same newscast, political debate, or sporting event. The world that we think, feel, and act in is our world. And the "I" that we see, feel, and act on is our conception of the "I." This can be seen in the least expected of places, for example "reality" television—"Regardless of what the *American Idol* judges say, I am really a good singer." It can also be witnessed in myopic rhetoric such as "Regardless of the facts, even if they suggest that I might be in error, I will continue to assert that my unwavering opinion of this individual, policy, or issue is the correct one."

When explaining how we are seen—self as object, or the second "I" in "I see I"—the strategy that has worked best for me is to understand one's constructed identity as a distinct, reasonably coherent entity existing across both space and time. Said another way, one's self-subjective conception of one's identity is manifest as a distinctive, amalgamated individuality that is deemed inherently interconnected and consistent.

In terms of interconnection, we have an identity to the extent that there is an "I" to see that is composed of associated, combinable attributes and is separate from other objects. That our parts form a discernable entity, or at least one amenable to labels and categorization. Notwithstanding that the self is often opaque and its qualities and connections elusive,[92] looking introspectively can reveal us, inductively or deductively, as the product of coherent collections of experiences and/or bundles of perceptions about them.[93] Of course, this collection can be more or less complex depending on the particular psychological, material, and/or spiritual focus of investigation. My hands don't do something; I do something. My eyes don't see something; I see something. My mind does not think something; I think something. My heart does not feel something; I feel something. Processes and outcomes transcend one particular aspect or fragment of us. The dimensions form the whole. The pixels construct the picture.

In terms of continuity, we have an identity to the extent that the "I" has some consistency over time. Of course, we change and this change can be more or less dynamic depending on the nature and degree of growth, or regression, or alteration, in its past, present, and future states. Identity is a constantly, cumulatively constructed stream of discovery and choice.[94] You are not the same as you were 25 years ago, or perhaps 25 minutes ago, but the iterations of you are just that—successive adaptations and (hopefully new and improved, albeit with bigger bellies and less hair—or is that just me?) versions of you. The entity evolves. The stages form the process. The acts propel the play. The scenes construct the cinema.

Together, across its various interconnected dimensions and interwoven stages, it makes a lot of sense to refer to a "narrative of the self"[95]—a more or less coherent self-image that is constituted in the various stories that we tell about ourselves, about who we are, how we got here, and where we are going—that unfolds with a sense of agency (I am acting) and ownership (I am experiencing). Thus, as per thinkers such as Bergson and Heidegger, there is a reflective, dynamic, and malleable character of the self that can come together within a process to achieve an authentic existence. Or, if one subscribes to Hegel's *The Philosophy of History*, when these two core aspects of self-consciousness are merged—the self as something that can know and the self as something that can be known—one can achieve a unity and through this resultant freedom realize one's potential.[96]

So let us add the postulation that there is a subjective self and that we can be conscious about who we are—that we have an "internal sense"[97] about the self and its manifest identity.

The introspective process of discovering self-knowledge is thus implied to be both functional and expressive.[98] That is to say, it allows us to interact with, and function in, the outside world (i.e., society). The better we understand ourselves, the better we can express our states and have meaningful conversations. The better we understand ourselves, the better we can fit, adapt, and manage our states to fulfill our roles and achieve our goals. Furthermore, looking within oneself reinforces the notion that there is a self from which to look inside or outside. Looking within oneself also provides a direct access to our nature and reveals a unique type of evidence of one's self-understanding that is not created, shaped, or retranslated by another.[99] And our subjective conceptions, by some accounts, can even serve to create or constitute ourselves.[100]

So let us add the postulation that we are active in acquiring and shaping our subjective selves and that this self-knowledge process is useful.

Evaluative

We might also address the question "Am I important?" from a philosophic perspective by next looking at it in the *evaluative: self-value* and *self-respect*.

Is my identity—all or part of it—good? This certainly relates to one's sense of Importance. When we consider the evaluative nature of one's self and its Importance, we must discuss what value is (and if we have any, and if so, how much).

One way of understanding the nature of value is to separate it into (a) intrinsic value—the inherent, non-derivative Importance that something has "in and of itself"[101] and (b) extrinsic value, or that which is important by association with or via instrumentality to derive something of intrinsic value. Thus one's subjective value is inexorably intertwined with a double assessment of what one values and the approximation of how the self (however conceived across dimensions, time, and context) maps on to these values. Said another way, subjective value is related to one's sentiments about, thoughts on, motivations to, attitude toward, and/or expressed emotions from oneself in totality or part.[102]

In terms of intrinsic value, Importance can relate to what one terms inherently good and bad (ethical), pleasurable and painful (hedonistic), intentional and humane (c.f., Kant and his categorical imperative), utile (c.f., Bentham, Mill), or a number of other anchors.[103] It is not my place here to pontificate on what you or anyone should value, only to highlight the interdependency therein of one's self and the determining criteria. Thus one's assessment of alternative potential ideals influences their designation of subjective value. In terms of extrinsic or instrumental value, Importance can be related to whatever pragmatically works, effectively and efficiently, to "get the job done" within a specific scenario and achieve one's desired ends, whatever they may be,[104] whatever is deemed within a defined context to be contingently or conditionally good or bad. Thus one's assessment of alternative potential paths to one's ideals also influences their designation of subjective value.

So let us add the postulation that the ascription of value is dependent on subjective intentionality (where one wants to go—desired ends) and subjective instrumentalities (how one wants to get there—desired means). Self-subjective value, therefore, will similarly be dependent on how one embodies/achieves desired ends and executes desired means.

We now take the final step of this section, connecting value with respect. Intuitively, it makes sense that the more you value something, including yourself, the more you would respect it. But this is not necessarily the case. Respect, particularly self-respect, comes in various shapes and sizes. Here we will consider how we see it cognitively in our proverbial head, how we feel it affectively in our proverbial heart, and how we conatively translate it into reality via our proverbial action.[105]

In short, we process respect differently; it varies in dimension.

Respect is first and foremost an attitude, the cognitive response of a person to an object. And self-respect is that attitude aimed at oneself, when we are the object of our attention and evaluation. Greater respect is associated with differential attention and acknowledgement, versus being oblivious or indifferent, as well as valuation and reverence, versus being depreciative and belittling. If we have greater respect for something, it registers with us, and it works for us. If we have greater self-respect, we see our self as worthy of attention and admiration. Respect is also a sentiment. We just don't have respect; we also feel respect. Our feelings of respect relate to our emotional reactions to our sense of subjective Importance. These may be positive (e.g., pride, love, admiration). These may be negative (e.g., embarrassment, loathing, fear). Both negative and positive forms of affective responses can vary in degrees. We also act with more or less respect. That is, respect is also a category of action. One can treat oneself with more or less respect. Behavioral dimensions of respect relate to our motivational and related dispositions. To support . . . or not. To help . . . or harm. To promote and defend . . . or denigrate and deprecate.

We also experience respect differently; it varies in type.[106]

Here we focus on "evaluative" or "appraisal" respect, which is basically a sense that something *deserves* (by virtue of what it is) or *earns* (by virtue of what it does) our favorable thoughts, feelings, and treatment. When "deserves" is pointed inward, this may translate into self-respect based on whom one is (I am important because I am a human), the role that one occupies (I am important because I am a mother/doctor/senator), or the character traits that one possesses (I am important because I am strong/smart/pretty/funny). When "earns" is pointed inward, this may translate into self-respect based on what one does in general (I am important because I act as a good human), in a role (I am important because I behave as a good mother/doctor/senator), or along a particular dimension (I am important because I perform with greater power and can move things, intelligence and can solve things, grace and can attract things, or humor and can please things).

Notwithstanding the source, respect can be universal (based on common traits, positions, or actions) or differential (based on superior traits, higher ranking position, more effective or efficient action).

Universal respect for persons is often expressed in terms of rights and duties. Perhaps the most influential arguments in this area are credited to Immanuel Kant, who argued that people, by virtue of their common humanity, deserve respect and have an inherent dignity.[107] Hence his categorical imperative—the duty to treat persons as ends in themselves (i.e., possessing inherent worth and value) and never as merely means. Dignity in his eyes is "incomparable worth" that cannot be ranked or reduced. Of course, the latter points can be debated by differentiating (a) equality and equal worth versus (b) equity and fair or just worth, based on the level or place of one's role, the perceived quantity and quality of one's performance, or on the perceived supply and demand for one's wares.[108] That is to say, some may deserve or earn more respect from others. They may also deserve or earn more respect from themselves.

Kant also speaks of the duty of self-respect, and others such as John Rawls[109] of the duty for organizations and institutions to design just systems that foster individuals' self-respect, and here we get to the heart of the matter. Self-respect is roughly equated with an internal sense of worthiness, mostly but not exclusively associated with moral character, or, dare we say, subjective Importance. It can be seen, from the previous conversation, as a way of knowing and valuing one's self-identity. It can be judged from (a) absolute, objective standards and the degree to which you are deemed to approximate them, or (b) relative, subjective perspectives and the degree to which your desired character, actions, and/or roles are in harmony with and/or express your actual ones. Insofar as we speak here about one's subjective sense of Importance, we will focus on the latter.

Also consistent with what we discussed before, you may respect yourself equally or differentially, and in the latter case the variability in your self-respect can come from valuations of who you are (characteristics based), what you do (performance based), where you are located/categorized (role based), how you are seen by others (relationship based), or who you are associated with (affiliations based). Are you the type of person that you should be? Do you do what you should do? Do you occupy or serve a good role? Are you regarded well? Are you well connected?

So let us add the postulation that respect, and more specifically subjective self-respect, is multidimensional and can be given (or not) in a variety of forms and amounts as well as for a variety of reasons.

Integration with Religious Perspectives

It would be remiss to discuss philosophical insights on Importance without considering the domain of organized religion. Religion, as per aggregated encapsulations publicly presented by the BBC,[110] "can be explained as a set of beliefs concerning the cause, nature, and purpose of the universe, especially when considered as the creation of a superhuman agency or agencies, usually involving devotional and ritual observances, and often containing a moral code governing the conduct of human affairs." In religion, some might find sanctioned paths to Importance via a merging of the philosophical and the spiritual. Insofar as religions represent systems of shared beliefs and rituals concerned with the realm of the sacred, and that these systems advocate a set of moral principles or ethics that guide and shape behavior across major as well as everyday life events, they can certainly be seen to intersect with spiritual (and institutional) ideas regarding significance and value.

In terms of the focal topic of our book, whereas the organized religions of the world evidence a great range of beliefs and systems, they can also be seen to offer some common (or at least roughly reconcilable) ideas regarding the descriptive and evaluative nature of Importance (again as per a rudimentary analyses of the aggregated BBC encapsulations):

- We are important. Life is inherently valuable, precious, and dear. This is suggested in teachings that we should do no harm (Buddhism), that life is given by God, and that we are created in God's image and possess an inherent dignity (Christianity), the principle of ahimsa or non-violence (Hinduism), that all human life is sacred because it is given by Allah (Islam), that all life is of infinite value so that whoever preserves a life is as if he preserved the whole world (Judaism), and that we are inexorably connected to the natural world and the universe (Taoism).
- This Importance extends beyond the transient life. This is suggested in teachings that highlight the endless cycle of being, rebirth, and reincarnation (Buddhism), that each life is a manifestation of God in the world (Christianity), that there is an Atman or eternal self-spirit-soul that is pervaded by a transcendent Brahman power (Hinduism), that humans should not interfere with the will of the eternal (Islam), that there is an omnipresent, omnipotent, eternal, and accessible God that works in the

world and is interested in each individual (Judaism), and that all things are unified and connected in and across time (Taoism).

- Right thinking, right feeling, and right action can enrich Importance. This is suggested in teachings advocating personal spiritual development (Buddhism), the unique capacity of people for rational existence and to see/live a life as close as possible to God's love (Christianity), the dharma or duty to act virtuously, fulfill obligations, and uphold the universe and society so that it might beget positive karma (Hinduism), the submission to the will of God and obedience to the revealed five pillars (Islam), the fulfillment of the covenant to keep God's laws and bring holiness to every aspect of their lives (Judaism), and that a person should take action by changing themselves and thus becoming an example of the good life to others by achieving harmony and unity (Taoism).

Summary

Taken together, the bottom line of such an inquiry might be that there are many factors—from a variety of transcendent perspectives and systems—that influence how we see and assess ourselves as an (important) philosophical and spiritual entity and how we form *philosophical and spiritual identities.*

Upshot of the Above

As we stated at the beginning of this chapter, what we know about Importance is based within and across many different areas of inquiry.

As a *physical* entity . . . to exist: We are important insofar as we reconcile our significance and value (a) within the natural sciences, as to our chemical/physical material essence, (b) within the life sciences, as to our biological/neurological organic essence, and (c) within the earth sciences, as to our ecological/geographical/meteorological systemic essence. Thus we can have more or less significantly valuable physical identities.

As a *psychological* entity . . . to be conscious: We are important insofar as we reconcile our significance and value (a) descriptively with regard to our personality and ability, (b) subjectively, with regard to our self-concept, values, and attitude, and (c) evaluatively, with regard to our self-assessment (including self-esteem, efficacy, and worth). Thus we can have more or less significantly valuable individual identities.

As a *social* entity . . . to be integrated: We are important insofar as we reconcile our significance and value (a) with our group(s) and our society(ies) and (b) with regard to the related roles, norms, power, status, and cultures that we as members are subject to. Thus we can have more or less significantly valuable social identities.

As a *functional/organizational* entity . . . to be managed: We are important insofar as we reconcile our significance and value (a) in a micro sense with

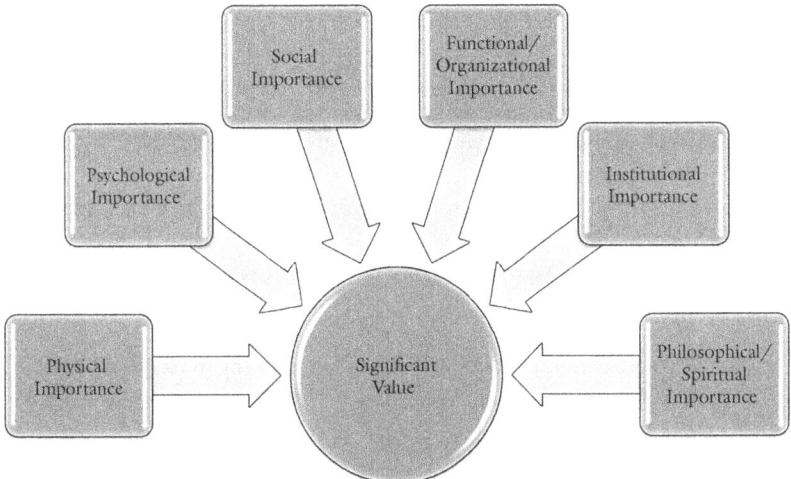

Figure 2.1   Diverse Perspectives on Significant Value.

our human capital (e.g., job-relevant knowledge, skills, and abilities), (b) in a meso sense with our participation in the management process (e.g., administration, practices, and roles), (c) in a macro sense with our contextual design (e.g., structure, culture, and systems), and (d) in a strategic sense with our orientation and engagement (e.g., competencies, advantage, and performance outcomes). Thus we can have more or less significantly valuable organizational identities.

As an *institutional* entity . . . to be established and codified: We are important insofar as we reconcile our significance and value with our political, economic, and legal context. Thus we can have more or less significantly valuable institutional identities.

As a *philosophical/spiritual* entity . . . to be realized: We are important insofar as we reconcile our significance and value (a) descriptively through our sense of self, identity, and self-knowledge and (b) evalutively, through our sense of intrinsic and extrinsic respect. Thus we can have more or less significantly valuable philosophical/spiritual identities.

As Figure 2.1 (above) suggests, all of the above pieces or perspectives of Importance must be considered for a proper understanding and treatment of one's significant value.

Informing an Integrated Model with the Above

The following chapters will draw from this aforementioned, and potentially synergistic, body of knowledge to systematically construct an integrated model of self- subjective Importance. We will do this by extracting, organizing, reconciling, and extending the previously discussed factors to make the following arguments:

- Conditions: There are different paths to Importance that are subject to different people's filters within their different contexts and as per their different criteria.
- Nature: These combine to influence different forces and different forms of Importance.
- Consequences: These can be used in different ways to facilitate different outcomes of Importance.

Drilling down deeper, the model will posit the following major factors at work within the above components.

Conditions

- Chapter 3: Our paths can be based on a variety of anchors, including characteristics, actions, acceptances, roles, and affiliations drivers.
- Chapter 4: Our profile can mediate the resonance of these paths based on a variety of dimensions, including values, motivations, abilities, personalities, and archetypes filters.
- Chapter 5: Our external context can moderate the above relationships based on a variety of factors, including locations, tasks, supports, and markets conditions.
- Chapter 6: Our internal criteria can moderate the above relationships based on a variety of factors, including scopes, times, frames, scales, and perspectives variables.

Nature

- Chapter 7: Our Importance can vary in force (valences and magnitudes), to be more or less balanced and grounded, and form (levels and stabilities), to be more or less fused and dynamic.

Consequences

- Chapter 8: We can use our Importance in more or less positive ways depending on the types of engagement, including their directions, functions, and expressions.
- Chapter 9: There are cognitive, affective, and conative/behavioral implications of our Importance that impact a variety of outcomes, including how we think, how we feel, and how we act.

So let us move forward and systematically consider these issues.

Part II

A Model of Importance

3

Path—The Drivers
of Importance

There are many different routes to Importance. One size does not fit all.

Chapter 3 presents the primary antecedents to Importance. In this chapter we will consider these different drivers or types of "paths." First, we will seek to UNDERSTAND how people traverse their particular path to pursue Importance through (a) characteristics, (b) actions, (c) acceptance, (d) roles, and (e) affiliations. The upshot of these choices will be reconciled along a continuum in terms of their relative internal and external focuses. Second, we will seek to IDENTIFY these different paths by sketching personal and professional case study illustrations. You might use them to see yourself (mirror) or others (window) more accurately. Third, we will seek to PERSONALIZE these different paths by presenting reflective exercises that you can use to relate them to your particular Importance journey. Fourth, we will seek to APPLY the above by deriving guided checklists that can help you make better personal choices and craft better management strategies.

UNDERSTAND . . .
The Different Paths to Importance

Why are some people obsessed with winning and being the best? Having a lot of money or a fancy title? Being smart or losing weight? Becoming popular or famous? Being seen on TV or going viral on YouTube?

This chapter will address these issues by taking up the underlying question "How do people feel important?" Stated plainly, "What are the drivers of Importance?" Stated technically, "What are the antecedents of Importance?" Stated colloquially, "How does one feel like a VIP?"

Or, in terms of our model, "What are the paths to Importance?"

Before we get started, a few points of clarification:

- POINT A: There are different paths to Importance. These drivers have fundamentally different features and gradients. They are distinct insofar as they represent different means to an end (i.e., different routes that one can take). Thus there is an equifinality to Importance.
- POINT B: The paths to Importance can be more internal or more external to a person, or in some instances a blend of both. Specifically, they can be primarily (via characteristics) or mostly (via actions) *internal* in nature, a mixture of the two (via acceptance), as well as mostly (via roles) or primarily (via affiliations) *external* in nature.
- POINT C: The paths to Importance are not mutually exclusive; even though they represent different routes, the paths may occasionally overlap or intersect. In fact, they (a) can be pursued simultaneously—a person can travel more than one at a time—and (b) may often be reinforcing—a person can use one (e.g., looks) to influence another (e.g., popularity). However, the paths are essentially independent because they are neither necessarily sufficient, inherently codetermined, nor universally or automatically correlated.
- POINT D: The paths to Importance can be conceived in either absolute or relative terms; to carry the metaphor forward, they can be single-lane or multi-lane boulevards. This is because they can be pursued and assessed (a) exclusively and absolutely, in and of themselves (e.g., excellent, pretty, centered, popular), or (b) relatively and comparatively, in relation to others' progress along common paths (e.g., more excellent, prettier, better centered, more popular).

Now for a discussion of the delineated paths (part one of the chapter).

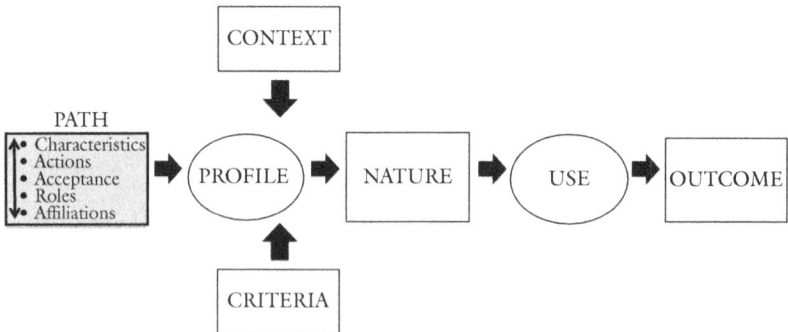

Figure 3.1   Antecedent Paths to Importance.

Path #1: Characteristics

First, you can pursue Importance through your *characteristics* (i.e., who you are—nouns and adjectives).

This is a completely *internal* path to significant value. It is just about you. So being a VIP is based inside yourself; it is about who you are. The message here is that some people pursue self-subjective significant value via the vehicle of their attributes. So you can become more important by improving your characteristics, or by being better. For example, a person can seek Importance via:

- Their figurative body: Based on physical stature and attributes
- Their figurative mind: Based on mental stature and attributes
- Their figurative soul: Based on spiritual stature and attributes

Physical
Some people seek Importance through their physical stature or attributes (i.e., body). Physical paths to Importance can take many forms, including a better look, better health, or better athleticism.

Perhaps if their body is *attractive* (good looks), people see themselves as important. So the better looking they are, the more significantly valuable they feel. In fact, many people have a passion for, and some even a near obsession about, their clothes, their hair, their makeup, their figures, their physical augmentations. And they might even evaluate others along this pathway (e.g., rating someone's looks on a scale, like "He's a ten . . . [or a two]"). Conceivably, this can be explained by evolutionary, innate, or even reinforced objectives to attract a mate. One's value rises with the greater number, and better quality, of partners that they can attract. Net net: Some measure their, and others', significant value by their looks. So they will feel of greater Importance when they look better (e.g., dressed nicely). Their sense of Importance will decline when they look worse (e.g., dressed raggedy).

Perhaps if their body is *healthy* (fit versus illness, disability, injury), people see themselves as important. So the healthier they are, the more significantly valuable they feel. In fact, many have a passion for, and some even a near obsession about, their food, their exercise, their weight, and their medical test numbers (High cholesterol! Low iron!). And they might even evaluate others along this pathway (e.g., commenting that "She's a fittie . . . [or a fattie]"). Conceivably, this can be explained by evolutionary, innate, or even reinforced objectives to increase "fitness" for breeding. One's value rises the better able they are to father or mother children. Net net: Some measure their, and others', significant value by their fitness (even consider the word itself: fit-ness). So they will feel of greater Importance when they feel well (e.g., after a good checkup). Their sense of Importance will decline when they feel ill (e.g., after a bad lab report).

Perhaps if their body is *athletic* (strong, fast, agile, etc.), people see themselves as important. So the more athletic they are, the more significantly valuable they feel. In fact, many have a passion for, and some even a near obsession about, their training, their workouts (reps, times, lifts, etc.), their practices, and their supplements. And they might even evaluate others along this pathway (e.g., commenting that "He's a starter/stud . . . [or a scrub/dud]"). Conceivably, this can be explained by evolutionary, innate, or even reinforced objectives to be a better hunter-gatherer or nurturer. One's value rises the better able they are to bring and maintain a supply of resources in the home. Net net: Some measure their, and others', significant value by their athleticism. So they will feel of greater Importance when they are able to play better (e.g., on a hot streak). Their sense of Importance will decline when their potential worsens (e.g., in a slump).

Taken together, if someone selects a physical characteristics path to Importance . . .

- Looks: They will tend to diet, dress nicely, and get made up.
- Fitness: They will tend to nourish their bodies and get their needed exercise.
- Athleticism: They will tend to train and practice hard.

And if their focus is more relative (versus absolute), it will be a priority to look *better* than others, to be *more* fit than others, and/or to train *harder* than others.

Mind you, people might do these things for other reasons as well. Not everyone who buys a nice outfit is doing so to feel important. However, the person who has defined their path to Importance in this manner will more likely pursue and emphasize these drivers.

So if you choose this path, then you will be a VIP when you are physically significant and valuable. VIPs here are driven by being more physically adept.

Mental
Some people seek Importance through their mental stature or attributes (i.e., mind). Mental paths to Importance can take many forms, including intelligence, cleverness, and wisdom.

Perhaps if their mind exhibits *intelligence* (smart, knowledgeable, brainy), people see themselves as important. So the smarter they are, the more significantly valuable they feel. In fact, many have a passion for, and some even a near obsession about, their grades, their studying, their reading, their learning. And they might even evaluate others along this pathway (e.g., commenting that "She's a brain . . . [or a dunce]"). Net net: Some measure their, and others', significant value by their intelligence. So they will feel of greater Importance when they feel smart (e.g., when their knowledge is validated). Their sense of Importance will decline when they feel dumb (e.g., when their ignorance is exposed).

Perhaps if their mind exhibits *cleverness* (witty, perceptive, shrewd), people see themselves as important. So the cleverer they are, the more significantly valuable they feel. In fact, many have a passion for, and some even a near obsession about, their debate, their arguments, their retorts, their wisecracks, their wiles. And they might even evaluate others along this pathway (e.g., commenting that "He's sharp . . . [or a dullard]"). Net net: Some measure their, and others', significant value by their wit. So they will feel of greater Importance when they feel clever (e.g., after a good joke or comment). Their sense of Importance will decline when they feel dull (e.g., when a retort flops).

Perhaps if their mind exhibits *wisdom* (sagacious, sound judgment), people see themselves as important. So the wiser they are, the more significantly valuable they feel. In fact, many have a passion for, and some even a near obsession about, their choices, their intuition, their gut, their expertise. And they might even evaluate others along this pathway (e.g., commenting that "She's a guru . . . [or a buffoon]"). Net net: Some measure their, and others', significant value by their wisdom. So they will feel of greater Importance when they feel prudent (e.g., when feeling assured about a decision). Their sense of Importance will decline when they feel careless (e.g., when feeling rash or reckless).

Taken together, if someone selects a mental characteristics path to Importance . . .

- Intelligence: They will seek to read, study, and digest data and information.
- Wit: They will seek to heighten their awareness and hone their intuition.
- Wisdom: They will seek to optimize their analytical and decision-making abilities.

And if their focus is relative (versus absolute), it will be a priority to know *more* than others, to see and react *better* than others, and/or to become *wiser* than others.

Again, people might do these things for other reasons as well. Not everyone who earns good grades is doing so to feel important. However, the person who has defined their path to Importance in this manner will more likely pursue and emphasize these drivers (and do well when playing along with the game show *Jeopardy*).

So if you choose this path, then you will be a VIP when you are mentally significant and valuable. VIPs here are driven by being more mentally adept.

Spiritual
Some people seek Importance through their spiritual stature or attributes (i.e., soul). Spiritual paths to Importance can take many forms, including peace, connection, and vitality.

Perhaps if their spirit is at *peace* (content, serene), people see themselves as important. So the more at peace they are, the more significantly valuable they feel. In fact, many have a passion for, and some even a near obsession about, their tranquility, their meditation, their calmness, their poise. And they might even evaluate others along this pathway (e.g., commenting that

"He's centered . . . [or off-kilter]"). Net net: Some measure their, and others', significant value by their inner peace. So they will feel of greater Importance when they feel serene (e.g., when meditating or deep in prayer). Their sense of Importance will decline when they feel restless (e.g., amidst a stressful or frantic episode).

Perhaps if their spirit is *connected* (embedded, linked), people see themselves as important. So the more in deep contact—with others, with transcendent beings and/or forces—they are, the more significantly valuable they feel. In fact, many have a passion for, and some even a near obsession about, their identification, their compassion, their service, their empathy. And they might even evaluate others along this pathway (e.g., commenting that "She's in tune . . . [or out of touch]" or maybe that "He's a giver . . . [or a taker]"). Net net: Some measure their, and others', significant value by their connection. So they will feel of greater Importance when they feel attached (e.g., when empathizing or understanding). Their sense of Importance will decline when they feel separated (e.g., when inner or outer conversations are not clicking).

Perhaps if their spirit is *vibrant* (energetic/alive), people see themselves as important. So the more vibrant they are, the more significantly valuable they feel. In fact, many have a passion for, and some even a near obsession about, their vim, their vigor, their energy, their enthusiasm. And they might even evaluate others along this pathway (e.g., commenting that "She's really alive, thriving, flourishing . . . [or lost, missing out, unengaged]"). Net net: Some measure their, and others', significant value by their vigor or élan. So they will feel of greater Importance when they feel alive (e.g., within a flow[1] state). Their sense of Importance will decline when they feel lifeless (e.g., when engulfed by apathy or ennui).

Taken together, if someone selects a spiritual characteristics path to Importance . . .

- Peaceful: They will try to reflect, be harmonious, and become more content.
- Connected: They will try to relate, be empathetic, and become more caring.
- Vibrant: They will try to exude, be engaged, and become more energized.

And if their focus is relative (versus absolute), it will be a priority to reflect *better* than others, to relate *better* than others, and/or to care *better* than others.

It is worth repeating a third time that people might do these things for other reasons as well. Not everyone who takes the time to reflect is doing so to feel important. However, the person who has defined their path to Importance in this manner will more likely pursue and emphasize these drivers.

So if you choose this path, then you will be a VIP when you are spiritually significant and valuable. VIPs here are driven by being more spiritually adept.

Path #2: Actions

Second, you can pursue Importance through your *actions* (i.e., what you do—verbs and adverbs).

This is *primarily,* but not exclusively, an *internal* path to significant value. It is mostly about you but also the interaction of you and your arena. Being a VIP is based on your deeds; it is about what you do. The message here is that some people pursue self-subjective significant value via the vehicle of their behaviors. So you can become more important by acting better. For example, a person can seek Importance via:

- "High" performance: Achieving behavior, excelling through your endeavors
- "Best" performance: Competing behavior, winning through your endeavors
- "Wide" performance: Participating behavior, experiencing through your endeavors

Achieving

Some people seek Importance by *achieving* a high level of performance (i.e., aiming to behave in an excellent or outstanding manner, to reach great heights). This is *not* a zero-sum game. A person assesses their actions independent of others. One person doing well does not mean that another did poorly or less well. Anyone can get an "A." Anyone can be important. It is simply a matter of walking the walk. The focus is absolute measurement of achievement—magnitude. There is a scale, and there exist better and worse parts on it. For example, getting a 95 percent is wonderful, but getting an 80 percent is less so. The goal is to strive. Do well. Be outstanding. This is reflected in the artist who creates a magnificent painting or song, or the scientist who discovers a penetrating truth. Net net: Some measure their, and others', significant value by their achievements. They will feel of greater Importance if they accomplish things up to their (high) standards (e.g., after receiving a good performance review). They will feel less Important if they do poorly (e.g., after being told that their work was wrong or subpar).

So if you choose this path, then you will be important when your actions allow you to achieve. VIPs here are driven by being high achievers.

Winning

Some people seek Importance by *winning* at a competitive level of performance (i.e., aiming to behave in a superior or victorious manner, to triumph). This *is* a zero-sum game. A person assesses their actions compared with others. If one person gains the prize, another does not. Only the best (or top percent) can get an "A." The victorious are important. It is simply a matter of winning the game. The focus is relative measurement of achievement—ranking. There is a curve, and there are superior/top and inferior/bottom parts on it. For example, getting a 95 percent is wonderful . . . only if others did not do as well (and it is not wonderful if they scored above you). The goal is to battle. Do better. This stands in sharp contrast to the "everyone gets a trophy" mentality. Net net: Some measure their, and others', significant value by their competitive ranking. They will feel of greater Importance if they win (e.g., coming in first place, besting the field, or beating a rival). They will feel less important if they lose (e.g., coming in second, third, or even last).

So if you choose this path, then you will be important when your actions allow you to win. VIPs here are driven by being winners.

Participating

Some people seek Importance by *participating* at any level of performance (i.e., aiming to behave in an active or enjoined manner, to dare to try). This is not per se a results-based game (although it could be if one were to compile and rate the quantity/quality of their check marks or compare them to others'). A person assesses their actions independent of a scored performance assessment. It is not a matter that one does well, it is only that one does something. Anyone who "throws their hat in the ring" and experiences life's opportunities can be important. It is simply a matter of getting involved. The focus is on involvement and exploration. There is a checklist, and there are completed/checked and incomplete/unchecked parts on it. For example, getting any grade is wonderful . . . as long as you endeavor to take the test. The goal is to experience. Do. Dare. This is reflected in Teddy Roosevelt's thoughts about crediting the man who moves off the proverbial sideline and wills himself to be "in the arena."[2] Net net: Some measure their, and others', significant value by their involvement. They will feel of greater Importance if they participate (e.g., when they ventured into the fray or got up on the dance floor). They will feel less important if they do not participate (e.g., when they stayed on the sidelines).

So if you choose this path, then you will be important when your actions allow you to participate. VIPs here are driven by being in the game.

Path #3—Acceptance

Third, you can pursue Importance through your *acceptance* (i.e., what you hear, how liked you are, type of feedback).

This is a harmonious blend or perfect *mix* of internal and external paths to significant value. It is about the reputation that others impart to you and, by extension, your characteristics and/or actions. It is based on how you are perceived and ultimately received or rejected by a focal social group.[3] As such, being a VIP is based on what other people think of you; it is about how you fit in. The message here is that some people pursue self-subjective significant value via the vehicle of their image. So you can become more important by elevating your reputation. For example, a person can seek Importance via:

- Intimate audience: How your closest family and friends see you
- Private audience: How your direct interactions see you
- Public audience: How your indirect peers and the general public see you

Intimate

Some people seek Importance by being well regarded by their intimate circle (i.e., closest family and friends). If the people closest to me like me and hold me in high esteem, I am important. This is a matter of your image within the central nucleus of your life (spouse, children, parents, relatives, best friends). The metric is core-circle acceptance and approval. Having high-quality relationships. Being/feeling "special." Symbols of this might include cherished notes/pictures and treasured heirlooms. Time might be spent interacting with, as well as hosting and visiting, the people closest to you. And your social media "friends" will be a small number of dear others. Net net: Some measure their, and others', significant value by their intimate acceptance. So they will feel of greater Importance if they have core approval (e.g., within a close-knit family). They will feel less Importance if they are not accepted in their central core (e.g., within a fractured family).

So if you choose this path, then you will be important when you gain acceptance within your intimate, immediate sphere. VIPs here are driven by being loved within their circle.

Private

Some people seek Importance by being well regarded in their personal or private relationships (i.e., colleagues, neighbors, and acquaintances). If the people that I interact with like me and hold me in high esteem, I am important. This is a matter of your image within the daily praxis of your life (coworkers, classmates, peers, customers and clients, service and product providers). The metric is proximal contacts and popularity. Having many online/network "friends" and "likes." Symbols of this might include social invitations and parties. Time might be spent interacting with, as well as hosting and visiting, local friendship networks, neighbors, and classmates. And your social media "friends" will be a medium number of past and present colleagues and acquaintances. Net net: Some measure their, and others', significant value by their private acceptance. So they will feel of greater Importance if they have network popularity (e.g., within a team of colleagues or a set of friendships). They will feel less important if they are not accepted in their network (e.g., within a tense or awkward group of reluctant associates).

So if you choose this path, then you will be important when you gain acceptance within your private, personal sphere. VIPs here are driven by being liked within their network.

Public

Some people seek Importance by being well regarded in their general or public renown (i.e., fans, followers). If the overall population (or a particularly relevant subset) likes me and esteems me, I am important. This is a matter of your eminence or prominence. The metric is general celebrity and fame. This is consistent with having a strong brand and creating an enduring legacy for all to see and admire. It is also frequently associated with being held apart in society. Symbols of this might include status recognition, media coverage, and even being granted special, uncommon privileges. Time might be spent visiting with news organizations, supporter and fan groups, and media outlets. And your social media "friends" will be a large (possibly enormous) number of everyone and anyone who will follow you and "like" you. Net net: Some measure their, and others', significant value by their public acceptance. So they will feel of greater Importance if they are famous (e.g., with a high number of Internet followers/likes or featured on the cover of a magazine). They will feel less important if they are not famous (e.g., with few followers/likes or when you Google yourself and get few hits).

So if you choose this path, then you will be important when you gain acceptance within the public, open sphere. VIPs here are driven by being revered in the public eye.

Path #4—Roles

Fourth, you can pursue Importance through your *roles* (how you are labeled, where you are placed, jobs/categories).

This is *primarily*, but not exclusively, an *external* path to significant value. It is about the inexorable interaction of your arena with you. Being a VIP is based on the centrality and criticality of your positions therein; it is about the parts that you play and the purpose that you serve. The focus is mainly on the role or office (e.g., president) and you as its "role occupant."[4] The more important the role is, by extension, the more important the person occupying it. The message here is that some people pursue self-subjective significant value via the vehicle of their formally, informally, or societally designated areas of responsibility and functionality (i.e., the degree to which they help people and other people rely on them). So you can become more important by elevating your place or position (e.g., level of tasks, duties, and authority). For example, a person can seek Importance via:

- Professional labels: Your place/position and responsibilities at work
- Personal labels: Your place/position and responsibilities at home
- Fundamental labels: Your place/position and responsibilities in society

Professional
Some people seek Importance by occupying an essential or prestigious role at work, serving a purpose, or helping people in a professional capacity. If I have a significant, valued (specific) job or (general) career, then I am important. For example some professional titles might be seen as more important than others, such as a doctor or lawyer. Some professional stages might be seen as more important than others, such as veteran as opposed to rookie. Some professional levels might be seen as more important than others, such as officer or executive. Notwithstanding, for all of these the metric is formal position. These distinctions can also be absolute (doctor, veteran, executive) or relative (specialty doctor, older veteran, upper executive). The people who set on this path will probably be proud of (and even display) symbols of their jobs and

careers, such as with business cards, desk nameplates, and titled signatures/ stationery. Net net: Some measure their, and others', significant value by their formal roles. So they will feel of greater Importance if they have an elevated or rising professional role status and impact (e.g., when they get a promotion). They will feel less important if their professional role is seen as lacking, disenfranchised, or declining in status and impact (e.g., when they are underemployed or lose their job).

So if you choose this path, then you will be important when you occupy important professional roles. VIPs here are driven by having significant, valuable positions at work.

Personal

Some people seek Importance by occupying an essential or prestigious role at home or in their community, serving a purpose or helping people in a personal capacity. If I play a significant, valuable (specific) part or (general) type of part, then I am important. For example some family roles might be seen as more important than others, such as parent or grandparent. Some social roles might be seen as more important than others, such as club director, party host, or block-party organizer. Some community roles might be seen as more important than others, such as advocate, coach, or pundit. Notwithstanding, for all of these the metric is informal position. These distinctions can also be absolute (sibling, organizer, coach) or relative (eldest sibling, lead organizer, head coach). The people who set on this path will probably be proud of (and even display) symbols of this, such as attire (#1 mom T-shirt, soccer coach windbreaker), bumper stickers, and photos. Net net: Some measure their, and others', significant value by their informal roles. So they will feel of greater Importance if they have an elevated or rising personal role status and impact (e.g., when their family standing improves or they are given a better proverbial or literal seat at the table). They will feel less important if their personal role is seen as lacking, disenfranchised, or declining in status and impact (e.g., when they are bumped to a side seat or relegated to the background).

So if you choose this path, then you will be important when you occupy important personal roles. VIPs here are driven by serving significant, valuable positions at home.

Fundamental

Some people seek Importance by occupying an essential or prestigious role in the general scope of things, serving a purpose or helping people in a fundamental capacity. If I occupy a significant, valuable (specific) position or (general) category or class, then I am important. For example, some generic categories might be seen as better than others. Some generic classes might be seen as better than others. Notwithstanding, for all of these the metric is basic place in the accepted societal hierarchy. This recalls the philosopher Plato's Republic and the differentiated tiers of citizenry[5] as well as projected distinctions based on general socioeconomic or other status. It is contrasted by the idea, voiced by Kant, King, and others, that every person or citizen warrants a common respect and deserves common rights.[6] These distinctions can also be absolute or relative (level or type of person or citizen). The people who set on this path will probably be proud of (and even display) symbols of this, such as class indicators, genealogical lineages, and so on. Net net: Some measure their, and others', significant value by their fundamental roles. So they will feel of greater Importance if they have an elevated or rising basic role status and impact (e.g., when they are listened to and their voice is heard or their vote is counted). They will feel less important if their basic role is seen as lacking, disenfranchised, or declining in status and impact (e.g., when their input and existence are belittled or ignored).

So if you choose this path, then you will be important when you occupy important fundamental roles. VIPs here driven by holding significant, valuable positions in society.

Path #5—Affiliations

Fifth, you can pursue Importance through your *affiliations* (i.e., where you are connected, associations or memberships).

This is an *external* path to significant value. It is about the outside organizations and causes that you connect yourself with. The focus is exclusively on them. The more important these connections and associations are, the more important the person feels. In essence, the Importance is second-hand. It is an imparted or once-removed path. Being a VIP is based on adopted or assumed Importance from someone or something else; it is about indirect proxies. The message here is that some people pursue self-subjective significant value via the vehicle of their attachments (i.e., the degree to which those other people, places, or things that you relate to are important). So you can become more important by connecting either explicitly or implicitly with a greater, more prominent, or more successful other. For example, a person can seek Importance via:

- Formal connections: Your official associations and memberships
- Informal connections: Your casual connections and proximities
- Vicarious connections: Your conjured, artificial identifications and affinities

Formal
Some people seek Importance by establishing official links with external others that they deem important. If I work at an important place, enroll in an important cause, or belong to an important club, then I am important. The metric is the Importance of the formal attachment. My company is important, so I am important. My country/state/town/school is important, so I am important. They might wear T-shirts or hats with their corporate logo or national flag. Net net: Some measure their, and others', significant value by their official associations. So they will feel of greater Importance if they have more important links and memberships (e.g., when they are a member of, or employed by, an A-list firm, lauded association, or esteemed organization).

They will feel less important if they lack these or have lesser attachments (e.g., when they are connected to a lower-level employer or an organization that is in decline).

So if you choose this path, then you will be Important when you create important formal associations and memberships. VIPs here are driven by being members of respected entities/organizations.

Informal

Some people seek Importance by establishing casual, less official connections with external things or others that they deem important. If I am seen with an important crowd or meet an important person, I am important. If I identify with—but not participate in per se—a particularly important cause or movement or traveled to (and was photographed at) an important place, then I am important. The metric is the Importance of the informal attachment. A family member is important, so I am important. My cause is important, so I am important. My friend/associate is important, so I am important. They might wear pins or use coffee mugs imprinted with their friends' formal connections, exhibit symbols of their hobbies and travels, or display and post photos of themselves with "important" others. Net net: Some measure their, and others', significant value by their casual associations. So they will feel of greater Importance if they have more important informal associations and connections (e.g., when they visit an important place or meet a "big shot" in the field). They will feel less important if their associations and connections are of smaller stature (e.g., when they have not visited places or met people of great repute).

So if you choose this path, then you will be Important when you create important informal connections and proximities. VIPs here are driven by being casually connected to respected entities/others.

Vicarious

Some people seek Importance by invoking sympathies with external others that they deem important. If I root for an important team (e.g., it is interesting to note that after a favorite team has emerged victorious from a game most fans typically proclaim "we" won) or wear the insignia of an important political or otherwise removed public personality, then I am important. The metric is the Importance of the conjured attachment. The sports team that I root for is important, so I am important. The musician/author/actor/politician that I follow on Twitter or like is important, so I am important. They might wear T-shirts or display posters with their favorite team, icon, or musician. Net net: Some measure their, and others', significant value by their manufactured or imagined associations. So they will feel of greater Importance if they create more important allegiances and sympathies (e.g., when their beloved professional sports team wins, preferred candidate gets elected, or their favorite band or movie receives an award). They will feel less Important if they have no allegiances or have lesser allegiances (e.g., when their adopted, artificial, and/or synthetic facade does not do well).

So if you choose this path, then you will be important when you create important vicarious identifications and affinities. VIPs here are driven by being allegiant with respected entities/things.

Upshot of the Above

I am important when . . .

> I *am* of significant value.
> I *do* things of significant value.
> I am *seen* by others as being of significant value.
> I serve a *function* of significant value.
> I am *affiliated* with an entity of significant value.

The following table illustrates the relationship between the different drivers or paths to Importance.

Table 3.1   Different Paths to Importance

INTERNAL <-------------------------------- MIX --------------------------------> EXTERNAL				
Characteristics	*Actions*	*Acceptance*	*Roles*	*Affiliations*
• Body	• Achieving	• Intimate	• Professional	• Formal
• Mind	• Winning	• Private	• Personal	• Informal
• Soul	• Participating	• Public	• Fundamental	• Vicarious

So some traverse more internally anchored paths to Importance, whereas others opt for more externally anchored paths to Importance. Notwithstanding, the greater the progress along your chosen path (characteristics, actions, acceptance, roles, affiliations), the stronger the path is to your self-subjective Importance.

An interesting example of the above can be found in the use of *money*. In our society, it is frequently felt that a sense of Importance can be gained, and even expanded, by money. Stated simply, a person is often deemed more significant and more valuable when they have more money. Money is certainly among the most malleable of objects (it can be exchanged for nearly all goods and services) and, as such, can afford someone esteem or power. However, it is our contention that, as is the case with most other tangible rewards and symbols, money may or may not reinforce any of the above paths. For instance, cast in a positive light, money might be interpreted:

- As a confirmation of one's *characteristics*: Money shows that I am smart, strong, together, and so on.
- As a measure of one's *actions* and performance: Money shows that I did a good job (and was compensated for it).
- As a social *acceptance* and status marker: Money shows that I am one who should be held in high regard and respected.

- As a legitimizer of a *role*: Money shows that my part/function is endorsed, impactful, and prioritized (note: there is sometimes an asymmetry between salary and job that causes us to question comparative pay scales, such as in the case of undercompensated teachers, parents, and public servants!).
- As access or entry to *affiliations*: Money gives me access and shows that I belong "here."

Alternatively, taking the contrary position, money is not seen the same way by everyone all the time in every place and under every circumstance. To various people and in various instances, it might have little to no associated or real correlation with the calibration of one's character, performance, status, role, or association. In addition, there are other types of less-tangible and non-financial symbols that might also, but again not automatically, feed into or validate any of these paths. Thus money in and of itself does not necessarily drive Importance but might serve as a convenient, salient (but not necessarily valid) heuristic for assessing and advancing oneself on one's chosen path.

IDENTIFY . . .
The Different Paths to Importance

In examining the following cases, please utilize them in the following ways:

1. In *general,* can you overlay the template from this chapter onto the scenes below and see the characters taking different paths to Importance?
2. Now, as a *mirror* (looking specifically at *you*): Do any of these characters remind you of you and help to reveal the paths to Importance that you choose?
3. Finally, as a *window* (looking at specific *others*): Do any of these characters remind you of someone else that you know and help to reveal the paths to Importance that they have chosen?

Case Study (Personal)

Dropping in at Home with the Normans

In the kids' playroom: Big sister is clearly very smart (characteristics/mind); she beams when she reads and writes. Young sister is very stylish and attractive (characteristics/body); she floats when she comes home from the mall with new clothes, hairdo, and makeup. Baby brother is very reflective (characteristics/ soul); nothing fazes him, and he is very content just being at peace in and connecting with the moment.

Around the dinner table: Uncle is very competitive (action/winning); he has to be better than you, do more than you, and have more than you. Aunt is very athletic (action/achieving); she broadcasts to all that will listen about her running every morning and working out every evening. Cousin is very well traveled (action/participating); she wears a T-shirt from her recent exotic trip and a hat from another one. Nephew is very popular (acceptance/ public); he spends much time honing his online profile brand and is always texting and checking social media pages for more "likes" and adding new "friends."

In the living room: Mom is very much into being "super-mom" (role/personal) with her school routines, bake-sale trays of fancy brownies, carpooling to extra-curricular activities, shared schedules, and ostentatious display of kids' home-made gifts. Dad is very much the proud teacher (role/professional); he wears a school pin symbolizing the university where he is a professor and insists that guests call him Dr., versus Mr., Norman. Grandpa is very much the "super-fan" (affiliation/vicarious), wearing his favorite team's jersey and talking about how if "we" get a new player, "we" will make it to the playoffs and again be world champions.

Case Study (Professional)

Behind the Scenes at the Gourmet Grille Restaurant

In the dining room: The regular waitstaff are all working tonight. The "brainy" waitress (characteristics/mind) is proud of the fact that she can recite the full menu and takes orders without using notes. The "hand-some" waiter (characteristics/body) relishes his perfect hair, a fashionable half beard, and a perfectly ironed uniform. The "laid-back" waitress (char-acteristics/soul) feels best when she calms the rambunctious children and relishes watching the beautiful sunset through the floor-to-ceiling bay win-dow. The regular customer beams with pride and takes every opportunity to share how long *his* restaurant has been here and how well *they* are doing (affiliation/vicarious).

At the bar: The senior bartender is very competitive (action/winning), bragging about his "signature" cocktails that are better and made faster than anyone else can do. The stock boy is a perfectionist (action/achieving), delighting in his perfectly piled provisions and real-time monitoring and supplying system to have the right amount of ice at the bar exactly when it is needed. The trainee is just glad to be here (action/participating) and can't wait to tell people how much she is doing and experiencing. The newly hired hostess (acceptance) talks to everyone, remembers their names, and joyfully greets them with a smile and a hug like they have been together all their lives.

In the kitchen: The grill-master clearly loves being a cook (role/professional); he is in heaven preparing food that nourishes and delights his customers and reflects well on his bosses. The salad chef (affiliation/formal) wears her Ivy League hat in place of the traditional white cook's hat with the logo prominently displayed, talking with whoever will listen about what the alma mater is doing and all the famous people who have graduated from it.

PERSONALIZE . . .
The Different Paths to Importance

This set of exercises gives you the opportunity to clarify your paths to significant value. A characteristics-based path measures your significant value based on who you are and have become. An actions-based path measures your significant value based on what you do. An acceptance-based path measures your significant value based on how you are seen. A role-based path measures your significant value based on the stature of your place/position. An affiliations-based path measures your significant value based on things that you associate yourself with. You can use this section to assess the degree to which you rely on different paths to significant value.

General

Come to grips with what drives your Importance and the paths that you take to pursue it.

At the most basic level, please rate the degree to which the following drivers are peripheral (low, say a "1") or central (high, say a "10") in determining your Importance. Please keep in mind that this is *not* what you want the truth to be—it should be an *honest* assessment of your reality as evidenced by your life story:

1. My characteristics: Who I am
2. My actions: What I do
3. My acceptance: What people think of me
4. My roles: The parts that I play
5. My affiliations: The things/others that I am associated with

Are you happy with your ratings? What would you change? How could you change this? Do your ratings suggest a more internal or external approach to Importance? Have the ratings changed as you have grown, experienced things, gone through life changes, or advanced in years? Is there any pattern to be found in these? Is there a sweet spot where everything fell into place? If so then how can you get (back) there?

Specific

Drill down further to isolate specific drivers and paths.

Now please note the degree to which you agree with the following ways for completing this sentence, from most to least descriptive of you:

I feel most important when I (am) . . .

Characteristics
- Body
  - Clad in nice clothes, look attractive and stylish
  - The best-looking person in the room or group
  - Eating well, exercising, and in good shape
  - The most athletic person on the team
- Mind
  - Knowledgeable about a topic
  - The smartest person in the room or class
  - Capable of making a wise decision about an issue
  - The most witty and clever person in the conversation
- Soul
  - At peace with myself
  - The most caring, connected person in the room or congregation
  - A vibrant champion of my beliefs and values
  - The most engaged, committed volunteer on the mission

Actions
- Achieving
  - Attaining high performance standards
  - Reaching set goals and objectives
  - Accomplishing outstanding results
  - Realizing excellence in my deeds and dealings
- Winning
  - Outpacing others and attaining higher performance standards
  - Prevailing above others and reaching greater goals and objectives
  - Defeating others and accomplishing superior results
  - Surpassing others and realizing greater degrees of excellence
- Participating
  - Striving to do my best
  - Daring to reach for goals and objectives
  - Experiencing new, different things and broadening my horizons
  - Taking steps to improve my deeds and dealings

Acceptance
- Intimate
  - Well regarded by my immediate family (parents, partner, children)
  - Liked by my extended family (cousins, aunts and uncles, in-laws)
  - Alerted to family news and invited to family events
  - Adored by my very best friend(s)
- Private
  - Well regarded by my peers and coworkers
  - Liked by my extended peers (e.g., online friends)
  - Alerted to social news and invited to social events
  - Adored by my circles and cliques

- Public
  - Well regarded in my area or neighborhood
  - Liked by the general public and press/media
  - Alerted to world news and invited to world events
  - Adored by people whom I have never met

Roles
- Professional
  - Work in a well-respected career or occupation
  - Hold a key position(s) and higher authority in my work organization
  - Have an impressive business title
  - Regarded as someone with meaningful job-related tasks, duties, and responsibilities
- Personal
  - Work in a well-respected family or interest group
  - Hold a key position(s) and greater status in my associations and groups
  - Have an impressive unofficial title or nickname
  - Regarded as someone with meaningful home-related tasks, duties, and responsibilities
- Fundamental
  - Work in a well-respected intention or cause
  - Hold a key position(s) and greater standing in my society
  - Have an impressive impression or image
  - Regarded as someone with meaningful societal tasks, duties, and responsibilities

Affiliations
- Formal
  - Directly belong to an organization that is regarded as important
  - Legitimately linked to a person, place, or thing that is regarded as important
  - A full-time member of what one sees as important
  - Officially recognized with something that is important
- Informal
  - Indirectly connected with someone who is regarded as important
  - Have experiences with a person, place, or thing that is regarded as important
  - A part-time participant with what one sees as important
  - Unofficially associated with something that is important
- Vicarious
  - Identify with someone or something that is regarded as important
  - Vaguely associated to a person, place, or thing that is regarded as important
  - A sympathetic supporter with what one sees as important
  - Casually or loosely coupled with something that is important

APPLY . . .
The Different Paths to Importance

From a personal perspective, your Importance is partly determined by the choices that you make about your path(s). From a professional perspective, your people's Importance is partly determined by the management strategies that you employ to help them shape the path(s) that they choose.

Please take a moment to apply the material from this chapter to make better choices and craft better strategies about the paths to Importance.

Making Personal Choices

Choice 1: You are, to varying degrees, in control of your path(s) to Importance.

That is to say, you can select a particular path, improve on its execution, and/or see it in a different light.

So target, enhance, and interpret your paths to optimize (not maximize per se—see Chapter 7) Importance.

Choice 1a: Choose to focus on *characteristics*, or not. If so, purposefully select and proactively, appropriately affect your focal characteristic(s).

> Is the *physical* most central to me? How will I (objectively) shape and then (subjectively) see my body? Can I look better? Can I like my looks? Can I become more fit? Do I feel OK with my fitness? Can I improve my athleticism? Is my athleticism fine?

> Is the *mental* most central to me? How will I (objectively) shape and then (subjectively) see my mind? Can I be smarter? Can I accept my level of intelligence? Can I become sharper? Do I feel OK with my wittiness and jocularity? Can I improve my decision making? Is my judgment fine?

> Is the *spiritual* most central to me? How will I (objectively) shape and then (subjectively) see my soul? Can I be more at peace? Can I accept my level of tranquility? Can I become more compassionate? Do I feel OK with my level of connection? Can I become more vibrant? Is my level of energy OK?

Choice 1b. Choose to focus on *actions*, or not. If so, purposefully select and proactively, appropriately affect your focal action(s).

> Is *achieving* most central to me? How will I (objectively) shape and then (subjectively) see my achievements? Can I do better? Can I like the way that I perform?

> Is *winning* most central to me? How will I (objectively) shape and then (subjectively) see my competitiveness? Can I rank better? Can I like the way that I rank?

> Is *participating* most central to me? How will I (objectively) shape and then (subjectively) see my participation? Can I be more involved? Can I like the level of my involvement?

Choice 1c. Choose to focus on *acceptance*, or not. If so, purposefully select and proactively, appropriately affect your focal acceptance(s).

Is the *intimate* most central to me? How will I (objectively) shape and then (subjectively) see my intimate relationships? Can I be more accepted in my core circle? Am I OK with the way that I am intimately accepted?

Is the *personal* most central to me? How will I (objectively) shape and then (subjectively) see my personal relationships? Can I be more accepted in my networks? Am I OK with the way that I am personally accepted?

Is the *public* most central to me? How will I (objectively) shape and then (subjectively) see my public relationships? Can I be more accepted in general? Am I OK with the way that I am publicly accepted?

Choice 1d. Choose to focus on *roles*, or not. If so, purposefully select and proactively, appropriately affect your focal role(s).

Is the *professional* most central to me? How will I (objectively) shape and then (subjectively) see my professional roles? Can I occupy better professional roles? Am I OK with the professional roles that I occupy?

Is the *personal* most central to me? How will I (objectively) shape and then (subjectively) see my personal roles? Can I occupy better personal roles? Am I OK with the personal roles that I occupy?

Is the *basic* most central to me? How will I (objectively) shape and then (subjectively) see my fundamental roles? Can I occupy better fundamental roles? Am I OK with the fundamental roles that I occupy?

Choice 1e. Choose to focus on *affiliations*, or not. If so, purposefully select and proactively, appropriately affect your focal affiliation(s).

Is the *formal* most central to me? How will I (objectively) shape and then (subjectively) see my formal affiliations? Can I create better formal affiliations? Am I OK with the formal affiliations that I create?

Is the *informal* most central to me? How will I (objectively) shape and then (subjectively) see my informal affiliations? Can I create better informal affiliations? Am I OK with the informal affiliations that I create?

Is the *vicarious* most central to me? How will I (objectively) shape and then (subjectively) see my vicarious affiliations? Can I create better vicarious affiliations? Am I OK with the vicarious affiliations that I create?

Crafting Management Strategies

Management Strategy 1: You can, to varying degrees, influence others' path(s) to Importance.

That is to say, you can facilitate or inhibit others' selected paths, their execution, and/or their interpretation. In a manner similar to the preceding section, you can help or hinder other people as they choose their paths, advance on their paths, and make sense of their paths.

This can happen at work, at home, or anywhere.

This can happen in any vertical direction—helping someone below or helping someone above. For example, flowing down, as a boss helping their reports, or a parent helping their kids, or a teacher helping their students, or a coach helping their players. It can also flow up, when you give a boost to those above you.

This can happen in any lateral direction—helping someone at the same level inside your organization or outside your organization. For example, where peers (colleagues, friends, neighbors, etc.) help or harm each other.

This can happen in any modality—helping someone directly one on one or indirectly via systematically designed and institutionalized practices. For example, regarding the latter, where you embed these into the prevailing designs, cultures, and selection, appraisal, and reward systems. For instance, if you establish a reporting hierarchy based on expertise, create a culture esteeming appearance or competiveness, or establish a reward system prioritizing popularity or experience.

So guide, boost, and encourage others' paths to optimize (not maximize per se—see Chapter 7) their Importance.

Strategy 1a. You can focus them on their particular *characteristic(s)*, or not. If appropriate, and if in need of encouragement (a) purposefully boost and/or (b) proactively and positively frame their physical, mental, or spiritual attributes. For example:

> Help them improve or feel better about their looks. Show them how they look or can look beautiful versus retarding their physical growth or saying something like "You look horrible."

> Help them improve or feel better about their intellect. Show them how they are or can be smart versus retarding their cognitive growth or saying something like "You are dumb."

> Help them improve or feel better about their peacefulness. Show them how they are or can be good versus retarding their spiritual growth or saying something like "You are bad."

Strategy 1b. You can focus them on their particular *action(s)*, or not. If appropriate, and if in need of encouragement (a) purposefully boost and/or (b) proactively and positively frame their levels of achievement, ranking, or involvement. For example:

> Help them achieve or feel better about their level of achievement. Show them how they did or can do great versus inhibiting their performance or saying something like "You can't do it; you always make mistakes."

Help them win or feel better about their competitiveness. Show them how they are or can be winners versus inhibiting their success or saying something like "You are a loser; so many people did so much better."

Help them engage or feel better about their involvement. Show them how they are or can be contributing versus inhibiting their involvement or saying something like "You are peripheral; you can never participate."

Strategy 1c. You can focus them on their particular *acceptance(s)*, or not. If appropriate, and if in need of encouragement (a) purposefully boost and/or (b) proactively and positively frame their intimate, private, or public liking. For example:

Help them strengthen or feel better about their circle. Show them how their family thinks or can think the world of them versus demeaning their core or saying something like "You are not worthy of love."

Help them strengthen or feel better about their network. Show them how they have or can have many friends versus demeaning their network or saying something like "You are not worthy of affection."

Help them strengthen or feel better about their reputation. Show them how they are or can be beloved versus demeaning their image or saying something like "You are not worthy of respect."

Strategy 1d. You can focus them on their particular *role(s)*, or not. If appropriate, and if in need of encouragement (a) purposefully boost and/or (b) proactively and positively frame their professional, personal, or fundamental roles. For example:

Help them enhance or feel better about their professional role(s). Show them how their (potential) career is or can be fantastic versus tearing down their profession or saying something like "Your work/job doesn't matter."

Help them enhance or feel better about their personal role(s). Show them how their (potential) parenting is or can be fantastic versus tearing down their home life or saying something like "Your family/friendship doesn't matter."

Help them enhance or feel better about their fundamental role(s). Show them how their (potential) contribution is or can be fantastic versus tearing down their fundamental stature or saying something like "Your existence/state doesn't matter."

Strategy 1e. You can focus them on their particular *affiliation(s)*, or not. If appropriate, and if in need of encouragement (a) purposefully boost and/or (b) proactively and positively frame their formal, informal, or vicarious affiliations. For example:

Help them build up or feel better about their organizations. Show them how they work or can work for a (potentially) great company or school versus disregarding their membership or saying something like "Your company or school is not that great."

Help them build up or feel better about their associations. Show them how they belong or can belong to a (potentially) great cause or interest group versus disregarding their connections or saying something like "Your cause or hobby is not so hot."

Help them build up or feel better about their affinities. Show them how their favored sports team or music band is or can be (potentially) outstanding versus disregarding their favorites or saying something like "Your favorite team or band is a failure."

Checkpoint

Now that we have concluded this chapter, it is appropriate to pause for a moment at this checkpoint and answer the following questions:

- Do you UNDERSTAND the different paths to Importance?
- Can you IDENTIFY the paths in personal and professional settings?
- Have you PERSONALIZED the paths by relating them to your own Importance journey?
- Will you APPLY the above to (a) develop your path-related plans and make better choices and (b) facilitate others' path-related plans and craft better strategies?

If not, circle back.

If so, let's move on to the next part of the model: *profile* and the filter-related mediators of Importance.

4

Profile—The Filters of Importance

*Your approach to Importance with be more resonant
when it is more customized and congruent.*

Chapter 4 presents the key mediators to Importance. In this chapter we will consider these different "profiles" to Importance. First we will seek to UNDERSTAND how people process the paths through their own particular:

- Value filters, including beliefs and priorities
- Motivation filters, including goals and needs
- Aptitude filters, including skills and abilities
- Personality filters, including traits and dispositions
- Archetype filters, including prototypes and stereotypes

The upshot of these choices will be reconciled in terms of their impact on, or regulation of, the impacts of the different aforementioned paths. Second, we will seek to IDENTIFY these filters by sketching personal and professional case study illustrations. You might use them to see yourself (mirror) or others (window) more accurately. Third, we will seek to PERSONALIZE these filters by presenting reflective exercises that you can use to relate them to your particular Importance journey. Fourth, we will seek to APPLY the above by deriving guided checklists that can help you make better personal choices and craft better management strategies.

UNDERSTAND . . .
The Different Filters of Importance

Why do people choose different paths to Importance? Are some choices inherently better than others? Can a path affect one person positively yet another negatively? One person more yet another person less? Is it possible for the same path to feel right for one person yet wrong for another?

This chapter will address these issues by taking up the underlying question "What makes a particular path to Importance work better or worse for a particular individual?" Stated plainly, "What are the personal factors influencing Importance?" Stated colloquially, "Why do certain factors make certain people feel like a VIP?"

Or, in terms of our model, "What are the mediators of Importance?"

Here we will advance the proposition that the power of our paths to impact our Importance is filtered through our *profile*. Therefore, the paths will impact different people differently. Lesson: Make sure that your path is consistent with who you truly are.

Before we get started, a few points of clarification:

- POINT A: People are different. We care about different things (values). We strive for different things (goals/needs). We are better at different things (abilities). We embody different preferences and patterns (personality). We model different categories and dimensions, both in terms of desired ideals (prototypes) and accepted/attributed pigeonholes (stereotypes and archetypes).
- POINT B: Consistency and congruency is key. It affects the degree to which a path will resonate with a person. Each person must construct their own path relative to their unique set of conscience and circumstance.[1] A path is more likely to lead to a healthy, sustainable self-subjective Importance where there is a better fit with our profile; it is less likely when there is a worse fit with our profile.
- POINT C: Our profiles are complex and can include a large variety of dimensions. They are also somewhat malleable and dynamic. Therefore, the following list of filters discussed in this chapter will *not* be comprehensive or definitive. However, they are presented here because they are seen as particularly potent and, at a given point in time as well as over time, should be in harmony with our path to produce positive results.

Now for a discussion of some key aspects of profile.

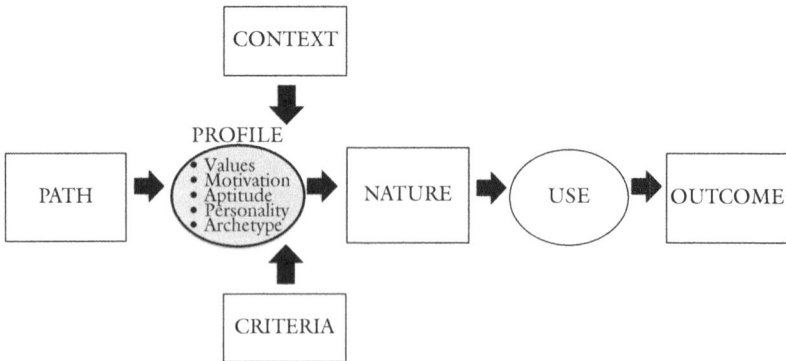

Figure 4.1   Profile Mediators of Importance.

Filter #1: The Aspect of Values—Our Beliefs and Priorities

First, our paths to Importance impact us differently depending on our *values*. As you recall from Chapter 2, personal values refer to the relatively stable sets of underlying principles that guide our choices and actions. Value sets include both the things that we want and the ways that we want to get them. That is to say, also per earlier discussion, they relate to our:

- Terminal values: Ends, where to go, content priorities
- Instrumental values: Means, how to get there, process priorities

The basic argument here is this: When a path is more consistent/congruent with our values, it is more resonant and, as such, amplifies or magnifies the impact of that particular driver. If a path gels with our desired ends and gets us to where we want to go, it will work better for us. If a path gels with our desired means and gets us there in the way that we want, it will work better for us.

For example, focusing first on terminal/content values:

Being athletic will be a resonant path to our significant value particularly when (a) we believe that *characteristics* are important and we prioritize them in our life, (b) we believe that *physical* aspects of characteristics are important and we prioritize them in our life, and (c) we believe that the *athleticism* aspects of physical characteristics are important and we prioritize them in our life.

Being fit and in shape will *not* be a resonant path to our significant value particularly when our beliefs and priorities are not consistent with a characteristics-based path (perhaps they are more action, role, acceptance, or affiliation based), or focus on a different aspect of characteristics (perhaps mental or spiritual based), or elevate a different embodiment of physical characteristics (perhaps attraction or health based).

The same logic applies to other types of paths as well. When someone believes more in deeds—the proverbial "actions speak louder than words"—they will be more likely to pursue an action path, and this path will bring to them the greatest "bang for the buck." Same for being smart. Same for being passionate about winning or being the best. Same for pursuing popularity. The point is that our paths work better for us when they are aligned with our elevated objectives and priorities.

So, in general, someone will be more likely to choose a path, and the path will be more likely to make them feel like a VIP, when it gels with their *terminal values*.

Now let's consider instrumental/process values:

If we believe that a home-centered, family-oriented path is the best means to Importance—and as such we prioritize characteristics, actions, roles, acceptance, and affiliations that are achieved through the family—approaching our paths in this way will work better for us. We will then feel of significant value, a proverbial VIP, when we travel the paths in a family-oriented manner. Family smart. Family wins. Family responsibilities. Family approval. Family networks.

If instead we believe that a work-centered, career-oriented life is a better means to Importance—and as such we prioritize characteristics, actions, roles, acceptance, and affiliations that are achieved through the job—approaching our paths in this way will work better for us. We will then feel of significant value, a proverbial VIP, when we travel the paths in a career-oriented manner. Career smart. Career wins. Career responsibilities. Career approval. Career networks.

We could add other examples of means to the mix as well. Conservatively or creatively traveling our paths. Aggressively or passively traveling our paths. Experimentally or consistently traveling our paths. Selfishly or benevolently traveling our paths. Honestly or manipulatively traveling our paths. Gregariously or solely traveling our paths. The point is that our paths work better for us when they are aligned with our preferred, prioritized processes.

So, in general, someone will be more likely to choose a path, and the path will be more likely to make them feel like a VIP, when it gels with their *instrumental values.*

Taken together, value filters shed light on Importance insofar as they show how a path will resonate more with a person when it supports their particular beliefs and preferences. Bottom line: VIPs are best propelled by paths that gel with their values.

Filter #2: The Aspect of Motivation—Our Goals and Needs

Second, our paths to Importance impact us differently depending on our *motivations.*

As you recall from Chapter 2, motivation is a gap-filling process whereby we seek to bridge a divide, or more specifically to move between where we see (a) our current position and (b) our desired position. In fact, the word "motivation" itself is derived from the root signifying "to move." Motivation is influenced by factors such as the way that we determine our desired position (that is, set our goals) and assess our current position (that is, target our needs). As such, also per earlier discussion, our motivation is thereby determined by a collection of factors including:

- Current state: Needs; assessed as per level and type of requirements
- Desired state: Goals; plotted as per level and type of intentions

The basic argument is this: When a path is more consistent/congruent with our motivations, it is more resonant and, as such, amplifies or magnifies the impact of that particular driver. If a path helps us fulfill our needs, helps propel us toward our goals, it will work better for us.

There are many theories of motivation that can be used to illustrate this. We choose a few below. We will focus first on current (need) states.

Our needs and strivings influence the character of the self.[2] According to classic needs theories,[3] people have different active needs, and they can be arranged along a continuum from lower-order (extrinsically satisfied) to higher-order (intrinsically satisfied) needs. If a path addresses a person's particular active needs—perhaps for some these are lower-order physiological, safety, and existence needs; perhaps for others these are middle-order social, relatedness, and affiliation needs; and perhaps for still others these are higher-order actualization, growth, and achievement needs—they will be more resonant. Alternatively, if paths address needs that are not active in a particular individual at a particular time (i.e., they miss the mark), they will have minimal attraction and impact.

For example, paths that satisfy actualization (c.f., Maslow), growth (c.f., Alderfer), or achievement (c.f., McClelland) concerns will impact a person's significant value, particularly when they are focused on these needs. Alternatively, if a person is focused on different sets of needs, the paths that emphasize them will be less desirable and of lesser impact. To this point, a person will *not* be attracted to or moved by a path that promises them more growth and development if they are motivated primarily by different sets of needs, such as eating or socializing. This explains two common mistakes that we make:

1. Assuming that everyone is similar and wants the same things—see the discussion below about "love." For example, not everyone wants to take a difficult class or be challenged at their job.
2. Assuming that everyone wants the same things that you want. When we project ourselves onto others, we fail to see them as individuals and constrain our ability to detect and satisfy their particular needs. For example, just because I care about becoming famous or being the center of attention doesn't mean that my coworkers share these desires and will want to pursue similar paths.

Take, for instance, the example of love. In the motivation literature love is frequently conceptualized as a type or category of need. For example, it is akin to Abraham Maslow's social/belongingness need and hierarchically speaking is placed above physical and security needs and below achievement and actualization needs. It is akin to Clayton Alderfer's modeling of relatedness need and lies between existence and growth needs. As per the previous paragraph, we can make similar arguments and cite like examples with regard to the criticality of fit for this need category. In short, if a person has a greater need for love (or related constructs such as affection, belongingness, etc.) in general or specific to a particular place and time, getting it will resonate more, and paths that satisfy this need will have a greater impact on their self-subjective Importance.

There are two additional points regarding love that are worthy of a brief mention. First, that it is a complex thing. In fact, psychologist Robert Sternberg developed a multi-component model consisting of three primary love types: intimacy, passion, and commitment.[4] If one ascribes to this or similar types of analyses, a person's need for love might vary with the type of love (e.g., some folks might have a higher need for intimacy, whereas other folks might require more passion or greater commitment). Thus the contingency between what we need and what will impact our significant value remains. It is just more complicated than immediately meets the eye. Second, some might argue—including a few people that I interviewed for this book—that we all need love, and as such that it is a universal need that makes everyone feel important. The Beatles went even further in their musical proclamation that *all* you really need is love. That is, love is not just universal but also a pre-eminent need. Notwithstanding, we contend that there are real differences in the intensity and dimensionality of love needs within and across individual . . . and thus continue to support motivation need-theory predictions that the extent to which something is an active, unfulfilled need for a particular person at a particular point in time will bear on a path's relative relevance and impact.

A similar argument holds when utilizing the logic of other needs and models, such as in Self Determination Theory and Job Characteristics Theory.[5] An intrinsic driver will resonate more if it satisfies an active need, such as providing competence and meaning or autonomy and discretion. Alternatively, a person will *not* be moved by such an intervention if their circumstances or dispositions create less of a need for these higher-order learning and growth opportunities.

So, in general, someone will be more likely to choose a path, and the path will be more likely to make them feel like a VIP, when it fulfills their *needs*.

In addition, we will now focus on desired (goal) states.

According to Goal Setting Theory,[6] if a path to Importance facilitates progress to one's desired state in a way that is (a) specific and quantifiable, (b) challenging and aspirational, and (c) accepted and interactive, they will be more resonant. Alternatively, if a path is too monotonous, too general, or too alien, it will have minimal attraction and impact.

Similarly, according to Expectancy Theory,[7] if a path to Importance facilitates progress to one's desired state in a way that supports (a) effort-to-performance efficacy, projecting the idea that one can do it, (b) performance-to-outcome instrumentality, projecting the idea that doing it will pay off, and (c) outcome-to-goal valence, projecting the idea that the payoff is desirable, it will be more resonant. Alternatively, if a path does not seem doable, profitable, or useful, it will have minimal attraction and impact.

So, in general, someone will be more likely to choose a path, and the path will be more likely to make them feel like a VIP, when it provides a (specific, challenging, and commitment-inducing) means for facilitating the steps (or, in terms of Expectancy Theory, strengthening the links) necessary for reaching their *goals*.

Taken together, motivational filters shed light on Importance insofar as they show how a path will resonate more with a person when it helps them to satisfy their particular needs and attain their goals. Bottom line: VIPs are best propelled by paths that gel with their motivations.

Filter #3: The Aspect of Aptitude—Our Skills and Abilities

Third, our paths to Importance impact us differently depending on our *aptitudes*.

As you recall from Chapter 2, aptitude is a multidimensional construct representing a host of capacity-based factors including:

- Overall *k*nowledge
- Specific, honed *s*kills
- Generalized competency-based *a*bilities

Together, the above three categories of aptitude form the elements of the acronym KSA.

The basic argument is this: When a path is more consistent/congruent with our KSAs, it is more resonant and, as such, magnifies the impact of that particular driver. That is to say, when we are better at something, we usually feel more significant, more valuable, and thus more important doing it. There are many theories of aptitude that can be used to illustrate this. We choose a few below.

According to classic human resource management models, we are attracted to positions and thrive in them when our KSAs match the tasks, duties, and responsibilities (TDRs) of that position, or to risk acronym overload, when our KSAs relate to the specific task at hand, when they are bona fide occupational qualifications (BFOQs). If a path is in our "sweet spot" or "wheelhouse," we are more likely to be recruited and selected into it, amenable to training and developments for it, assessed positively in it, compensated (in money, praise, attention, etc.) by it, and grow along it. For instance, if we are paired well with a physical job (stamina and long-distance running, explosive strength and the shot put) or a mental job (cognitive intelligence and analysis, emotional intelligence and diplomacy), our self-subjective Importance will be amplified. Similarly, as per research on efficacy and "confidence,"[8] when the demands of a path's requirements fit the supply of our aptitudes, we do it naturally, easily, and assuredly; we do it proactively, engagedly, and resiliently; and we do it in a virtuous, upward-sloping, self-reinforcing (versus viscous, downward-sloping, self-destructive) cycle.

Thus when a path is more consistent/congruent with our aptitude, it is more resonant and, as such, amplifies or magnifies the impact of that particular driver. When added to considerations of motivation—what a person *will* do—the argument for aptitude complements it by emphasizing fit based on what a person *can* do.

So, in general, someone will be more likely to choose a path, and the path will be more likely to make them feel like a VIP, when it feeds into their *aptitudes*.

Taken together—along with values and motivations—aptitudes filters shed light on Importance insofar as they show how a path will resonate more with a person when it aligns with what they are good at. Bottom line: VIPs are best propelled by paths that gel with their aptitude.

Filter #4: The Aspect of Personality—Our Traits and Dispositions

Fourth, our paths to Importance impact us differently depending on our *personality*.

As you recall from Chapter 2, personality comprises the conglomeration of characteristics and propensities that make you who you are. The basic argument here is this: When a path is more consistent/congruent with our predilections and preferences, it is more resonant and, as such, amplifies or magnifies the impact of that particular driver. That is to say, when we are more comfortable at something, we usually feel more significant, more valuable, and thus more important doing it.

There are many theories of personality that can be used to illustrate this. Looking at the previously discussed Big Five or Five-Factor model, we can identify several distinct but related personality dimensions:

- Extraversion: Are you more outgoing or reserved?
- Agreeableness: Are you more cooperative or critical?
- Conscientiousness: Are you more reliable or carefree?
- Emotional stability: Are you more secure or anxious?
- Openness to experience: Are you more curious or conventional?

It is axiomatic that a subject can fit better or worse with their context. In the social sciences, we see this where a person is happier and more productive when they have a good fit with their job. In the hard sciences, we see this when a serum has a good fit with its host or a vehicle has a good fit with its terrain. The same logic applies to person-"ality" and path. For example, utilizing the above framework, those who are higher on the extraversion dimension might feel relatively more important when traveling on more externally oriented paths (e.g., socially oriented roles, outwardly directed affiliations) that emphasize, and reward, their more outgoing, talkative, and bold nature. Alternatively, those who are lower on this dimension (i.e., more withdrawn, quiet, and shy) might feel less important when traveling on these paths.

As an additional example, those who are higher on the agreeable dimension might feel relatively more important on more "absolute" and objectively defined paths (e.g., intelligence, excellence) that emphasize and reward their cooperative sympathetic nature, whereas those who are lower on this dimension (i.e., more competitive) might prefer more "relativistic" and comparatively defined paths (smarter, better).

Similarly, we can examine other dimensions of personality to construct even more focused arguments. As a third example, as per research on locus of control,[9] those who ascribe their success and failure to more internal causes might prefer internally reliant and contingently rewarded paths (e.g., characteristics and actions, particularly performance- or commission-based endeavors), whereas those who attribute outcomes to more external causes might feel more important when traveling on relatively defined, detached, or outwardly sanctioned paths.

Thus it is readily apparent that a path will be more consistent/congruent with our preferred patterns of interaction when it is more resonant and, as such, amplifies or magnifies the impact of that particular driver.

So, in general, someone will be more likely to choose a path, and the path will be more likely to make them feel like a VIP, when it feeds into their *personality.*

Taken together, personality filters shed light on Importance insofar as they show how a path will resonate more with a person when it aligns with their disposition. Bottom line: VIPs are best propelled by paths that gel with their personality.

Filter #5: The Aspect of Archetype—Our Categories,
Prototypes, and Stereotypes

Fifth, our paths to Importance impact us differently depending on our *archetype.* That is to say, how we typecast ourselves, which may or may not be influenced by how we are typecast.[10] As you recall from Chapter 2, cognitive categories are the mental labels that we put on things . . . including ourselves. As such, by virtue of the categories that we ascribe to ourselves, they influence our self-identities. Drilling down further, these labels can take the form of:

- Prototypes: Intended, desired models
- Stereotypes: Perceived, differentiated models

The basic argument here is this: When a path is more consistent/congruent with our current (stereotypical) or aspirant (prototypical) category labels, it is more resonant and, as such, amplifies or magnifies the impact of that particular driver. If a path fits with our identity, helps us fulfill our prescribed intention/purpose or perceived lot/fate, it will work better for us. There are various theories relating to identity, demography, and discrimination that can be used to illustrate this. We choose a few below.

Our archetypes influence our identity. Regarding personal identity formulation, people tend to define themselves by their identified categories and their associated schemata, which can be based on internally oriented individualized experiences and/or externally oriented social embeddedness. These category attributions might be related to distinct characteristics, traits, and action patterns (e.g., smart, strong, achiever, high potential). Or these category attributions might be related to interdependent clusters (e.g., member of the A or B, race, gender, nationality, club, team, society, firm, class). The different types of self-construals will be discussed more in Chapter 7. However, suffice it to say that we form identities around how we, and others, label ourselves.

To the extent that we choose (or are "cued" to focus on) salient paths that are consistent with, and support, our identities, they are likely to have a more positive impact on our self-subjective Importance. For instance, pursuing a path that fits well with (versus works against) our adopted "tech-geek" or "athletic-jock" labels. In addition, when we ascribe more desirable labels *within* these categories, such as those suggesting a higher level (better geek- or jock-related characteristics, actions, acceptances, roles, affiliations), our perceived Importance is elevated. This makes intuitive as well as logical sense insofar as the labels are highly significant to us (they resonate) and the labels connote greater value within these areas (they elevate).

Moreover, our archetypes influence our experiences. Regarding Organizational Demography theory,[11] our experiences in the world and in the workforce are profoundly impacted by our demographic (salient, attributed categorical memberships and distributions) characteristics such as age, gender, generation, and income level. According to the "cohort effect," people who share a similar, and potent, defining moniker will tend to have shared experiences, similar views and attitudes, and as a consequence, stronger and more similar bonds than they will with others. This would naturally include those toward significance and value (i.e., Importance).

Thus, insofar as experiences impact a person's identity and aspirations, one might expect more correspondences in people of similar age groups, genders, generations, levels, and professions. For instance, a teenage male in the 1950s born of a poor family might very well have different views of actual and potential Importance, and as such react differently to its alternative paths, than a forty-something female in 2015 who was born into great wealth. If a person "acts their age," or in a manner consistent with their office or title, thereby modeling projected, and accepted, standards and expectations associated with the customary practices of their identified category, their paths tend to receive greater validation. Of course, it is well beyond the scope of this book to hazard predictions on the complex contingencies that might make someone young/old, male/female, upper/lower socioeconomic status, or poor/rich income level more likely to prioritize and pursue a path built on characteristics, actions, acceptance, roles, or affiliations. Notwithstanding, the overall thrust of the argument is compelling—our drivers are influenced to some degree, but of course not entirely, by our demography.

Moreover, our archetypes influence our comparisons and, in some cases, our resultant discriminations. A similar argument to the above can be made with regard to the adoption of others' external generalized category expectations. If we are placed in categories that are consistent with, and support, our identities, they are likely to have a more positive impact on our perceived Importance. In addition, when we are ascribed more desirable labels or levels within these categories, our perceived Importance is elevated. Social Identity Theory[12] further suggests that these labels can create (a) in-group prototypes or ideals that we seek to approximate and (b) out-group stereotypes with other categories that we seek to differentiate. To the former point, we often see our group memberships exerting cohesive pressures on us to adopt its norms. To the latter, we frequently make prejudicial evaluations and adopt discriminatory attitudes/practices that seek to elevate our category's Importance at the expense of other categories' labels. Therefore, there is increased pressure to promote category-specific paths and demean those that are related to other categories.

Thus, if a path is more consistent/congruent with our archetype, it is more resonant and, as such, amplifies or magnifies the impact of that particular driver.

So, in general, someone will be more likely to choose a path, and the path will be more likely to make them feel like a VIP, when it feeds into and elevates their *archetype*.

Taken together—along with values, motivations, aptitudes, and personality—archetype filters shed light on Importance insofar as they show how a path will resonate more with a person when it aligns with their attached expectations and aspirations. Bottom line: VIPs are best propelled by paths that gel with their archetype.

Upshot of the Above

Our paths to Importance (how we seek to "shine" via enhanced self subjective significant value from: characteristics or who I am, actions or what I do, acceptance or degree that I am liked, roles or how I am placed, and affiliations or where I am connected) will be more or less resonant depending on the personal filter/prism that this shine must pass through. In general, it is probably safe to say that:

I am important when . . .	I shine (am, do, liked, placed, connected) in a way that supports my *values.*
	I shine (am, do, liked, placed, connected) in a way that supports my *motivations.*
	I shine (am, do, liked, placed, connected) in a way that supports my *aptitudes.*
	I shine (am, do, liked, placed, connected) in a way that supports my *personality.*
	I shine (am, do, liked, placed, connected) in a way that supports my *archetype.*

In terms of our model, profile filters act as a mediator between path and Importance. So:

- If my paths are not aligned with my filters, the mediator "regulator" is *low.* This is akin to being stopped by a red traffic light. The inconsistency results in a thick, impermeable barrier, triggers a blockage, renders the driver irrelevant, and ultimately does not impact Importance. The filter is clogged or closed.
- If my paths are moderately/selectively aligned with my filters, the mediator "regulator" is in an intermediate or, to simplify, *moderate* position. This is akin to being slowed by a yellow traffic light. The measured consistency results in a semi-porous barrier, enables only a partial flow or seepage, renders the driver tangenital, and minimally impacts Importance. The filter is restricted or semipermeable.

Table 4.1   Key Filters of Importance

FILTER	MEDIATOR DEGREE OF ALIGNMENT		
	Low (Red Light)	Moderate (Yellow Light)	High (Green Light)
	CLOSED	RESTRICTED	OPEN
• Values	Inconsistent	Somewhat Congruent	Synergistic
• Motivations	Thick Filter	Semiporous Filter	Clear Filter
• Abilities	Blocked Flow	Partial Flow	Free Flow
• Personality	Irrelevant	Tangential	Resonant
• Archetype	No Impact	Some Impact	Powerful Impact

- If my paths are well aligned with my filters, the mediator "regulator" is *high*. This is akin to being expedited by a green traffic light. The synergistic consistency results in a thin or negligible barrier, triggers a free flow, renders the driver resonant, and powerfully impacts Importance. The filter is free flowing, or open.

The table above illustrates the relationship between the different drivers or paths to Importance.

IDENTIFY . . .
The Different Filters to Importance

In examining the following cases, please utilize them in the following ways:

1. In general, can you overlay the template from this chapter onto the scenes below and see the characters using different filters on their paths to Importance?
2. Now, as a *mirror* (looking specifically at *you*): Do any of these characters remind you of you and help to reveal your filters to Importance and the resonance of your paths?
3. Finally, as a *window* (looking at specific *others*): Do any of these characters remind you of someone else that you know and help to reveal their filters to Importance and the resonance of their paths?

Case Study (Personal)

Visiting the Normans' Local Country Day Public High School

In the classroom: Two neighborhood sisters walk to school. Bev walks purposefully and enthusiastically; she really cares about education, learning, and individual achievement. When Monday comes around, she feels ten feet tall. Kris slinks to school dragging her feet and looking for any distraction; she does not share the above *values* and could not care less about doing well in school, either in and of itself or as a path to something else in the future. She feels very small on school days.

Soon they arrive in homeroom: Bev is tweeting (posting and reading messages via the social media tool Twitter) with her classmates; she is feeding her relationship needs; she feels in control and autonomous, that social media is meaningful, that tweeting (following and being followed by a high quantity and quality of others) gives her esteem, that she is capable of doing it, and that this meets her social goals; she is constantly rewarded by the audiovisual stimulation. Kris is ignoring her phone; the above *motivations* just don't click for her.

Later in advanced math class: Bev, the quant jock, feels like a star and a critical contributor to the class, answering the questions and projecting their answers; Kris, the verbal type, does not have the *aptitude* so feels like a nobody and thinks the class would be better off without her lame self dragging the discussion down.

After school: Band practice attracts about 45 students to the music room. The sisters play the two first trombones and sit in the front row . . . but one clearly enjoys the spotlight more than the other; smiling Bev is extroverted, likes the conscientious practice sessions, and is open to new experiences, whereas the downcast Kris is the polar opposite *personality*.

At the pep rally: Cheerleader Bev smiles ear to ear. She fits the dominant *archetype*; she really looks peppy, and her profile gels with the scene. Kris is locked into a perpetual frown. She clearly does not fit the prototypical cheerleader image; her introverted and reserved nature is the perfect contrast to the "enthusiastic supporter" the event is looking for.

Whose profile makes their path more resonant? As a result, who probably feels of more significant value? How would you leverage the situation for Bev? How would you remedy the situation for Kris? Alter her profile? Alter her path?

Case Study (Professional)

Behind the Scenes at the Towne Bank

In the lobby: Two classmates, Jack and Mike, were hired by the bank and started work at the same time, being placed in their job rotation program. The aggressive, financially based *values* of Jack (nicknamed the Shark)—he wants to make a lot of money and do so in a high-risk, high-reward manner—make the investment desk a heaven to be, whereas the opposite values make it a living nightmare for Mike.

Jack is highly *motivated* by his time at the loan department—it meets his needs, looks like it could provide a path to fulfill his career goals, allows him to work hard and self-determine his bonus, and provides many opportunities for learning and personal growth. In contrast, Mike is affected in the exact opposite way—it does not in any way satisfy his needs or help accomplish his goals; he winds up severely disincentivized and even contemplates quitting.

Jack is great at calculations, so he is like a fish in water working with the mortgage refinance expert—he is even called "indispensible" by the seasoned manager— whereas Mike does not have the *aptitude* for this and feels rather useless.

At the teller desk: Jack's outgoing *personality* makes this an ideal place to shine, whereas for the more introverted Mike every awkward customer interaction is like having an impacted tooth pulled—he hates it, he is bad at it, and he feels awkward and trifling every time he does it.

At the weekly awards ceremony: Jack makes a grand entrance, sharply present- ing himself like the *archetypical* banker (he even has the pinstripes, wingtips, and power tie to prove it), whereas frumpy, tieless, loafer-wearing Mike simply does not look like he should be here . . . and acts like he knows it.

Whose profile makes their path more resonant? As a result, who probably feels of more significant value? How would you leverage the situation for Jack? How would you remedy the situation for Mike? Alter his profile? Alter his path?

PERSONALIZE . . .
The Different Filters to Importance

This set of exercises gives you the opportunity to clarify how your filters medi- ate the paths to significant value to make them more or less resonant. All together, the more your paths align with your values, motivations, aptitudes, personality, and archetype, the greater and more positive their impact on your Importance. You can use this section to assess the degree to which your paths suit you well or need to be altered.

General

Come to grips with the filters that mediate your paths to Importance.
    At the most basic level, please rate the degree to which the following filters are closed and out of line (low, say a "1") or open and in line (high, say a "10") with the path(s) to Importance that you have chosen. Recall that you identi- fied these paths in the exercise from our previous chapter.

1. My values
2. My motivations
3. My aptitudes
4. My personality
5. My archetype

Are you happy with your scores? What would you change? How could you change this? Does your ranking suggest a more or less resonant approach to Importance? Has the ranking changed as you have grown, experienced things, gone through life changes, or advanced in years? Is there any pattern to be found in these? Is there a sweet spot where everything fell into place? If so then how can you get (back) there?

Specific

Drill down further to isolate specific filters and how they mediate the resonance of your paths.

Now please note the degree to which you agree with the following ways for completing this sentence, from most to least descriptive of you:

My paths to Importance . . .

- Are in line with my values
  - ○ Support and are supported by my terminal values
  - ○ Are consistent with what I care about
  - ○ Sync with my end-state priorities
  - ○ Support and are supported by my instrumental values
  - ○ Are consistent with what I feel comfortable doing
  - ○ Sync with my means/process priorities
- Are in line with my motivations
  - ○ Support and are supported by my specific objectives
  - ○ Are consistent with what I strive toward
  - ○ Address my main goals
  - ○ Support and are supported by my strongest desires
  - ○ Are consistent with what I require
  - ○ Fulfill my main needs
- Are in line with my aptitudes
  - ○ Support and are supported by my knowledge and expertise
  - ○ Work well with what I know
  - ○ Support and are supported by my specific skill sets
  - ○ Work well with what I have learned and am confident doing
  - ○ Support and are supported by my general abilities
  - ○ Work well with the things that I am normally good at
- Are in line with my personality
  - ○ Support and are supported by my general disposition
  - ○ Gel with how I tend to orient myself toward others—outgoing or reserved
  - ○ Gel with how I tend to get along with others—cooperative or critical
  - ○ Gel with how I tend to approach tasks—reliable or carefree
  - ○ Gel with how I tend to deal with events—secure or anxious
  - ○ Gel with how I tend to experience things—curious or conventional

- Are in line with my archetype
  - Support and are supported by my idealized definition for success
  - Consistent with my perfect role models
  - Sync with the type of person that I want to be
  - Support my adopted guidelines, norms, and standards
  - Consistent with how I view my "category" or "label"
  - Sync with the type of person that I am expected to be

APPLY . . .
The Different Filters to Importance

From a personal perspective, your Importance is partly determined by the choices that you make about your filtered path(s). From a professional perspective, your people's Importance is partly determined by the management strategies that you employ to help them shape their filtered path(s).

Please take a moment to apply the material from this chapter to make better choices and craft better strategies about the filters of Importance.

Making Personal Choices

Choice 2: You are, to varying degrees, in control of your Importance path-profile resonance. That is to say, you can customize/match your path to align with your filters. Or you can alter/change your profile to fit with your path.

Choice 2a. You can choose to align your path with your *values* or alter your values to suit your chosen path.

> Does my path line up with my terminal and instrumental priorities? Should I change my path? Or perhaps reconsider my priorities?

Choice 2b. You can choose to align your path with your *motivations* or alter your motivations to suit your chosen path.

> Does my path line up with my goals and needs? Should I change my path? Or perhaps refocus my goals and needs?

Choice 2c. You can choose to align your path with your *aptitudes* or alter your aptitudes to suit your chosen path.

> Does my path line up with my knowledge, skills, and abilities? Should I change my path? Or perhaps enhance my knowledge, skills, and abilities?

Choice 2d. You can choose to align your path with your *personality* or alter your personality to suit your chosen path.

> Does my path line up with my predilections and patterns? Should I change my path? Or perhaps alter my predilections and patterns?

Choice 2e. You can choose to align your path with your *archetype* or alter your archetype to suit your chosen path.

> Does my path line up with my categories and labels? Should I change my path? Or perhaps redefine my categories and labels?

Crafting Management Strategies

Management Strategy 2: You can, to varying degrees, make others' Importance paths-profiles more resonant.

That is to say, you can try to align others' paths with their profiles. In a manner similar to the preceding section, your efforts might facilitate or impede the degree to which their choices fit with their values, motivations, aptitudes, personalities, and archetypes.

This can happen at work, at home, or anywhere.

Strategy 2a. You can move them on a path that gels with their particular *values*. For example:

> Help them identify their terminal and instrumental priorities. Explore the degree of alignment with their path to see if they resonate. Optimize fit by asking, "Is this the right path for you? Or do you have the appropriate priorities for what you are doing?"

Strategy 2b. You can move them on a path that gels with their particular *motivations*. For example:

> Help them identify their goals and needs. Explore the degree of alignment with their path to see if they resonate. Optimize fit by asking, "Is this the right path for you? Or do you have the appropriate goals and needs for what you are doing?"

Strategy 2c. You can move them on a path that gels with their particular *aptitudes*. For example:

> Help them identify their knowledge, skills, and abilities. Explore the degree of alignment with their path to see if they resonate. Optimize fit by asking, "Is this the right path for you? Or do you have the appropriate knowledge, skills, and abilities for what you are doing?"

Strategy 2d. You can move them on a path that gels with their particular *personalities*. For example:

> Help them identify their predilections and personality patterns. Explore the degree of alignment with their path to see if they resonate. Optimize fit by asking, "Is this the right path for you? Or do you have the appropriate predilections and patterns for what you are doing?"

Strategy 2e. You can move them on a path that gels with their particular *archetypes*. For example:

> Help them identify their categories, expectations, and labels. Explore the degree of alignment with their path to see if they resonate. Optimize fit by asking, "Is this the right path for you? Or do you have the appropriate categories, expectations, and labels for what you are doing?"

Checkpoint

Now that we have concluded this chapter, it is appropriate to pause for a moment at this checkpoint and answer the following questions:

- Do you UNDERSTAND the different filters to Importance?
- Can you IDENTIFY how the filters make our paths more or less resonant in personal and professional settings?
- Have you PERSONALIZED the filters by relating them to your own Importance journey?
- Will you APPLY the above to (a) align your paths with your filters to make better choices and (b) align others' paths with their filters to craft better strategies?

If not, circle back.

If so, let's move on to the next part of the model: *context* . . . and the external-moderator contingencies of Importance.

Context—The External Contingencies to Importance

You should be aware of (good), flexibly adapt to (better), or strategically create (best) the environment where you locate your Importance.

Chapter 5 presents the landscape moderators to Importance. In this chapter we will consider these different external contingencies to Importance. First, we will seek to UNDERSTAND the impact of the context or environment in which we are positioned, in particular our:

1. Location factor, including societal, organizational, and group norms
2. Task factor, including activities and jobs
3. Situation factor, including treatment and support
4. Market factor, including relative dependency, power, and advantage

The upshot of these choices will be reconciled in terms of how their respective external "On or Off switches" bear on the different path-nature relationships. Second, we will seek to IDENTIFY these external/contextual moderators by sketching personal and professional case study illustrations. You might use them to see yourself (mirror) or others (window) more accurately. Third, we will seek to PERSONALIZE these external/contextual moderators by presenting reflective exercises that you can use to relate them to your particular Importance journey. Fourth, we will seek to APPLY the above by deriving guided checklists that can help you make better personal choices and craft better management strategies.

UNDERSTAND . . .
The Context of Importance

Will a person's path be just as attractive in any circumstances? Will a person's path work just as well in any circumstances? If not, why does the same person's path fit better or worse in different contexts/places?

This chapter will address these issues by taking up the underlying question "What makes a person's particular path to Importance work better or worse in different situations?" Stated plainly, "What are the contextual factors influencing Importance?" Stated colloquially, "Why do certain places make certain people feel more or less like a VIP?"

Or, in terms of our model, "What are some of the key external moderators of Importance?"

Here we will advance the proposition that the power of our drivers to impact our Importance is contingent on their *context*. Therefore, the impact of people's filtered paths will depend on the environment or circumstances that they are in. Lesson: Different situations can help or hinder your particular path to Importance.

Before we get started, a few points of clarification:

- POINT A: Importance is not situation neutral. It depends on the context (i.e., the landscape or general environment where we operate).
- POINT B: Contexts are different. They bring with them different overlapping sets of cultures and norms, different types of dominant activities and tasks, different overarching treatment and support conditions, and different essential dependency and power relationships. These are critical, non-trivial distinctions of how context can alter parameters.
- POINT C: Context moderates Importance. It is impossible to understand one's self-subjective Importance until the venue in which it takes place is understood. If the circumstances change, our Importance can change accordingly. That is to say, we can pursue significant value differently in different environments as per the dimensions and demands of the situations that we find ourselves in.
- POINT D: If you *understand* context, you will be able to see why things happen . . . but still be at its mercy (low control). If you *adapt* to your context, you will be able to amend yourself to facilitate or find fit (moderate control). If you proactively, strategically regulate context—adapt it to you[1]—you will be able to *transform* your world to create fit (high control).

Now for a discussion of some of the key external, context-related factors bearing on Importance.

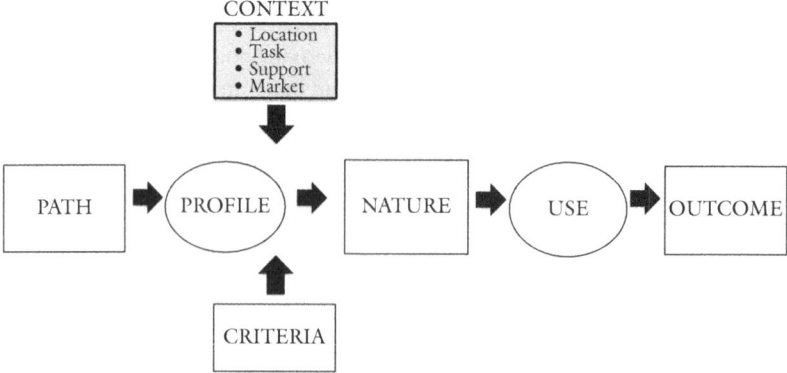

Figure 5.1   External Context Moderators of Importance.

Factor #1: Our Location

First, the prevailing *cultural norms* impact the way in which Importance will be determined.

The message here is that the more our personal paths align with our location's cultural context, the more positive their impact on significance and value. Or said another way, the paths to Importance will vary depending on the culture that the person is operating in.

Culture is multidimensional and is the composite of overlapping layers, for example:

- Societal culture: Based in macro-context
- Organizational culture: Based in meso-context
- Group culture: Based in micro-context

Societal Culture

Importance is often society specific. Significant value can mean different things depending on the society that you are in. As per much research, we know that societal culture is not the same in every corner of the world. Instead it varies by country and, in many cases, within different regions of the same political entity. In short, societies have been found to share general belief systems (c.f., Kluckhohn and Strodtbeck) based on their historically transmitted patterns and webs of meanings (c.f., Geertz) that define the conceptions of desirable and undesirable actions and attitudes (c.f., Schwartz) and "program the mind" (c.f., Hofstede) to experience the world in different ways.[2]

Recalling the discussion from Chapter 2, some of Hofstede[3] and colleagues' most striking findings are that societies can put relatively more or less emphasis on:

- The individual or the collective
- The quantitative or the qualitative
- The risky or the certain
- The hierarchical or the equitable
- The present or the future

In relatively more *individualistic* cultural contexts, one might find that Importance is attributed to and by people who support norms of loosely connected, self-serving orientations. As such, focusing on more internally defined drivers like personal characteristics and actions might be popular, sanctioned paths here. Alternatively, in relatively more collectivist contexts, significant value might be assessed and ascribed when conforming to norms that put an emphasis on strong group ties and collaborative, cohesive action. For example, paths focusing on the more externally defined drivers of roles and affiliations might be prioritized in this type of context.

In relatively more *qualitative* cultural contexts, one might find that Importance is attributed to and by people who support norms of prototypically masculine preferences for assertive, competitive standards and material rewards.

As such, focusing on winning might be a popular, sanctioned path here. Alternatively, in relatively more quantitative or prototypically feminine contexts, significant value might be assessed and ascribed when conforming to norms that put an emphasis on more modest, caring standards and aesthetic rewards. For example, focusing on spirituality and connection-related paths might be prioritized in this type of context. This is reminiscent of Dr. Martin Luther King's argument[4] that "if you want to be important, wonderful. If you want to be recognized, wonderful. If you want to be great, wonderful. But recognize that he who is greatest among you shall be your servant."

In relatively more *risk-seeking* cultural contexts, one might find that Importance is attributed to and by people who support norms of flexibility and adaptiveness as well as a generally relaxed comfort with ambiguous situations. As such, focusing on more results-oriented drivers such as judgment and achievement might be a popular, sanctioned path here. Alternatively, in relatively more risk-averse contexts, significant value might be assessed and ascribed when conforming to norms that put an emphasis on rigidity and orthodoxy, as well as a generally conservative approach to future uncertainties. For example, more process-oriented paths such as health maintenance and general participation might be prioritized in this type of context.

In relatively more *hierarchical* or high power-distance cultural contexts, one might find that Importance is attributed to and by people who support norms of unequal distributions and implicit, clear-cut differentiations of power. As such, more formal and defined (affiliations, roles) drivers might be popular, sanctioned paths here. Alternatively, in relatively more egalitarian or low power-distance contexts, significant value might be assessed and ascribed when conforming to norms that put an emphasis on harmonized distributions of power and fluid, consensual responsibilities. For example, less formal and defined paths might be prioritized in this type of context.

Finally, in relatively more *short-term* cultural contexts, one might find that Importance is attributed to and by people who support norms of immediate gratification and predilections for acting and spending. As such, time- and situation-specific (action-based) drivers might be popular, sanctioned paths here. Alternatively, in relatively more long-term contexts, significant value might be assessed and ascribed when conforming to norms that put an emphasis on restricted indulgences and predilections for planning and saving. For example, more stable and enduring (e.g., characteristics-based) paths might be prioritized in this type of context.

In addition to societal values, the structure of a society—as embodied in its political, economic, and legal climate—bears on its culture. That is to say, and as discussed in Chapter 2, the way that a society designs its institutions can impact its citizens' Importance journeys. It therefore stands to reason that societies with more democratic, capitalistic, and legally protective systems might endorse different paths to significant value (e.g., with regard to personal competition and achievement) than those that are less so. This is evidenced to some extent in the proliferation of different mythological tales and pop-culture heroes that emerge from different societies' histories and propagate throughout their varied trajectories. Indeed, research supports the link between how a culture explicitly or implicitly signals its endorsed values with the manifest preferences and predilections of its leaders and peoples.[5]

All together, when a filtered path is a better fit with one's society, it is reinforced and, as such, magnifies the impact of that particular driver. When it is a poor fit, the impact of that driver is reduced. Thus, VIPs tend to fit their societal context.

Organizational Culture
Importance is also organization specific. Significant value can mean different things depending on the organization that you are in. As per much research, we know that culture is not identical in every formal and informal association. Instead, culture varies by company and, in many cases, within different divisions of the same corporate entity.

At its essence, organizational culture is a pattern of shared tacit assumptions, manifest in core taken-for-granted values and identifiable via surface artifacts that it adopts to meet its challenges and that it communicates to its members as the correct way to see, think, and feel when doing their work.[6] In a sense, it describes an organization's "personality" (no, I am not entering the political/legal debate here about whether corporations are people, simply making a useful, relatable analogy)—that which it has evolved to adapt and survive in its environment.

Some of the most striking findings are that firms can have diverse levels and types of culture as seen in their:

1. Assumptions: Fundamental postulates on the meaning of success
2. Values: Beliefs and standards that they apply to evaluating the rightness and goodness of actions
3. Artifacts: Tangible symbols, rites, language, and other displays of their underlying culture

At the heart of an organization's culture are its assumptions. When organizations adopt different assumptions, they then implicitly define paths to the realization, attribution, and calibration of Importance. Examples of assumptions are the way that a firm might view the nature of business and profit, the fundamental patterns of human dynamics and relationships, and as such its reason for existence as ingrained in its core statements of mission and purpose. Different views of reality, mission, and purpose naturally beget different conceptions of significance and value.

An organization's values follow from its assumptions. When organizations adopt different values, they explicitly sanction different paths to the realization, attribution, and calibration of Importance. Indeed it has been found that organizations tend to be most effective when they have stronger cultural values guiding and governing their central activities.[7] As per the Competing Values framework, these values would then address standards of effectiveness (e.g., dynamic flexibility, change, and organic adaptability versus stability, predictable order, and mechanistic control) as well as different processes (e.g., efficiency and congruent internal processes versus positioning and competitive external relationships).[8] It is therefore clear from the above discussion that different firm values would logically be associated with varied paths to endorsing and rewarding members' self-subjective Importance.

An organization's artifacts are the salient manifestations of its culture that aid in its identification, communication, and sustenance. Here one would observe different *symbols* of Importance, different *stories* about Importance, different *rituals* around Importance, and different *language* of Importance. For example, one might understand the dominant approaches to significant value when witnessing employees:

- Wearing pins or displaying awards that emphasize seniority versus sales versus innovation
- Reminiscing about the legendary entrepreneurial risk takers versus steady-handed peacemakers, or salespeople versus visionary trailblazers, or tech gurus versus sociable people-persons in the firm's history
- Partaking in cutthroat promotional competitions versus broad-based profit-sharing or trial-by-fire initiations versus compassionate mentoring practices
- Referring to key corporate buzzwords like meetings as "workouts," problem solving as "threshing," assessment as "rank and yank," employees as "cast members," project management as "blue chipping," or interpersonal relations as a process of "respecting the spirit"

Thus cultural indicators signal different defined, sanctioned paths to significance and value.

Another set of key findings is that the aforementioned nature of an organizational culture is fluid (for some companies this is more true than for others) insofar as it is influenced by a variety of factors. Therefore, when a company appoints new leaders (insiders or outsiders), moves into new industries (more or less regulated), experiences new levels of performance (success or failure), establishes new structures and designs (more or less bureaucratic), and acquires new businesses (traditional or high-tech, products or services), it makes sense that it might experience a shift in culture. When assumptions, values, and artifacts change, so might sanctioned paths to Importance.

All together, when a filtered path is a better fit with one's organization, it is reinforced and, as such, magnifies the impact of that particular driver. When it is a poor fit, the impact of that driver is reduced. Thus, VIPs tend to fit their organizational context.

Group Culture
Importance is also group specific. Significant value can mean different things depending on the group that you are in. Countries and companies do not always have a perfectly uniform culture. Instead, there are often groups within them, each with its own subculture and normalities. There is a sizable amount

of research on the nature and function of group norms.[9] Rather than recounting it all here, we select a few interesting findings that shed unique light on our topic.

As per the discussion in Chapter 2, group norms are, by and large, social standards regarding the appropriate attitudes and behavior of its members. They govern both nouns, such as appearances, and verbs, such as behaviors. For example, regarding appearance, norms might give people an indication of what grooming and attire will make them feel and seem more important in the group. As an additional example, regarding behavior, they might describe the actions that will help them be more effective or adaptive (i.e., significantly valuable) in the group as well as prescribe the approved or disapproved manners of behavior that would subsequently beget reinforcement or punishment by the group.

It is also worth mentioning that these group norms can be more homogenous (or tight) or heterogeneous (or loose), as well as more explicit (stated) or implicit (implied). It therefore stands to reason that Importance would be more clearly delineated in explicit, homogenous contexts and less so in their opposite. A group's tolerance for deviance from its norms might therefore vary accordingly, as well as the range of sanctioned paths to Importance.

All together, when a filtered path is a better fit with one's group, it is reinforced and, as such, magnifies the impact of that particular driver. When it is a poor fit, the impact of that driver is reduced. Thus, VIPs tend to fit their group context.

Taken Together
We can see from the above discussion that Importance is location specific. The more your filtered paths are in line with your location, the more positive their impact on your Importance.

More specifically, societal, organizational, and group norms can be seen to moderate the relationship between the conditions, nature, and eventual consequences of Importance.

So you will feel more like a VIP when you choose a path that is favored by your location. Alternatively, you will feel less like a VIP when your chosen path does not fit your location.

Factor #2: Our Tasks

Second, the prevailing *tasks* impact the way in which Importance will be determined.

The message here is that the more our personal paths align with our jobs, duties, and responsibilities, the more positive their impact on significance and value. Or said another way, the paths to Importance will vary depending on the activity that the person is engaged in. Importance is often task specific.

Tasks are multidimensional and are comprised of many facets, for example:

- Their scope or breadth
- Their intensity or depth

Task Breadth

Importance can be influenced by person–job fit. Regarding task scope or breadth, this fit is partially determined across its range of components. As introduced in Chapter 2, Human Capital Theory[10] tells us that people possess personal knowledge, skill, and abilities that are derived from natural (genetic) and experience-based (education, training, travel) sources and explain in some part their variation in performance, productivity, and compensation. The extent to which a person has the skills and competencies necessary to complete a job can influence their potential to successfully complete a job. When they do not, they are likely to experience negative internal (frustration, shame) and external (demotion, termination) outcomes.

Simply put, we are more likely to feel important when we are working in our areas of strength and less likely when we are engaged in endeavors outside of our training and comfort zones. So to extend the prior line of reasoning, when a person aligns their KSAs with their tasks, duties, and responsibilities (TDRs), they possess bona fide occupational qualifications (BFOQs). This will align their filtered paths with the horizontal range of their context. When the two mesh, their Importance will be magnified; when they clash, it will be diminished. Thus when a path is accentuated by task demands, it is reinforced and, as such, supports the impact of that particular driver. Moreover, in this world of frequently shifting responsibilities and requirements, it is all the more critical that a dynamic alignment is maintained through constant reflection, reorientation, and reeducation. Thus, VIPs tend to fit their task range.

Task Depth

Regarding task intensity, Importance can be influenced by a person's fit with the deep-seated nature of a job's components.[11] If a person engages merely at the surface level of a job, what Hertzberg referred to as hygiene factors, the fit would not be as profound as if they were in sync with its deeper, intrinsic factors that truly touch the worker and enrich (versus merely enlarge) the experience. This is explained even more thoroughly through Job Characteristics Theory, which identifies the components of a job that enhance its inherent meaningfulness (e.g., tasks that stretch one's capacity, enable identity, and help others), experienced responsibility (e.g., tasks that enable freedom and discretion), and cybernetic learning (e.g., tasks that provide knowledge and feedback to facilitate growth and enable adjustments).

Simply put, we are more likely to feel important when our degrees of expertise and unfolding experiences are sufficient to match the nature of our endeavors (i.e., we are not proverbially "over our heads" or "out of our vertical depth"). So to extend the prior line of reasoning, when a person aligns their intrinsic psychological states with their deep task's dimensions, they will be more satisfied and effective and will thrive. This will bring into line their filtered paths with the callings of their context. When the two mesh, their Importance will be magnified; when they clash, it will be diminished. Thus, when a path is accentuated by task characteristics, it is reinforced and, as such, supports the impact of that particular driver. Thus, VIPs tend to fit their task depth.

Taken Together

We can see from the above discussion that Importance is task specific. The more your filtered paths are in line with your task, the more positive their impact on your Importance.

More specifically, task breadth and depth can be seen to moderate the relationship between the conditions, nature, and eventual consequences of Importance.

So you will feel more like a VIP when you choose a path that is favored by your task. Alternatively, you will feel less like a VIP when your chosen path does not fit your task.

Factor #3: Our (Management) Support

Third, the prevailing *treatment* or management style impacts the way in which Importance will be determined.

The message here is that the more our personal paths align with the way we are treated, the more positive their impact on significance and value. Or said another way, the paths to Importance will vary depending on the management style the person is subject to; Importance is often dyad specific.

Management support is multidimensional and is composed of many facets, for example:

- Prevailing attitudes
- Level of care
- Degree of inclusion
- Type of treatment

Prevailing Attitudes

A person's self-subjective Importance can be influenced by the way their managers view them (i.e., their prevailing management approach or projected attitude). In a broader sense, this relates to what some refer to as "humanistic" management[12] or the valuing and developing of human needs, dignity, and growth. As per Douglas McGregor,[13] managers make implicit or explicit assumptions about their employees, which can be simplified and bifurcated as a) a generally pessimistic view (Theory X) that workers are inherently lazy, limited, and untrustworthy (i.e., viewed like children or simple machines); versus b) a generally optimistic view (Theory Y) that they are industrious, substantial, and responsible (i.e., viewed with respect and support). Moreover, we know from research on the self-fulfilling prophecy[14] that the way managers view their employees influences a chain of events whereby they treat them differently, elicit different levels of motivation, development, and commitment, and ultimately bias the outcomes in favor of their original assumptions (i.e., perceptions and treatment create their very reality). That is to say, these attitudes tend to be self-reinforcing insofar as managers will often get what they expect, turning their people into the very types of lowly or capable employees that they conjured. Thus, how managers see someone makes it more likely that they will rise or fall to their expectations.

It thus stands to reason that individuals' sense of significant value will be impacted by these attitudes. When managerial attitudes accentuate versus devalue particular paths to Importance, they will support the impact of that driver. However, in general, a more positive managerial attitude will result in an amplified impact of one's filtered path. Thus, VIPs tend to be supported by received management attitudes.

Level of Care
A person's self-subjective Importance can also be influenced by the way their managers actually care for them.[15] As per the above, managers can, to different degrees, promote the growth, potential, and dignity of the employee. When managers adopt an "X" type of attitude, they tend to show less care—exert tight control, close supervision, and disconnected, depersonalized mechanistic practices. In this scenario, a lack of humanity might degrade into purely instrumental relationships or even abusive and exploitative practices. Alternatively, when managers adopt a "Y" type of attitude, they tend to show more care—allow for looser controls, more personal supervision, and customizable and empowered delegation. This amounts to different realizations of the manager–employee partnership. Here it is designed more as synergistic co-stakeholders who are mutually interdependent and, as such, jointly responsible for the other's welfare. In this scenario, a person would more likely experience holistic results oriented not just compliant to the myopically linear maximization of efficient returns but instead committed to a broader simultaneous pursuit as represented by the proverbial "triple bottom line," grounded in process and outcome fairness, that synergistically balances profit with humane and broader ethical concerns.

It thus stands to reason that individuals' sense of significant value will be impacted by these behaviors. When the level of care accentuates versus devalues particular paths to Importance, it will support the impact of that driver. However, in general, a more positive level of care will result in an amplified impact of one's filtered path. Thus, VIPs tend to be supported by received management care.

Degree of Inclusion
A person's self-subjective Importance can also be influenced by the way their managers include versus exclude them and encourage their participation. As per Leader-Member Exchange (LMX) Theory,[16] managers can develop high-quality or low-quality groupings with workers, which in turn has a major impact on their attitudes and behaviors. In the former type of arrangement, where a person is included in the manager's "in-group," their short-term needs and long-term growth potential are prioritized, resulting in greater engagement and commitment, satisfaction and positivity, task effectiveness,

and career success. Alternatively, in the latter type of arrangement, where a person is excluded and effectively cast off into an "out-group," the process dynamics and outcomes are reversed and correspondingly negative outcomes ensue.

It thus stands to reason that individuals' sense of significant value will be impacted by these different arrangements. When inclusion accentuates versus devalues particular paths to Importance, it will support the impact of that driver. However, in general, a more open, high-quality level of inclusion will result in an amplified impact of one's filtered path. Thus, VIPs tend to be supported by received management inclusion.

Type of Treatment

A person's self-subjective Importance can also be influenced by the way their managers treat them. As well documented by the multitude of research on "servant leadership" [17] managers can treat their people as if (a) the employees are figurative pawns to simply serve the manager's whims and directives, or instead, (b) the manager is there to serve and grow their employees. Invoking the sentiments of Immanuel Kant (discussed in Chapter 2), the former treats people merely as a means, whereas the latter treats them as ends in themselves. Servant leaders put their people first and focus on providing followers with the tools and support they need to do their jobs and reach their full potential. Individuals who are treated in this manner tend to have greater loyalty, confidence, citizenship, creativity, and performance. Alternatively, when a person is treated merely as an instrumental means, they tend to experience less positive outcomes, even becoming alienated from the work, and as such regressing into negative spirals of dissatisfaction and failure.

It therefore stands to reason that individuals' sense of significant value will be impacted by these different patterns of treatment. When treatment accentuates versus devalues particular paths to Importance, it will support the impact of that driver. However, in general, a more servant-oriented type of treatment (where individuals are regarded as ends in and of themselves) will result in an amplified impact of one's filtered path. Thus, VIPs tend to be supported by received management treatment.

Taken Together

We can see from the above discussion that Importance is support dependent. The more your filtered paths are supported by your management—their attitudes, their care, their inclusion, and their treatment—the more positive their impact on your Importance.

More specifically, management support can be seen to moderate the relationship between the conditions, nature, and eventual consequences of Importance.

So you will feel more like a VIP when your chosen path is supported by the management context. Alternatively, you will feel less like a VIP when your chosen path is not supported by the management context.

Factor #4: Our Market

Third, the prevailing *market* conditions impact the way in which Importance will be determined.

The message here is that the more our personal paths are in demand (relative to their supply) the more positive their impact on significance and value. Or said another way, the paths to Importance will vary depending on the power and dependency (im)balances the person is subject to; Importance is often market specific.

Power is multidimensional and is comprised of many facets, for example:

- Dependency dimensions
- Power bases
- Relative competitive advantage

Market Dependency

Importance can be influenced by market dependency.[18] It is axiomatic in the field of economics that the significant value of a resource, including human resources, is partially determined by the interaction of their relative supply (*scarcity*) and relative demand (*criticality*). In the market price system, a resource is more important, and can thus command a higher price, when it is in high demand (hot) or short supply (rare). Alternatively, it is less important, and can thus only command a diminished price, when it is in soft demand (passé) or bloated supply (plentiful). In addition, scarcity and criticality are impacted by the extent to which the resource has viable or prospective substitutes—this is called *elasticity*. If a resource's functionality cannot be duplicated or reasonably approximated, say human blood, its Importance would be more durable than one that can be replaced, say a generic flavored soft drink. In such a system of dynamic dependency, the "invisible hand" of the market determines value, calibrates its significance, and then allocates resource Importance accordingly.

In general, when dependency conditions favor particular paths to Importance, the context will support the impact of that specific driver. For example, this would hold true with regard to the demand, supply, and elasticity of a particular characteristic, action, acceptance, role, or affiliation. More specifically, in your "market," if your filtered path to Importance (e.g., a particular characteristic such as mathematical acumen or occupied role such as social media project manager) is in high or growing demand, is in short or shrinking supply, and is invulnerable or inelastic to proxies, your contextualized significant value will be amplified. Thus, VIPs tend to create greater dependency.

Market Power

Importance can also be influenced by market power.[19] As per French and Raven's classic framework, social power is conceptualized as the potential influence one person can have to change the actions or beliefs of another person. A person interacting with others in a system of ideas, exchanges, and so on, can draw on positional power sources, personal power sources, or a combination of both. With regard to people's predominantly positional sources, they can have:

- Legitimate power: Usually granted to a person via their hierarchical position in an organization and conveying a sanctioned zone of authority within which they possess a right to influence others
- Reward power: Granted to a person to control sources of reinforcement and benefit that they can disperse at their discretion to raise others' utility
- Coercive power: Granted to a person to dispense contingencies of punishment at their discretion to reduce others' utility

With regard to people's predominantly personal sources, they can have:

- Expert power: Derived from a person's capacities, alacrities, and talents to solve problems and seize opportunities
- Referent power: Derived from a person's earned admiration, identification, and personal charisma that others attribute to them

Power is not universal or unidirectional, instead it is relative and fluid depending on the particular relationships. In such a system of dynamic power, the nature of the interaction (versus any "objective" arbiter) defines and determines value, calibrates its significance, and allocates influence accordingly.

In general, when power conditions favor particular paths to Importance, the context will favorably support the impact of that specific driver. For example, this would hold true with regard to the relative power of a particular characteristic, action, acceptance, role, or affiliation. Different paths then, to the extent that they allow people to tap into and leverage these contextualized sources of influence, would become more or less vigorous and provide individuals more freedom, resources, and so on, to strengthen, grow, and progress. More specifically, in your arena, if your filtered path to Importance is relatively more potent—and by virtue of it you can command, reward, punish, advise, or inspire others—then your contextualized significant value will be amplified. Thus, VIPs tend to hold greater power.

Market Advantage
Importance can also be influenced by market competency and relative competitive advantage.[20] As per the seminal work of Michael Porter and others introduced in Chapter 2, we know that firms (and people) can create distinct competencies. They do this through path-dependent accumulations of resources and routines that enable them to sense, seize, and transform opportunities. These competencies can in turn create relative competitive advantages if they allow the focal parties to successfully navigate the structural forces of their environment (e.g., customers, suppliers, rivals, new entrants, and potential substitutes), occupy unique and defensible strategic positions

within it (e.g., broadly based or focused, based in high-end differentiation or low-end cost), customize its value-creative activities around it (primary and supporting), and outperform its rivals over a sustained period of time.

In general, when conditions favor particular paths to Importance, the context will support the impact of that specific driver. For example, this would hold true with regard to the relative position and advantage created by one's characteristics, actions, acceptances, roles, or affiliations. More specifically, in your "market," if your filtered path to Importance is relatively more distinctive, functional, and well positioned (e.g., it can better advance your organization's interests or make your firm money), your contextualized significant value will be amplified. Thus, VIPs tend to construct greater advantage.

Taken Together

We can see from the above discussion that Importance is market specific. The more your filtered paths are in line with your market, the more positive their impact on your Importance.

More specifically, market conditions such as dependency (criticality, scarcity, and non-substitutability), power (positionally and/or personally based), and advantage (competitively positioned) can be seen to moderate the relationship between the conditions, nature, and eventual consequences of Importance.

So you will feel more like a VIP when you choose a path that is favored by your market. Alternatively, you will feel less like a VIP when your chosen path does not fit your market.

Upshot of the Above

Our paths to Importance will be more or less resonant depending on where they are located (e.g., the contextual moderators that these paths are subject to). In general, it is probably safe to say that:

I am important when . . .   The prevailing *location* fits/favors/emphasizes my path.
The prevailing *task* fits/favors/emphasizes my path.
The prevailing *support* fits/favors/emphasizes my path.
The prevailing *market* fits/favors/emphasizes my path.

In terms of our model, context filters act as an external moderator between path and Importance. So:

- If my filtered paths do not fit with, and are not favored or emphasized by, the external context, the figurative moderator "switch" is set to Off—the inconsistency results in a dysfunctional, hostile, and punishing dynamic that creates a *negative* relationship between independent and dependent variables in the conceptual model.

Table 5.1   External Context and Importance

CONTEXT	EXTERNAL MODERATOR SWITCH	
	OFF	ON
• Location	Non-Supportive	Supportive
• Task	Low Regard	High Regard
• Support	Punished	Rewarded
• Market	More Villainous	More Heroic
	Hostile/Opposing	Symbiotic/Reinforcing
	Dysfunctional	Functional
	Contrary	Consistent
	Negative Image	Positive Image
	Removed/Estranging	Intrinsic/Involving
	Debilitating and Restrictive	Enriching and Helpful
	Peripheral/Weak/Undesirable	Critical/Powerful/Desirable
	Disadvantageous	Advantageous

- If my filtered paths fit with, and are favored and emphasized by, the external context, the figurative moderator "switch" is set to On—the consistency results in a functional, symbiotic, and rewarding dynamic relationship that creates a *positive* relationship between independent and dependent variables in the conceptual model.

Of course, as the present chapter suggests, this resembles more of a multi-dimensional collection of continuums, but for illustrative purposes we have simplified the rendering to clearly show the moderating power of external context.

The table above illustrates the relationship between external context and Importance.

IDENTIFY . . .
The Context of Importance

In examining the following cases, please utilize them in the following ways:

1. In general, can you overlay the template from this chapter onto the scenes below and see the impact of the characters' contexts on their Importance?
2. Now, as a *mirror* (looking specifically at *you*): Do any of these characters remind you of you and help to reveal the impact of your contexts on your Importance?
3. Finally, as a *window* (looking at specific *others*): Do any of these characters remind you of someone else that you know and help to reveal the impact of their contexts on their Importance?

Case Study (Personal)

Following the Middle Norman Child (Annie) When She Attends
State University as a Freshman

In the dorm: Annie loves to travel, so she signed up to live in International House and is assigned to a suite with several international exchange student roommates. The three young women from the collectivist *culture* love and are elevated by all the group assignments and team-based grades of the required freshman seminar, whereas Annie, from an individualist culture, cannot stand them and feels like a fish out of water. The roommates are all excited about how academic standards are really emphasized at the university, that is, except for Annie who wanted to go to a more laid-back "party school" and was dissuaded by her parents. The other schoolgirls form a study group and agree on common norms for the suite, including lights out and no music after 11 p.m., and post the list on the refrigerator . . . these rules are not suiting Annie well.

In the science lab: Annie has dreaded the required science lab ever since she saw it on her schedule. That this is her first class ever does not bode well for her enthusiasm, image, or GPA. Annie feels confined by the strict guidelines and procedures of the *tasks*—she particularly does not like doing the long, detailed weekly write-ups, she gets no intrinsic joy or reinforcement from the material, and she is ill suited to what is asked of her (e.g., she just can't bring herself to dissect that frog).

In the library: For the freshman English paper all students work one on one with an upper-class research assistant who is assigned to *support* them. Annie heard about the tutor, who is fun, patient, organized, and service oriented. Her students look like they are walking on air after returning from a session. Of course she got assigned to the other one with the reverse profile. He makes her spend more time slaving away on his own project than working on hers. She has never felt so abused, ignored, used, and disempowered by this uncaring, inhumane non-mentor.

In the career-planning center: Annie signs up for the teachers-prep program and wants to enter the *market* to work at a local day care center. However, it seems like everyone else also wants the same job . . . and there are only two positions. During the initial interview stage, it becomes painfully clear that other applicants have better credentials, advanced knowledge, more unique skills, and some even have established connections with the industry. Whereas she used to feel OK about her prospects, she now feels that in this cohort her services are comparatively marginal and peripheral.

Do you see how context influences Importance? Is Annie's path supported by her context? As a result does she feel of significant value? How would you help Annie to see the context? Adjust to it? Change it?

Case Study (Professional)

Behind the Scenes at Apex Insurance Company's Sales Office

In the headquarters: The global marketing team is thinking about how to sell their insurance policies in the expanding international markets. Anil knows that different *cultures* have different norms and adapts his presentation to account for this—emphasizing, for example, individualistic motives for one place and collectivist motives for another. He also connects his pitch to the company's culture of cooperation and innovation. It really seems to connect with the audience. On the other hand, Yani is culturally oblivious and commits several faux pas in his talk, including the misuse of words, colors, and symbols that run counter to, and even offend, the deep norms and foundational practices of his clients.

In the field office: The web design team is busy on the assigned *task* of updating the firm's cyber presence. Kumar is not keen on the newest software and, because he is all the way upstream in the process, he is forced to work with strict cookie-cutter procedures and clear programmatic guidelines. He feels like a simple cog in the machine, and this proverbial round peg is having problems fitting into the defined square hole. On the other hand, Nadia loves the downstream freedom her part of the process gives her—she can make many decisions, do a variety of things, see how the implementation impacts her clients, and has even been heard singing at her desk as she enthusiastically engages to solve problems and beat deadlines.

In the call center: Maggio's boss is nicknamed the Ogre—he is always complaining, constantly grumpy, only gives help to his "favorite" employees (a group to which Maggio does *not* belong), and treats Maggio like a slave doing his bidding. Too bad he doesn't work for Cleo's *supportive* boss—she is always positive, cheerful, encouraging, caring, helpful, a good listener, and will do anything for her employees . . . who in turn will do anything for her. Maggio is made to feel insignificant and valueless. Cleo and her colleagues feel that their sense of Importance has never been higher.

In the weekly sales meeting: Jon has skillfully plotted a learning curve and established great longstanding relationships within the hottest and fastest-growing *market* sectors of the business. He is now the only one who has really mastered the cutting-edge technologies, systems, and sectors that drive an increasingly greater percentage of profits. As such, he feels like he is on the way up, literally and figuratively. When Jon talks in meetings, people listen. Stevie is on the opposite end of the spectrum. He is just one of 13 coworkers working in the same windowless back-office location with the same semi-outdated skill sets and expertise that the industry has already begun phasing out. He has no voice in things. Jon sits tall in his chair and is held in high regard, whereas no one really heeds Stevie or notices the increasingly sad, disconnected stare on his face, and it would be unlikely that they would even know if he was missing. Come the next round of layoffs, he probably will be.

Do you see how context influences Importance? Are Anil and Yani's, Kumar and Nadia's, Maggio and Cleo's, and Jon and Stevie's paths differentially supported by their context? As a result, do they feel of significant value? How would you help those who are not supported to see their context? Adjust to it? Change it?

PERSONALIZE . . .
The Context of Importance

This set of exercises gives you the opportunity to clarify how your external context moderates the filtered paths to significant value. All together, the more your paths are supported by the context of your location, your task, your management, and your market, the greater and more positive their impact on your Importance. You can use this section to assess the degree to which your significant value is moderated by your external context.

General

Come to grips with the external factors that moderate your paths to Importance.
   At the most basic level, please rate the degree to which the following contextual factors are incompatible/barriers (low, say a "1") or supportive/facilitators (high, say a "10") of your path(s) to Importance. Recall that you identified these paths in the exercise from a prior chapter.

   1. My location
   2. My task
   3. My support
   4. My market

Are you happy with your scores? What would you change? How could you change this? Does your ranking suggest better or worse contextual fit with Importance? Has the ranking changed as you have grown, experienced things, gone through life changes, or advanced in years? Is there any pattern to be found in these? Is there a sweet spot where everything fell into place? If so then how can you get (back) there?

Specific

Drill down further to isolate specific contextual factors and how they moderate your filtered paths.
   Now please note the degree to which you agree with the following ways for completing this sentence, from most to least descriptive of you:
   My filtered path(s) to Importance . . .

   - Are aligned with my location
     ○ Are supported by my society
     ○ Fit with the prevailing global/national/regional culture and norms

- ○ Are supported by my organization
- ○ Fit with the prevailing corporate culture and norms
- ○ Are supported by my group
- ○ Fit with the prevailing team culture and norms
- Are aligned with my task
  - ○ Are supported by my task breadth
  - ○ Fit the range of TDRs of what I am asked to do
  - ○ Relate to my area or proverbial "wheelhouse"
  - ○ Are supported by my task depth
  - ○ Fit the core characteristics of the jobs I am asked to do
  - ○ Provide meaning, responsibility, and growth opportunities
- Are aligned with my management
  - ○ Are supported by my manager(s)
  - ○ Fit my preferred management style
  - ○ Provide to me positive attitudes
  - ○ Provide to me genuine care
  - ○ Provide to me real inclusion
  - ○ Provide to me service-oriented, client-focused, prioritized treatment
- Are aligned with my market
  - ○ Are supported by my market
  - ○ Are in short, and shrinking, supply
  - ○ Are in great, and growing, demand
  - ○ Create dependency and allow me to influence others
  - ○ Convey to me greater levels of power
  - ○ Construct for me relative (competitive) advantage

APPLY . . .
The Context of Importance

From a personal perspective, your Importance is partly determined by the choices that you make about the contexts of your filtered path(s). From a professional perspective, your people's Importance is partly determined by the management strategies that you employ to help them shape the context of their filtered path(s).

Please take a moment to apply the material from this chapter to make better choices and craft better strategies about the context of Importance.

Making Personal Choices

Choice 3: You are, to varying degrees, in control of your Importance's external fit. That is to say, you can approach external context in at least three ways:

1. First (good): Be mindful of your context. Here you can see why things happen . . . but still be at their mercy. This is low control. It is passive. Knowing is generally better than not knowing (ignorance here is *not* bliss), but it does not matter per se if nothing is changed.

Table 5.2   Different Approaches to Managing Context

CONTEXT	APPROACH		
	Understand *(Good)*	*Adapt* *(Better)*	*Regulate* *(Best)*
• Location	Low Control	Moderate Control	High Control
• Task	Passive	Reactive	Proactive
• Support	Minimal Involvement	Sporadic Involvement	Active Involvement
• Market	Insight	Flexibility	Mastery
	See It	Flow with It	Create It
	No Change	Change Self	Change Context
	Hope for Best	Adjust for Fit	Customize for Fit

2. Second (better): Flexibly acclimate yourself to your context. Here you can adapt or modify yourself to facilitate or find fit. This is moderate control. It is reactive. Your strategy is adaptive.
3. Third (best): Strategically create your context. Here you can regulate or select and shape your context to create fit. This is high control. It is proactive. Your strategy is enactive.[21]

These approaches are illustrated in the table above.

More specifically, in terms of the latter two active options (versus a passive but unaffected understanding):

Choice 3a. You can choose to align your filtered path with your *location*—by altering your path to suit the context, or changing your context, or altering the context to suit your chosen path.

> Are my paths favored by the prevailing locational norms? Should I change my path? Advocate for or create a change in norms? Relocate to a different cultural (society, organization, and/or group) environment?

Choice 3b. You can choose to align your filtered path with your *task*—by altering your path to suit the context, or changing your context, or altering the context to suit your chosen path.

> Are my paths favored by the prevailing tasks? Should I change my path? Advocate for or create a change in my (breadth and/or depth of) tasks? Move to a different task environment?

Choice 3c. You can choose to align your filtered path with your *support*—by altering your path to suit the context, or changing your context, or altering the context to suit your chosen path.

> Are my paths favored by the prevailing managerial support? Should I change my path? Advocate for or create a change in my management (attitude, care, inclusion, and/or treatment)? Move to a different management environment?

Choice 3d. You can choose to align your filtered path with your *market*—by altering your path to suit the context, or changing your context, or altering the context to suit your chosen path.

> Are my paths favored by the prevailing market conditions? Should I change my path? Advocate for or create a change in the market (dependency, power, advantage) arrangements? Move to a different market environment?

Crafting Management Strategies

Management Strategy 3: You can, to varying degrees, influence fit between others' people's filtered Importance paths and their external context. That is to say, you can try to align others' contexts with their drivers by changing context or changing drivers. In a manner similar to the preceding section, your efforts might facilitate or impede the degree to which their choices are reinforced by prevailing norms, tasks, support, and market conditions.

The impact will not only be a static, one-time occurrence but can be magnified over time. This is due to the effects of its inherent path dependency (based on successively accumulated, more objective changes in state and corresponding trajectories) as well as potential self-fulfilling prophecy (based on successively accumulated, more subjective changes in perception and corresponding responses).

This can happen at work, at home, or anywhere.

Strategy 3a. You can create circumstances so their particular paths mesh with prevailing *locational* norms. For example:

> Help them identify the norms of the societal, organizational, and group locations in which they are embedded. Explore the degree of alignment with their path to see if they are synergistic. Optimize fit by asking, "Is this the right path for you here? If not, what should be changed? Or is this the right place (cultural environment) for your path? If not, where should you go?"

Strategy 3b. You can create circumstances so their particular drivers mesh with prevailing *tasks*. For example:

> Help them identify the breadth and depth of the tasks in which they engage. Explore the degree of alignment with their path to see if they are synergistic. Optimize fit by asking, "Is this the right path for you here? If not, what should be changed? Or is this the right place (task environment) for your path? If not, where should you go?"

Strategy 3c. You can create circumstances so their particular drivers mesh with prevailing *support*. For example:

> Help them identify the management context in which they function. Explore the degree of alignment with their path to see if they are synergistic. Optimize

fit by asking, "Is this the right path for you here? If not, what should be changed? Or is this the right place (management environment) for your path? If not, where should you go?"

Strategy 3d. You can create circumstances so their particular drivers mesh with prevailing *markets*. For example:

> Help them identify the market conditions in which they operate. Explore the degree of alignment with their path to see if they are synergistic. Optimize fit by asking, "Is this the right path for you here? If not, what should be changed? Or is this the right place (market environment) for your path? If not, where should you go?"

Checkpoint

Now that we have concluded this chapter, it is appropriate to pause for a moment at this checkpoint and answer the following questions:

- Do you UNDERSTAND the different external moderators of Importance and how they make it context specific?
- Can you IDENTIFY the external moderators in personal and professional settings?
- Have you PERSONALIZED the external moderators by relating them to the environment(s) in which you locate your own Importance journey?
- Will you APPLY the above to (a) develop your external moderator-related "fit" to make better choices and (b) facilitate others' external moderator-related "fit" to craft better strategies?

If not, circle back.

If so, let's move on to the next part of the model: *criteria* . . . and the internal-moderator contingencies of Importance.

6

Criteria—The Internal Contingencies to Importance

You should be aware of (good), flexibly adapt to (better), or strategically create (best) the lens that you use to assess your Importance.

Chapter 6 presents the lens moderators to Importance. In this chapter we will consider these different internal contingencies to Importance. First, we will seek to UNDERSTAND the impact of the criteria that we emphasize, including the:

- Scope dimension, in particular our cross-sectional Importance lens "snapshot"
- Time dimension, in particular our longitudinal Importance lens "cinema"
- Frame dimension, in particular our Importance lens "zoom"
- Scale dimension, in particular our Importance lens "anchors" or benchmarks
- Perspective dimension, in particular our Importance lens "clarity"

The upshot of these choices will be reconciled in terms of how their respective internal On or Off switches bear on the different path-nature relationships. Second, we will seek to IDENTIFY these internal/criteria moderators by sketching personal and professional case study illustrations. You might use them to see yourself (mirror) or others (window) more accurately. Third, we will seek to PERSONALIZE these internal/criteria moderators by presenting reflective exercises that you can use to relate them to your particular Importance journey. Fourth, we will seek to APPLY the above by deriving guided checklists that can help you make better personal choices and craft better management strategies.

UNDERSTAND . . .
The Criteria of Importance

Will a person's Importance be evaluated the same way regardless of the method that is used to measure it? Or, if not, is Importance inherently dependent on the approach to assessment that a person selects? Does this mean that different paths to Importance will vary in attractiveness, and be deemed more or less successful, based on the criteria that we choose to apply?

This chapter will address these issues by taking up the underlying question "Do different criteria make a person's particular path to Importance look better or worse?" Stated plainly, "What are the measurement factors influencing Importance?" Stated colloquially, "Why do certain lenses make certain people feel more or less like a VIP?"

Or, in terms of our model, "What are some of the key internal moderators of Importance?"

Here we will advance the proposition that the power of our drivers to impact our Importance is also contingent on our *criteria*. Therefore, the impact of people's filtered paths will also depend on the metrics they apply. Lesson: Different "lenses" can make us assess Importance in different ways. If we think about criteria as the means that we choose to assess or judge Importance, it is critical that we recognize that these different "judges" can render different verdicts.

Before we get started, a few points of clarification:

- POINT A: Importance is not measurement neutral. It depends on our criteria (i.e., the lens that we use to view ourselves).
- POINT B: Measurements (criteria) are different. They vary in breadth and scope. They vary in length and time. They vary in emphasis and focus. They vary in scale and comparison/calibration benchmarks. They vary in perspective and clarity. These are critical, non-trivial distinctions of how criteria can influence assessment.
- POINT C: Criteria moderates Importance. It is impossible to understand one's self-subjective Importance until the means of assessment itself is understood. If the criteria change, our Importance can change accordingly. That is to say, we can assess our significant value differently when we use different measurement approaches, employ different perspectives, and utilize different standards.
- POINT D: If you *understand* the Importance criteria that you use, you will be able to understand why you see yourself in a certain manner . . . but still be at their mercy (low control). If you flexibly *adapt* your criteria, you will be able to incrementally modify your self-perceived significant value (moderate control). If you *regulate* criteria, you will be able to proactively enact your world and create your fundamental reality (high control).

Now for a discussion of some of the key internal, criteria-related dimensions bearing on Importance.

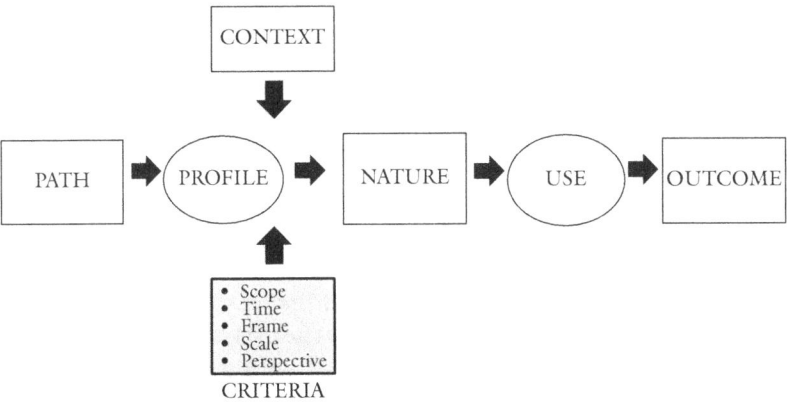

Figure 6.1   Internal Criteria Moderators of Importance.

Dimension #1: Scope—The Cross-Sectional Snapshot

First, the prevailing *scope*, or cross-sectional orientation of the lens, impacts the way in which Importance will be determined.

The message here is that the more our personal paths align with our scope, the more positive their impact on significance and value. Or said another way, the paths to Importance will vary depending on the inclusiveness of the measurement lens that the person applies to assessing it.

Importance is therefore scope specific. For example, you can assess your Importance by looking at your total self or, alternatively, different selected parts of yourself:

- Holistic (total) selves
- Component (partial) selves

Scope = Holistic/Total
A holistic (broad) scope involves looking at the entire range of oneself. It is akin to taking a broad full-body scan. It sees the entire person—your big picture, your proverbial "forest." This is a more objective way to structure the scope of one's lens than looking at any particular or arbitrarily selected part. If the cross-sectional scope is more inclusive, Importance will be assessed in a more descriptive (i.e., complete and potentially more true) manner. That is to say, if you subject the entire "you" to an assessment of significant value, the more comprehensive criteria set would capture a more accurate picture and yield a more representative analysis. For example, utilizing a broad holistic scope, you can consider the combined, amalgamated conglomerate of the full ranges of your characteristics, actions, acceptance, roles, and affiliations. It is a full assessment. It does not vary much with conscious, or unconscious, changes in any particular dimension.

So, ask yourself, when considering Importance, do you look at your whole self? The whole of others?

Scope = Component/Part

A component (narrow) scope involves looking at a select range of one's self. It is akin to taking a focused close-up scan. It sees only a chosen pinpoint section of the self—only selected parts of you, your proverbial "trees." This is a more subjective (if random) or strategic (if purposeful) way to structure the scope of one's lens as compared to a holistic consideration. If the cross-sectional scope orientation is less inclusive, Importance will be assessed in a less descriptive, more idiosyncratic (or strategic?) manner. Since the self is complex, the range of facets that one could select are multifarious. It also stands to reason that there would be more or less flattering parts that would reflect oneself in a different light and portray a different image.

Said another way, if only a subset or facet of "you" is subject to an assessment of significant value, the more selective criteria set would capture a less accurate picture and yield a more skewed, and less stable, analysis. If the cross-sectional scope emphasizes more favorable aspects, Importance will be assessed in a more positive manner. Alternatively, if the selective scope emphasizes less favorable aspects, Importance will be assessed in a more negative manner. For example, utilizing a narrow component scope, you can look at only one particular dimension of one particular path. As such, assessment varies greatly with a change in the focal dimension. It also varies when you consciously, or unconsciously, shift the focus from one dimension to another.

So, ask yourself, when considering Importance, do you look at only part of yourself? If so, what parts do you look at? Only select parts of others? If so, what parts do you look at?

Taken Together

We can see from the above discussion that Importance is scope specific. A broader scope is more holistic and stable. A narrower scope is more idiosyncratic, selective, and capricious. Ultimately the more that your paths are favored by your lens's scope orientation, or its cross-sectional dimension, the more positive their impact on your Importance.

More specifically . . . the scope of your criteria—whether holistic or component—can be seen to moderate the relationship between the conditions, nature, and eventual consequences of Importance. When the scope of your criteria fits with your filtered path, it magnifies the impact of that particular driver. When there is a poor fit, the impact of that driver is restricted or reduced. Thus, VIPs harmonize their consideration of scope and their path.

So you will feel more like a VIP when you reconcile holistic-component aspects of criteria and choose a path that is favored by the scope of your assessment . . . or if you adopt a scope that favors your chosen path. Alternatively, you will feel less like a VIP when your criteria scope neither reconciles nor favors your chosen path.

Dimension #2: Time—The Longitudinal Cinema

Second, the prevailing *time*, or longitudinal orientation of the lens, impacts the way in which Importance will be determined.

The message here is that the more our personal paths align with our time, the more positive their impact on significance and value. Or said another way, the paths to Importance will vary depending on the temporal emphasis of the measurement lens that the person applies to assessing it.

Importance is therefore time specific. For example, you can assess your Importance by looking at different temporal benchmarks—your past (legacy), your present (state), or your future (potential) selves.[1]

- The past: Historical record
- The present: Here and now
- The future: Potential and prospects

Time = Past
Looking at the past embodiment of oneself is akin to conducting a historical review. It sees what one has been or has done. That is to say, significant value is conceptualized as a matter of established record and accumulated metrics. In visual terms, your treasured, attic-stored sepia photo album could represent this past-based visioning of Importance. If the longitudinal dimension is more past-oriented, Importance will be assessed in a more retrospective, nostalgic, resume-like manner.

Thus the relevant question here is "Have I demonstrated Importance?" And the temptation would be to then "live in the past." Using a musical analogy, you might sing the song "Glory Days."[2] Using a sports analogy, you might deem the old veteran player who paid their dues as meriting the highest assessment of Importance. Ultimately, utilizing a past-based time lens, you primarily consider the *historical* up-and-down trends of your relevant characteristics, actions, acceptances, roles, and affiliations.

So, ask yourself, when considering Importance, do you look at your past self? The past selves of others?

Time = Present
Looking at the present embodiment of oneself is akin to conducting a current, real-time assessment. It sees what one is or is doing. That is to say, significant value is conceptualized as a matter of current account and real-time metrics. In visual terms, your daily or hourly social media posting—Twitter, Facebook, Instagram, Snapchat —could represent this present-based visioning of Importance. If the longitudinal dimension is more present oriented, Importance will be assessed in a more here-and-now, practical, recent (marginal) value manner.

Thus the relevant question here is "Am I important at this specific instant?" And the temptation would be to "be in the now." Using a musical analogy, you might sing the song "Live for Today"[3] or chant "Carpe Diem," which refers to a preference for living in the moment and roughly translates into the popular phrase "seize the day."[4] Using a sports analogy, you might deem the current star player in their prime as meriting the highest assessment of Importance. Ultimately, utilizing a present-based time lens, you primarily consider the current, *real-time* ups and downs of your relevant characteristics, actions, acceptances, roles, and affiliations.

So, ask yourself, when considering Importance, do you look at your current self? The current selves of others?

Time = Future

Looking at the future embodiment of oneself is akin to conducting a probabilistic forecast. It sees what one might be or do. That is to say, significant value is conceptualized as a matter of future account and projected metrics. In visual terms, your prognostic, planning-based, or possibilities-frontier rendering could represent this future-based visioning of Importance. If the longitudinal dimension is more future oriented, Importance will be assessed in a more prospective, hypothetical, growth-curve manner.

Thus the relevant question is "Am I likely to be important going forward?" And the temptation would be to "invest in tomorrow." Using a musical analogy, you might sing the song "The Future's So Bright I Gotta Wear Shades."[5] Using a sports analogy, you might deem the emerging young prospect with tremendous upside as meriting the highest assessment of Importance. Ultimately, utilizing a future-based time lens, you primarily consider the *potential* or predicted ups and downs of your relevant characteristics, actions, acceptances, roles, and affiliations.

So, ask yourself, when considering Importance, do you look at your future self? The future selves of others?

Taken Together

We can see from the above discussion that Importance is time specific. The more your paths are favored by your lens's time orientation, or its longitudinal dimension, the more positive their impact on your Importance. Moreover, the leverage points for each are different. A past-time orientation is more retrospective and open to interpretation. A current-time orientation is more experiential and open to alteration. A future-time orientation is more prospective and reliant on projection and forecasting.

More specifically, the time of your criteria—whether past, present, or future—can be seen to moderate the relationship between the conditions, nature, and eventual consequences of Importance.

From an objective angle (and akin to the prior argument regarding scope), if the time orientation is more inclusive—taking into account past, present, and future concerns—Importance will be assessed in a more descriptive (i.e., complete, and potentially more representative and truer) manner. Alternatively, if the time orientation is less inclusive, Importance will be assessed in a less descriptive manner. From a strategic angle, if the time orientation is slanted toward more favorable aspects of oneself (e.g., if you happen to have a relatively more distinguished past, impressive present, or rosy future), Importance will be assessed in a more positive manner. Either way, when the time orientation of our criteria fits with our filtered path, it magnifies the impact of that particular driver. When there is a poor fit, the impact of that driver is restricted or reduced. Thus, VIPs harmonize their consideration of time and their path.

So you will feel more like a VIP when you reconcile past-present-future aspects of criteria and choose a path that is favored by the time orientation of your assessment . . . or if you adopt a time orientation that favors your chosen path. Alternatively, you will feel less like a VIP when your criteria time orientation neither reconciles nor favors your chosen path.

Dimension #3: Frame—The Zoom

Third, the prevailing *frame*, or focus of the lens, impacts the way in which Importance will be determined.

The message here is that the more our personal paths align with our frame, the more positive their impact on significance and value. Or said another way, the paths to Importance will vary depending on the nature of the lens that the person applies to assessing it.

Importance is therefore frame specific.

For example, you can assess your Importance by fading or zooming in (to put yourself more prominently in the picture, or front and center). Alternatively, you can assess your Importance by fading or zooming out (to put yourself less prominently in the picture, or in the background).

- Large frame = Zoom-out panorama
- Small frame = Zoom-in focus

To further clarify this distinction, please consider the following text from a movie scene featuring the late Robin Williams reading a selection of Walt Whitman's prose:[6]

> To quote from Whitman: "O me, O life of the questions of these recurring. Of the endless trains of the faithless. Of cities filled with the foolish. What good amid these, O me, O life? Answer: That you are here. That life exists and identity. That the powerful play goes on, and you may contribute a verse."

Which part of the quote did you emphasize . . . the massive "play" (zoom-out large frame, where your existence is more trivial) or your unique "verse" (zoom-in small frame, where your existence is more prominent)?

In addition, please also consider the following quotes and see which ones speak more directly to you:

> Zoom-out panorama—David Hume:[7] "The life of man is of no greater importance to the universe than that of an oyster." Leo Tolstoy:[8] "How good is it to

remember one's insignificance: that of a man among billions of men, of an animal amid billions of animals; and one's abode, the earth, a little grain of sand
in comparison with Sirius and others, and one's life span in comparison with
billions on billions of ages."

Upshot . . . in a grand, expansive reality, we can loom small and can be seen as
relatively unimportant.

Zoom-in focus—Blaise Pascal:[9] "The least movement is of importance to all
nature. The entire ocean is affected by a pebble." Nelson Mandela:[10] "What
counts in life is not the mere fact that we have lived. It is what difference we
have made to the lives of others that will determine the significance of the life
we lead."

Upshot . . . in our focal arena, and in a highly interdependent system, we can
loom large and be seen as very important.

If it was the Hume/Tolstoy quotes that resonated more with you, this suggests a zoom-out, panoramic frame. If it was the Pascal/Mandela quotes that
spoke more directly to you, this suggests a zoom-in, focused frame. Let us
now consider them in turn.

Frame = Panoramic Zoom-Out
When you place yourself within a larger frame, you appear smaller.
    Perhaps here you are seen as just a face in the crowd. Or perhaps through
this frame you are conceptualized as a single person among so many, in a
small place amidst so much, for a short life span amid such a long history. Or
pushing it further perhaps as merely a tiny mite-like organism (person) on a
tiny pebble (Earth) existing for a tiny nanosecond (life span) in an unfathom-
ably massive universe (or collection of multiverses) that has been around for
indeterminably billions upon billions of years and is part of something even
greater that we cannot even come close to understanding.
    If the criteria frame is larger—the play, the ocean—and you as a result are
smaller, Importance will be assessed in regard to a more epic arena and in a
less concentrated manner. Here you see your significant value as akin to a
single note in a colossal opus. Or as a single chapter in a massive book. Or
as a single scene in an epic movie. The emphasis is less on the fidelity of your
note/chapter/scene per se but instead breaking down discernable boundaries to examine its (your) niche and impact in the often inconceivably grand
scheme of things.
    So, ask yourself, when considering Importance, do you look at yourself in
relation to the larger, infinite picture? The infinite selves of others?

Frame = Focused Zoom-In
In contrast, when you place yourself within a smaller frame, you appear larger.
    Perhaps here your single face is the entire focus of the picture, and
the crowd is merely fuzzy background noise. What matters is that the

considered frame—this moment (now!), this place (here!), this relationship, this episode—is the entire relevant world.

If the criteria frame is smaller—the verse, the pebble—and you as a result are larger, Importance will be assessed in regard to a more defined arena and in a more concentrated manner. Here you see your significant value as the singer of a beautiful note (e.g., the "song of me") or as the author of an enthralling chapter (e.g., the "book of me") or as the star of a fantastic scene (e.g., the "movie of me"). The emphasis is less on the grand scheme of things per se but instead looking within discernable boundaries to examine its (your) distinct niche and impact.

So, ask yourself, when considering Importance, do you look at yourself in relation to the smaller, intimate picture? The intimate selves of others?

Taken Together

We can see from the above discussion that Importance is frame specific. The more your paths are favored by your lens's frame, the more positive their impact on your Importance. A zoomed-out broad frame positions you as a relatively minor element of a massive multidimensional panorama. Importance is determined in relation to the inconceivably infinite. A zoomed-in narrow frame positions you in the proverbial front and center of the relevant shot. Importance is determined in relation to the saliently intimate.

More specifically, the frame of your criteria—whether panoramic or focused—can be seen to moderate the relationship between the conditions, nature, and eventual consequences of Importance. Significance and value are dependent on the frame of the lens. When the frame of our criteria fits with and favors our filtered path, it magnifies the impact of that particular driver. When there is a poor fit, the impact of that driver is restricted or reduced. Thus, VIPs harmonize their consideration of frame and their path.

So you will feel more like a VIP when you reconcile panoramic-focused aspects of criteria (i.e., the "infinite" with your "intimate") and choose a path that is favored by the frame of your assessment . . . or if you adopt a frame that favors your chosen path. Alternatively, you will feel less like a VIP when your criteria frame neither reconciles nor favors your chosen path.

Dimension #4: Scale—The Benchmarks

Fourth, the prevailing *scale*, or benchmarks within the lens, impacts the way in which Importance will be determined.

The message here is that the more our personal paths align with our scale, the more positive their impact on significance and value. Or said another way, the paths to Importance will vary depending on the nature of the comparison points or gradients in the measurement lens that the person applies to assessing it. Self-evaluation is in part, and similar to that voiced by William James, dependent on the ratio of our successes relative to our pretentions.[11]

This is consistent with much research on perception and decision making, where one's reference point determines perceived relative positive and negative comparative assessments.[12] For example, a five-and-a-half-foot person looks tall when standing next to a four-foot child and short when standing instead next to a seven-foot basketball player. If you score an 80 percent on an exam you feel good if your comparison (benchmark or reference point) is someone who earned a 60 percent, and you feel bad if your comparison instead is someone who earned a 95 percent. If you receive a $10,000 raise it looks like you did poorly or lost money if you were expecting a $25,000 increase, and it looks like you did well or gained money if you were instead expecting a $1,000 increase.

Importance is therefore relative or scale specific.

For example, you can assess your Importance by comparing yourself to more or less favorable others, more or less similar others, as well as higher or lower trending others, using a relative gain or loss reference point.

Benchmark Favorability
Regarding favorability, when you use higher gradients on the relevant continuum—great looking (characteristics), extraordinary achieving (actions), extremely famous or popular (acceptance), highly ranking (roles), or well-connected (affiliations) people for your comparison points, you are more likely to look worse than if you selected standards who were less of the above. As suggested earlier, you look larger when you stand next to infants . . . and you look smaller when you stand next to sumo wrestlers. If the scale is steeper, and you as a result appear worse on it, Importance will be assessed in a less favorable manner. In contrast, if the scale is lower, and as a result you appear better on it, Importance will be assessed in a more favorable manner. Bottom line: Significant value is unavoidably assessed in comparison to some anchors or standards; it looks larger when measured against lesser gauges and smaller against greater gauges.

So, ask yourself, when considering Importance, do you assess yourself in relation to higher or lower comparisons? Do you assess others in relation to higher or lower comparisons?

Benchmark Similarity
Regarding similarity, when you use more similar gradients on the relevant continuum—identically looking, achieving, popular, ranked, or connected people—as comparison points, you are more likely to look less unique than if you selected standards who were dissimilar on the above. You blend in when you are redundant (e.g., a "duplicate" or doppelgänger) and stand out when you are distinctive (e.g., an "original" or one-of-a-kind). If the scale is uniform, and you as a result appear common on it, Importance will be assessed in a less prominent, more generic manner. In contrast, if the scale is eclectic, and a result you appear salient on it, Importance will be assessed in a more favorable manner. Bottom line: Importance is assessed in comparison to others; significant value looks less special (i.e., cookie-cutter, generic; becomes lost and blends in) when measured against similar others

and more special (distinctive, unique; stands out and "pops") against different others.

So, ask yourself, when considering Importance, do you assess yourself in relation to more or less similar comparisons? Do you assess others in relation to more or less similar comparisons?

Benchmark Relativity
Regarding relativity, when you use positive deviations on the relevant continuum—upward-sloping/inclined curve of incrementally better-looking, achieving, popular, ranked, or connected people—as reference points, you are more likely to be seen differently than if you selected standards who emphasized the decline of the above. You appear progressive (and perhaps more important) when you are *gaining* ground and, conversely, appear degenerative (and perhaps less important) when you are *losing* ground. If the scale is relatively expanding, and you as a result appear to be falling or going lower on it, Importance will be assessed in a less favorable manner, say against a proverbial "rising star." In contrast, if the scale is relatively receding, and you as a result appear to be climbing or going higher up on it, Importance will be assessed in a more favorable manner, say against someone that is past his or her peak path. Bottom line: Significant value is assessed in comparison to the movements of those around you; it looks positive when measured against shrinking others and negative against growing others.

So, ask yourself, when considering Importance, do you assess yourself in relation to rising or falling comparisons? Do you assess others in relation to rising or falling comparisons?

Taken Together
We can see from the above discussion that Importance is scale specific. The more your paths are favored by your lens's benchmarks, the more positive their impact on your Importance.

More specifically, the scale of your criteria—whether utilizing favorable, similar, or relatively consistent benchmarks—can be seen to moderate the relationship between the conditions, nature, and eventual consequences of Importance.

From an objective angle, and akin to the prior arguments, if the scale orientation is more inclusive—taking into account, and balancing, all of the above factors—Importance will be assessed in a more descriptive (i.e., more complete, and in a potentially more representative and truer) manner. Alternatively, if the scale is less inclusive, Importance will be assessed in a less descriptive manner. From a strategic angle, if the scale is slanted toward more favorable aspects of oneself (e.g., to look big, special, or trending upward), Importance will be assessed in a more skewed and positive manner. For example, when choosing one's benchmark: a) Importance might be calibrated against laggards to look good, peers to look average, or aspirants to look negative; b) Importance might also be calibrated against clones to look common and blend in, or opposites to look unique and stand out; c) Importance might also be calibrated against those growing at a slower rate or even shrinking to look like one is progressive and gathering steam and on the upside (an up-and-comer?), or at a faster rate to look like one is receding and fading out and on the downside (over the hill?). Either way, when the scale of our criteria fits and favors our filtered path, it magnifies the impact of that particular driver. When there is a poor fit, the impact of that driver is restricted or reduced. Thus, VIPs harmonize their consideration of scale and their path.

So you will feel more like a VIP when you reconcile favorability-similarity-relativity aspects of criteria and choose a path that is favored by the scale of your assessment . . . or if you adopt a scale that favors your chosen path. Alternatively, you will feel less like a VIP when your criteria scale neither reconciles nor favors your chosen path.

Dimension #5: Perspective—The Quality

Fifth, the prevailing *perspective* quality, or clarity/transparency of the lens, impacts the way in which Importance will be determined.

The message here is that the more our personal paths align with our perspective, the more positive their impact on significance and value. Or said another way, the paths to Importance will vary depending on the clarity of the measurement lens the person applies to assessing it.[13]

Importance is therefore perspective specific.

For example, your perspective of your Importance can be influenced by:

- Attention clarity
- Perception clarity
- Intention clarity

Attention Clarity
Regarding clarity of attention, we can be more or less cognizant about our Importance. This is a matter of awareness. Can you see it? Is your significant value explicit and salient?

On the one hand, if attention is more sensitive, Importance will be assessed in a more representative manner. On the other hand, if attention is less sensitive, it will be more vulnerable to biases in attention (i.e., systematic errors in what you happen to notice, what grabs your attention, at a given point in time). For example, salience is influenced by a variety of factors such as a) object, or what you are looking at (e.g., its novelty, brightness, dominance, or movement) as well as b) subject, or who is doing the looking (e.g., your interests, expectations, preferences). Take for instance the "soul" aspect of the "characteristics" path. If we have a greater or lesser ability to really examine our soul, to be aware of it, to appreciate it, to fully attend to it, then its degree and fidelity of impact on our Importance will vary accordingly. Even more specifically, if peacefulness were a more elusive dimension of character to a particular person, then they would be less likely to truly prioritize or ultimately excel along this path. Bottom line: What we attend to is far from universal or objective.

A particular aspect of a particular path (e.g., of our characteristics of body, mind, soul; actions; acceptance and audience; roles; affiliations) will have a greater impact on our self-subjective significance and value depending on the degree to which it can be attended to or seen by the relevant party. Paths are more likely to be selected, to resonate, and to lead to positive outcomes when they are more *salient*.

So, ask yourself, when considering Importance, do you notice all aspects of yourself with equal clarity? Do you clearly notice all aspects of others?

Perception Clarity

Regarding clarity of perception, we can be more or less discerning about our Importance. This is a matter of accuracy. Can you see it correctly? Is your significant value precise?

On the one hand, if attention is sharper, Importance will be assessed in a more accurate manner. On the other hand, if attention is less sharp, it will be more vulnerable to biases in perception (i.e., systematic errors in how you happen to notice things, what determines their meaning at a given point in time). Indeed, it is well documented that a broad range of cognitive biases and heuristics often act upon us to skew our perception.[14] Take for instance the "fundamental" aspect of the "roles" path. If we have a greater or lesser ability to make sense of our roles, to crystalize them with precision, then their degree and fidelity of impact on our Importance will vary accordingly. Even more specifically, if "citizen" were a more distorted and biased dimension of role to a particular person, then they would be less likely to truly prioritize or ultimately excel along this path. Bottom line: How we make sense of what we attend to is far from universal or objective.

A particular aspect of a particular path (e.g., of our characteristics of body, mind, soul; actions; acceptance and audience; roles; affiliations) will have greater impact on our self-subjective significance and value depending on the way in which the relevant party sees it. Paths are more likely to be selected, to resonate, and to lead to positive outcomes when they are *precise*.

So, ask yourself, when considering Importance, do you perceive all aspects of yourself with equal clarity? Do you clearly perceive all aspects of others?

Intention Clarity

Regarding clarity of intention, we can be more or less honest about our Importance. This is a matter of sincerity. Can you see it earnestly? Is your significant value genuine?

On the one hand, if attention is more candid, Importance will be assessed in a more sincere manner. On the other hand, if attention is less candid, it will be more vulnerable to biases in intention (i.e., systematic errors in how you [mis]use what you notice, what determines their purpose at a given point in time). Indeed, it is well documented that a range of psychological processes often act upon us to skew our intentionality.[15] Take for instance the "achieving" aspect of the "actions" path. If we have a greater or lesser ability to openly and honestly make use of our achievements, to pursue them sincerely and positively, then their degree and fidelity of impact will vary accordingly. Even more specifically, if "accomplishments" were a less candidly and earnestly calibrated dimension of achieving to a particular person, then they would be less likely to truly prioritize or ultimately excel along this path. Bottom line: How we intend what we see and interpret is far from universal or objective.

A particular aspect of a particular path (e.g., of our characteristics of body, mind, soul; actions; acceptance and audience; roles; affiliations) will have a greater impact on our self-subjective significance and value depending on the way in which the relevant party intends it. Paths are more likely to be selected, to resonate, and to lead to positive outcomes when they are *earnest*.

So, ask yourself, when considering Importance, do you interpret all aspects of yourself with equal clarity? Do you clearly interpret all aspects of others?

Taken Together

We can see from the above discussion that Importance is perspective specific. The more your paths are favored by your lens's clarity, the more positive their impact on your Importance.

More specifically, the quality of your criteria perspective—whether more or less clear in attention, perception, and intention—can be seen to moderate the relationship between the conditions, nature, and eventual consequences of Importance.

From an objective angle (and akin to the prior arguments), if the criteria is more clear—across all of the above factors—Importance will be assessed in a more descriptive (i.e., complete, and potentially more representative and truer) manner. Alternatively, if the scale is less clear, Importance will be assessed in a less descriptive manner. From a strategic angle, if perspective is slanted toward more favorable aspects of oneself (e.g., to see selectively, interpret optimistically, or intend in a self-serving, biased manner), Importance will be assessed in a more positive manner. Either way, when the perspective quality or clarity of our criteria fits with our filtered path, it magnifies the impact of that particular driver. When there is a poor fit, the impact of that driver is restricted or reduced. Thus, VIPs harmonize their consideration of perspective and their path.

So you will feel more like a VIP when you reconcile attention-perception-intention clarity aspects of criteria and choose a path that is favored by the perspective of your assessment . . . or if you adopt a perspective that favors your chosen path. Alternatively, you will feel less like a VIP when your criteria perspective neither reconciles nor favors your chosen path.

Upshot of the Above

Our paths to Importance will be more or less resonant depending on how we measure it (e.g., our criteria moderators that these paths are subject to). In general, it is probably safe to say that:

I am important when . . .   The lens's *scope* fits/favors/elevates my path.
                                 The lens's *time* fits/favors/elevates my path.
                                 The lens's *frame* fits/favors/elevates my path.
                                 The lens's *scale* fits/favors/elevates my path.
                                 The lens's *perspective* fits/favors/elevates my path.

In terms of our model, criteria filters act as an internal moderator between path and Importance. So:

- If my filtered paths do not fit or are not supported by the internal criteria, the figurative moderator "switch" is Off—the inconsistency results in a dysfunctional, hostile, and punishing dynamic that creates a *negative* relationship between independent and dependent variables in the conceptual model.
- If my filtered paths fit or are supported by the internal criteria, the figurative moderator "switch" is On—the consistency results in a functional, symbiotic, and rewarding dynamic relationship that creates a *positive* relationship between independent and dependent variables in the conceptual model.

Of course, and again as the present chapter suggests, this resembles more of a multidimensional collection of continuums, but for illustrative purposes we have simplified the rendering to more plainly show the moderating power of internal criteria.

The following table illustrates the relationship between internal criteria and Importance.

Table 6.1   Internal Criteria and Importance

CRITERIA	INTERNAL MODERATOR SWITCH	
	OFF	ON
• Scope	Low Regard	High Regard
• Time	Reduced	Magnified
• Frame	Spurious	Central
• Scale	Looms Smaller	Looms Larger
• Perspective	De-emphasized	Emphasized
	Negative Spin	Positive Spin
	Regressing	Progressing
	Obscure/Diminishes	Salient/Highlights
	Inaccurate	Accurate
	Insincere	Sincere

Identify . . .
The Criteria of Importance

In examining the following cases, please utilize them in the following ways:

1. In *general*, can you overlay the template from this chapter onto the scenes below and see the impact of the characters' lens/criteria on their Importance?
2. Now, as a *mirror* (looking specifically at *you*): Do any of these characters remind you of you and help to reveal the impact of your lens/criteria on your Importance?
3. Finally, as a *window* (looking at specific *others*): Do any of these characters remind you of someone else that you know and help to reveal the impact of their lens/criteria on their Importance?

Case Study (Personal)

In the Community—Watching the Normans in Their Local Activities

In the Sunday service (re: *scope*): They sit near a neighboring family. Mother assesses her church worthiness by how she lives her life 24/7 from morning to night. Father assesses it by how he lives this particular two hours only. She will feel of significant value if her entire being is aligned. He will be OK if he merely stays awake, sings in tune, and gives a nice tithe. When they pull out of the parking lot, they cut off another car to beat the light—she winces whereas he is oblivious.

In the Saturday little league (re: *time*): The father coaches his son's baseball team. What influences him is how the kids carry themselves, put out effort to play, and enjoy the current here-and-now experience. His assistant coach fathers take somewhat different approaches. One seems to be trying to relive his past "glory days" and struts around the field house like he is walking on water. The other is constantly focusing on how the experience will position the kids for long-term personal development and projected professional careers.

In the Friday town hall meeting (re: *frame*): As the Normans sit in the audience, they see one of the council members completely focused on the town and everything within its borders. Nothing could be more imperative to her than the new tree-planting initiative at the park or the debate as to whether the speed limit on Main Street should be 25 or 30 mph. Another of the council members cares more about matters concerning the bigger state, the entire country, the geopolitical world events, and even the cosmological questions raised by physicists in the latest science magazine about the beginning and end of the universe as well as the potentially interdependent, embedded systems of multiverses. Needless to say, he zones out and disconnects from what is deemed a relatively trivial tree-planting and speed-limit conversation.

In the annual July Independence Day parade and December holiday season festivals (re: *scale*): In the summer, as the Normans march through the town with their daughters' Girl Scout troupe on the sunny Fourth of July morning, they see several people working on their lawns. One house has an OK yard but the owner beams because it clearly looks better than the weedy lot next door. Another house down the road has a beautifully manicured yard but its owner seems to slink as he compares it to the professionally landscaped, picture-perfect uber-lawn that he once saw in a magazine. Later in the winter, during the Christmas sleigh ride, the Normans again evidence different levels of pride and contentment when their neighbors are putting up their holiday decorations. The house across the street looks better than it ever has, and the improvement clearly makes its owner proud. However, the one next to it, even though it sports a dazzling Griswold-worthy[16] display of choreographed light-shows and mechanized armies of figurines, makes the owner sulk as he was not able to find some of last year's displays and as a result the display does not shine as brightly as it once did.

In the PTA annual school barbeque (re: *perspective*): The Normans walk around the gymnasium sampling some of the local fare. Some of the cooks astutely pick up on the nuances of the different foods and really grasp what it means to add certain spices or prepare the beef and rubs in different ways. They also seem really honest about their own plates and are happy to compliment others when they did a good job. On the other hand, some of the other cooks do not have such sensitivity, perspective, or good intentions. Instead they evidence limited palates, display skewed perceptions, and are unashamedly overly positive about their food while being overly critical about others' dishes.

Do you see how different criteria can influence one's sense of Importance? What happens when people adopt different scopes, times, frames, scales, and perspectives? How would you remedy situations where the above factors reduce people's significance and value to help them see their criteria? Adjust to it? Change it?

Case Study (Professional)

Behind the Scenes at the Hospital Emergi-Care Facility

In the emergency room (re: *scope*): One doctor assesses her medical worthiness by how she lives her life 24/7 from morning to night. She will feel of significant value if her entire being is aligned. Another assesses it by how he acts only during this particular shift. He will be OK if he stays awake, gives good care, and doesn't get sued. When they both see a man limping into another hospital wing in obvious pain she winces and approaches to help, whereas he is oblivious and tends only to his limited domain and defined desk area.

In the semi-private treatment rooms (re: *time*): The on-call doctor is most influenced by how the patients respond to her daily therapy treatments each and every time they are administered. Her colleagues take somewhat different approaches. One seems to be trying to relive his past med-school days as the valedictorian star student and, as such, struts around the ward from room to room like a proverbial big man on campus. The other is constantly focusing on how the patients' stays will help them later in life as well how the different experiences will position her for a long-term medical career and future professional advancements.

In the post-op care units (re: *frame*): One of the nurses is completely focused on the list of patients assigned to him. Nothing could be more important to him than the specific individuals under his care. They are all that matter. This is his entire (relevant) world. Another of the nurses is more concerned about the proverbial bigger picture, including new aesthetic and technological upgrades to the floor that will enhance her capacity for care. In addition, her mind frequently goes to the financial state of the hospital, the overall levels of societal health and wellness, and the new advancements described by researchers in the latest medical magazine about evolving diseases and their advanced treatments.

In the administrative support areas (re: *scale*): After they receive the middle-level, passing grade of the local medical board licensing committee, the two managers on duty react quite differently. One beams because it is definitely better than the shoddy hospital across town, whereas the other slumps when comparing it to the elite stature of the Mayo Clinic along with the other top most innovative facilities in the country.

In the hospital's machine repair shop (re: *perspective*): Some of the technicians really pick up on the nuances of the medical instruments and really get what it means to tweak or recalibrate them in different ways. They also seem exceedingly honest about their capabilities and are happy to send the products out or defer to other specialty centers when they can do a better job. Other technicians do not have such sensitivity, awareness, or good intentions. Instead they have limited diagnostic awareness, inaccurate perceptual abilities, and are overly braggadocious about their skills and unwarrantedly pessimistic about the quality of others' services.

Do you see how different criteria can influence one's sense of Importance? What happens when people adopt different scopes, times, frames, scales, and perspectives? How would you remedy situations where the above factors reduce people's significance and value to help them see their criteria? Adjust to it? Change it?

PERSONALIZE . . .
The Criteria of Importance

This set of exercises gives you the opportunity to clarify how your lens, or internal criteria, moderates the filtered paths to significant value. All together, the more your paths are supported by your criteria scope, time, frame, scale, and perspective, the greater and more positive their impact on your Importance. You can use this section to assess the degree to which your significant value is moderated by your internal criteria.

General

Come to grips with the internal criteria (lens) factors that moderate your paths to Importance.

At the most basic level, please rate the degree to which the following criteria dimensions are denigrating/barriers (low, say a "1") or amplifying/facilitators (high, say a "10") of your path(s) to Importance. Recall that you identified these paths in the exercise from a prior chapter.

1. Scope
2. Time
3. Frame
4. Scale
5. Perspective

Are you happy with your scores? What would you change? How could you change this? Does your ranking suggest better or worse criteria fit with Importance? Has the ranking changed as you have grown, experienced things, gone through life changes, or advanced in years? Is there any pattern to be found in these? Is there a sweet spot where everything fell into place? If so then how can you get (back) there?

Specific

Drill down further to isolate specific criteria-related (e.g., lens) factors and how they moderate your filtered paths.

Now please note the degree to which you agree with the following ways for completing this sentence, from most to least descriptive of you:

In assessing my filtered path(s) to Importance, I . . .

- Align them with my criteria scope
  - ○ Reconcile holistic and component considerations
  - ○ Integrate a broader, entire-person view
  - ○ Am cast in a favorable light by a broader-scope appraisal
  - ○ Integrate a narrower, partial-person view
  - ○ Am cast in a favorable light by a narrow-scope appraisal
  - ○ Choose my lens's scope dimension strategically
  - ○ Represent the real me
- Align them with my criteria time
  - ○ Reconcile past, present, and future considerations
  - ○ Integrate, and am cast in a favorable light by, a historical view
  - ○ Integrate, and am cast in a favorable light by, a here-and-now view
  - ○ Integrate, and am cast in a favorable light by, a prospective view
  - ○ Choose my lens's time dimension strategically
  - ○ Represent the real me

- Align them with my criteria frame
  - ○ Reconcile large-frame and small-frame considerations
  - ○ Integrate a zoomed-out, panoramic lens
  - ○ Am cast in a favorable light by a large-frame appraisal
  - ○ Integrate a zoomed-in, focused lens
  - ○ Am cast in a favorable light by a small-frame appraisal
  - ○ Choose my lens's frame dimension strategically
  - ○ Represent the real me
- Align them with my criteria scale
  - ○ Reconcile favorability, similarity, and relativity considerations
  - ○ Integrate, and am cast in a favorable light by, higher/lower benchmarks
  - ○ Integrate, and am cast in a favorable light by, unique/generic benchmarks
  - ○ Integrate, and am cast in a favorable light by, improving/receding benchmarks
  - ○ Choose my lens's scale dimension strategically
  - ○ Represent the real me
- Align them with my criteria perspective
  - ○ Reconcile attention, perception, and intention considerations
  - ○ Integrate, and am cast in a favorable light by, clear and salient attentions
  - ○ Integrate, and am cast in a favorable light by, clear and precise perceptions
  - ○ Integrate, and am cast in a favorable light by, clear and sincere intentions
  - ○ Choose my lens's perspective dimension strategically
  - ○ Represent the real me

APPLY . . .
The Criteria of Importance

From a personal perspective, your Importance is partly determined by the choices that you make about the criteria (lens) that is applied to your filtered path(s). From a professional perspective, your people's Importance is partly determined by the management strategies that you employ to help them shape the criteria (lens) applied to their filtered path(s).

Please take a moment to apply the material from this chapter to make better choices and craft better strategies about the criteria of Importance.

Making Personal Choices

Choice 4: You are, to varying degrees, in control of your Importance's internal fit. That is to say, just as in the prior chapter (with regard to external context moderators), you can approach internal criteria moderators in at least three ways:

1. First (good): Be mindful of your lens. Here you can see why things are assessed the way they are . . . but still be at the mercy of the criteria. This is low control. It is passive. Knowing is generally better than not knowing but matters less if nothing is changed.
2. Second (better): Flexibly adjust yourself to your lens. Here you can adapt or modify yourself to facilitate or find fit with the employed criteria. This is moderate control. It is reactive. Your strategy is adaptive.
3. Third (best): Strategically create/enact your lens. Here you can regulate or select and shape your criteria to create fit. This is high control. It is proactive. Your strategy is enactive.

These approaches are illustrated, again mirroring the prior chapter, in the table at the bottom of this page.

More specifically, in terms of the latter two active options (versus a passive but unaffected understanding):

Choice 4a. You can choose to align your filtered path with your *scope*—or cross-sectional (snapshot) orientation of the lens—by altering your path to suit the criteria or altering the criteria to suit your chosen path.

> Does the prevailing scope accurately assess/favor my paths? Should I change my path? Or perhaps emphasize a different criteria scope (holistic or component, and if the latter, which component)?

Choice 4b. You can choose to align your filtered path with your *time*—or longitudinal (cinema) orientation of the lens—by altering your path to suit the criteria or altering the criteria to suit your chosen path.

> Does the prevailing time accurately assess/favor my paths? Should I change my path? Or perhaps emphasize a different criteria time (past, present, or future)?

Choice 4c. You can choose to align your filtered path with your *frame*—or amount of "zoom" on the lens—by altering your path to suit the criteria or altering the criteria to suit your chosen path.

Table 6.2 Different Approaches to Managing Criteria

CRITERIA	APPROACH		
	Understand *(Good)*	*Adapt* *(Better)*	*Regulate* *(Best)*
• Scope	Low Control	Moderate Control	High Control
• Time	Passive	Reactive	Proactive
• Frame	Minimal Involvement	Sporadic Involvement	Active Involvement
• Scale	Insight	Flexibility	Mastery
• Perspective	See It	Flow with It	Create It
	No Change	Change Self	Change Criteria
	Hope for Best	Adjust for Fit	Customize for Fit

Does the prevailing frame accurately assess/favor my paths? Should I change my path? Or perhaps emphasize a different criteria frame (wide-angle: big picture/infinite or close-up: focused/intimate)?

Choice 4d. You can choose to align your filtered path with your *scale*—or comparative benchmarks within the lens—by altering your path to suit the criteria or altering the criteria to suit your chosen path.

Does the prevailing scale accurately assess/favor my paths? Should I change my path? Or perhaps emphasize a different criteria scale (re: favorability—against aspirant, peer, or laggard benchmarks; re: similarity—against more common or more unique benchmarks; relativity—against more progressive or more regressive benchmarks)?

Choice 4e. You can choose to align your filtered path with your *perspective*— or clarity/quality of the lens—by altering your path to suit the criteria or altering the criteria to suit your chosen path.

Does the prevailing perspective accurately assess/favor my paths? Should I change my path? Or perhaps emphasize a different criteria perspective (re: attention, perception, and/or intention)?

Crafting Management Strategies

Management Strategy 4: You can, to varying degrees, influence fit between others' filtered Importance paths and their internal criteria. That is to say, you can try to align others' lenses with their drivers by changing lenses or changing drivers. In a manner similar to the preceding section, your efforts might facilitate or impede the degree to which their choices are reinforced by scope, time, frame, scale, and perspective.

Again, the impact will not only be a static, one-time occurrence but can be magnified over time. This is due to the effects of its inherent path dependency (based on successively accumulated, more objective changes in state and corresponding trajectories) as well as potential self-fulfilling prophecy (based on successively accumulated, more subjective changes in perception and corresponding responses).

This can happen at work, at home, or anywhere.

Strategy 4a. You can create lenses so their particular drivers mesh with prevailing *scopes*. For example:

Help them identify the scope of the criteria embedded implicitly or explicitly in their significant value assessment methodology. Explore the degree of alignment with their path to see if they are synergistic. Optimize fit by asking, "Is this the right scope for you? Is the criteria appropriately holistic or component? If not, is it better to change your path or change your scope?"

Strategy 4b. You can create lenses so their particular drivers mesh with prevailing *times*. For example:

Help them identify the time orientation of the criteria embedded implicitly or explicitly in their significant value assessment methodology. Explore the degree of alignment with their path to see if they are synergistic. Optimize fit by asking, "Is this the right time orientation for you? Is the criteria appropriately past, present, or future focused? If not, is it better to change your path or change your time orientation?"

Strategy 4c. You can create lenses so their particular drivers mesh with prevailing *frames*. For example:

Help them identify the frame of the criteria embedded implicitly or explicitly in their significant value assessment methodology. Explore the degree of alignment with their path to see if they are synergistic. Optimize fit by asking, "Is this the right frame for you? Is the criteria appropriately wide-angle/panoramic or close-up/focused? If not, is it better to change your path or change your frame?"

Strategy 4d. You can create lenses so their particular drivers mesh with prevailing *scales*. For example:

Help them identify the scale of the criteria embedded implicitly or explicitly in their significant value assessment methodology. Explore the degree of alignment with their path to see if they are synergistic. Optimize fit by asking, "Is this the right scale for you? Is the criteria appropriately favorable, similar, or trending? If not, is it better to change your path or change your scale?"

Strategy 4e. You can create lenses so their particular drivers mesh with prevailing *perspectives*. For example:

Help them identify the perspective of the criteria embedded implicitly or explicitly in their significant value assessment methodology. Explore the degree of alignment with their path to see if they are synergistic. Optimize fit by asking, "Is this the right perspective for you? Is the criteria appropriately attentive, perceptive, and intended? If not, is it better to change your path or change your perspective?"

Checkpoint

Now that we have concluded this chapter, it is appropriate to pause for a moment at this checkpoint and answer the following questions:

- Do you UNDERSTAND the different internal moderators of Importance and how they make it criteria specific?

- Can you IDENTIFY the internal moderators in personal and professional settings?
- Have you PERSONALIZED the internal moderators by relating them to the lens(es) with which you assess your own Importance journey?
- Will you APPLY the above to a) develop your internal moderator-related "fit" to make better choices and b) facilitate others' internal moderator-related "fit" to craft better strategies?

If not, circle back.

If so, let's move on to the next part of the model: *nature* . . . and the forces and forms of Importance.

Nature—The Qualities of Importance

Strive for a healthy sense of Importance across its
(balanced and grounded) forces and (fused and dynamic) forms.

Chapter 7 presents the nature of Importance. In this chapter we will consider its different types or qualities. First, we will seek to UNDERSTAND the nature of Importance, in particular the two prime components that come together to create its force and form: (a) force, including valence and magnitude, and (b) form, including level and stability. The upshot of these choices will be reconciled in terms of how they can create a more or less "healthy" self-subjective sense of Importance that varies in the degree to which its force is balanced and grounded (i.e., near the sweet spot of Figure 7.2) as well as to which its form is fused and dynamic (i.e., near the bull's-eye of Figure 7.3). Second, we will seek to IDENTIFY the nuanced nature of Importance by sketching personal and professional case study illustrations. You might use them to see yourself (mirror) or others (window) more accurately. Third, we will seek to PERSONALIZE the nature of Importance by presenting reflective exercises that you can use to relate them to your particular Importance journey. Fourth, we will seek to APPLY the above by deriving guided checklists that can help you make better personal choices and craft better management strategies.

UNDERSTAND . . .
The Nature of Importance

Is it always better to feel more important? If not, what are the different forces of Importance . . . and might it have an optimal valence and magnitude? In addition, is there only one basic type of Importance? If not, what are its different forms . . . and might it have an optimal level and stability?

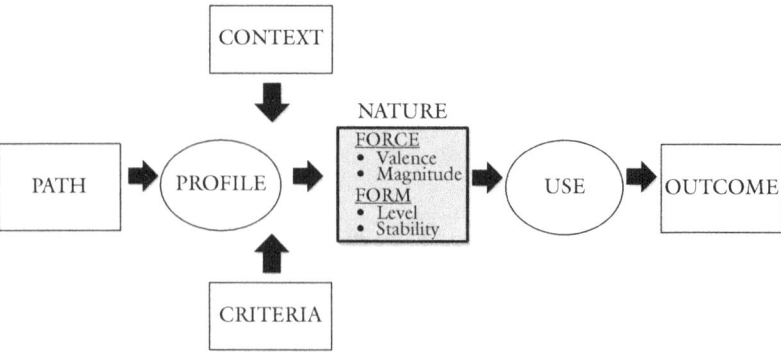

Figure 7.1   Nature of Importance.

This chapter will address these issues by taking up the underlying question "What are the different modes of Importance?" Stated plainly, "What are some of the key qualities of Importance?" Stated colloquially, "What does it really mean for people to say that they feel like a VIP?"

Or, in terms of our model, "What is the nature of Importance?"

Here we will advance the proposition that there are different *forces* and *forms* of Importance. Therefore, there is not one predetermined place where the paths, mediated by profile and moderated by context and criteria, lead. Different combinations thereof can affect differentiated, nuanced Importance(s) in different ways. Lesson: There are important distinctions in the manifestations of Importance.

Before we get started, a few points of clarification:

- POINT A: Importance varies in *force*. This force is a function of its valence (positive versus neutral or negative) and magnitude (large versus moderate or small). In an equation: Force = Valence × Magnitude. Force can be more, or less, balanced and grounded.
- POINT B: Importance varies in *form*. This form is a function of its level (independent versus interdependent) and stability (fixed versus variable). In an equation: Form = Level × Stability. Form can be more, or less, fused and dynamic.
- POINT C: Importance comes in different varieties. Combining the first and second points, it is accurate to say that there are more and less healthy types of Importance.

Now for a discussion of some of the force and form of Importance.

The Force of Importance

We begin by discussing some of the key elements that define the force of your Importance.

Since Importance was previously defined as a combination of significance and value, or in equation form $I = V * S$, we focus here on drilling down further to explore and delineate these two functional components—force and form. We will first take up the issue of force.

For the sake of simple correspondence, force is broken down in a consistent manner along the following lines:

- Valence: Represents a question of value, qualitatively probes whether self-subjective Importance is seen as relatively positive, neutral, or negative
- Magnitude: Represents a question of significance, quantitatively probes (as to the amount of the above positivity or negativity) whether self-subjective Importance is seen as relatively large, moderate, or small

Each will now be discussed in turn.

Force Valence

First, regarding force *valence*, we can say that the quality of Importance can be relatively more positive, neutral, or negative. Again, this describes the "value" (V) part of the $I = S * V$ Importance function.

Positive Valence. If the quality of your self-perceived Importance is positive, we could say that you have an affirming sense of Importance. You tend to appreciate your Importance. Thus, you feel as if you possess favorable value. You hold yourself in good regard. You are inherently worthy and desirable. In a way, positive valence meshes with, to some extent and under some contingencies, an encouraging sense of identity, esteem, efficacy, worth, and a generally optimistic outlook regarding oneself. A positive valence means that you see yourself as an agent of good. You are (more of) a virtue. You make things better. You lighten your world. You are of benefit, functional, helpful, a facilitator. Bending this back to the literatures introduced in Chapter 2, you embody a more positive physical, psychological, social, organizational, institutional, and spiritual/philosophical identity.

In terms of the Importance model, specifically your mediated and moderated paths (i.e., the conditions of Importance), you see yourself to have decidedly good characteristics, actions, roles, acceptance, and/or affiliations.

Neutral Valence. If the quality of your self-perceived Importance is *neutral*, we could say that you have an "indifferent," "indeterminate," or even "unclear" sense of Importance. That is, you feel as if you possess immaterial or uncertain net value. You hold yourself in neither good nor bad regard. You are neither inherently worthy nor unworthy, desirable nor undesirable. In a way, neutral Importance meshes with, to some extent and under some contingencies, a temperate sense of identity, esteem, efficacy, worth, and a generally dispassionate outlook regarding oneself. A neutral valence means that you see yourself as neither an agent of good nor bad. You don't make things better or worse. You don't lighten or darken your world. You are neither of benefit nor detriment, functional nor dysfunctional, helpful nor harmful, a facilitator nor a hindrance.

In terms of the Importance model, specifically your mediated and moderated paths (i.e., the conditions of Importance), you see yourself to have neither decidedly good nor bad characteristics, actions, roles, acceptance, and/or affiliations.

Negative Valence. If the quality of your self-perceived Importance is *negative*, we could say that you have a disconfirming sense of Importance. You tend to disparage and depreciate your value. That is, you feel as if you possess unfavorable value. You hold yourself in bad regard. You are inherently unworthy and undesirable. In a way, negative Importance meshes with, to some extent and under some contingencies, a discouraging sense of identity, esteem, efficacy, worth, and a generally pessimistic outlook regarding oneself. A negative valence means that you do *not* see yourself as an agent of good. You are (more of) a vice. You make things worse. You darken your world. You are of detriment, dysfunctional, harmful, a hindrance. Again, bending this back to the literatures introduced in Chapter 2, you embody a more negative physical, psychological, social, organizational, institutional, and spiritual/philosophical identity.

In terms of the Importance model, specifically your mediated and moderated paths (i.e., the conditions of Importance), you see yourself to have decidedly unworthy and undesirable characteristics, actions, roles, acceptance, and/or affiliations.

Force Magnitude

Second, regarding force *magnitude*, we can say that the quantity of Importance can be low, moderate, or high. This describes the "significance" (S) part of the $I = S * V$ Importance function.

Small Magnitude. If the quantity of your self-perceived Importance is *small*, we could say that you see yourself as representing a relatively minor deviation from a zero/baseline sense of Importance. That is, you feel as if you have little significance. You have a slight impact. You are a tad good or bad. Nominally virtuous or malevolent. If your valence is of positive (beneficial) value, your effect is of trivial benefit or help. Contrarily, if your valence is of negative (detrimental) value, your effect is of trivial hindrance or harm.

In terms of the model, specifically your mediated and moderated paths (i.e., the conditions of Importance), you see yourself to have marginal characteristics, actions, roles, acceptance, and/or affiliations.

Moderate Magnitude. If the quantity of your self-perceived Importance is *moderate*, we could say that you see yourself as representing a relatively medium or average deviation from a zero/baseline sense of Importance. That is, you feel as if you have ordinary significance. You have a mediocre impact. You are sorta/kinda good or bad. If your valence is of positive (beneficial) value, your effect is of some benefit or help. Contrarily, if your valence is of negative (detrimental) value, your effect is of some hindrance or harm.

In terms of the model, specifically your mediated and moderated paths (i.e., the conditions of Importance), you see yourself to have unexceptional, common characteristics, actions, roles, acceptance, and/or affiliations.

Large Magnitude.   If the quantity of your self-perceived Importance is *large*, we could say that you see yourself as representing a relatively large deviation from a zero/baseline sense of Importance. That is, you feel as if you have extraordinary significance. You have a major impact. You are really good or bad. Extremely virtuous or malevolent. If your valence is of positive (beneficial) value, your effect is of substantial benefit or help. Contrarily, if your valence is of negative (detrimental) value, your effect is of substantial hindrance or harm.

In terms of the model, specifically your mediated and moderated paths (i.e., the conditions of Importance), you see yourself to have astoundingly potent characteristics, actions, roles, acceptance, and/or affiliations.

$$Force = Valence \times Magnitude$$

To reiterate, the force of your Importance is determined by the qualitative valence of your self-subjective value multiplied by the quantitative magnitude of your self-subjective significance. Combining the two, we will make the argument that one's force of Importance can be (a) too low—overly timid, self-depreciating, or deflating), b) too high—arrogant, overly indulgent, or inflating, or c) as the astrophysicist community, and nursery rhyme fans, might say—in the "Goldilocks" (just right[1]) zone—healthy, balanced, and grounded.

So you will be a true VIP if you realize a healthy, balanced force of Importance. We plot this graphically in Figure 7.2 (see below).

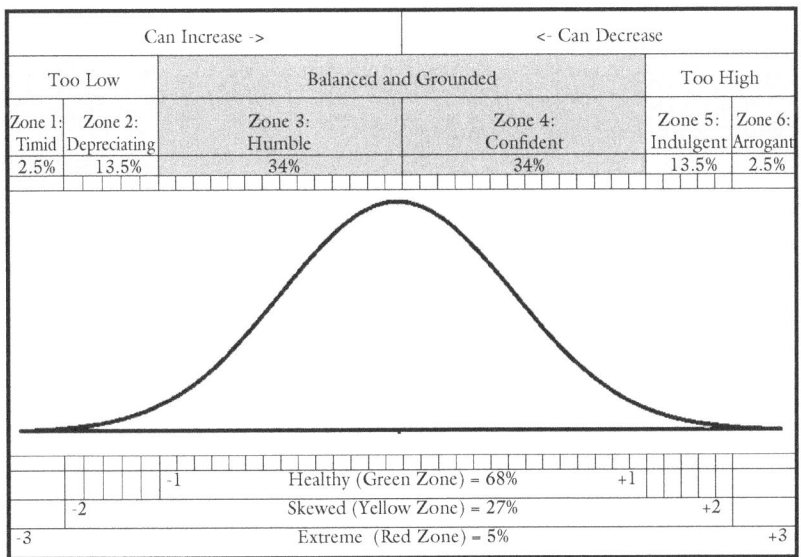

Figure 7.2   Force of Importance.

When Force of Importance Is Too Low

If your force of Importance is *too low*, you will most likely overemphasize the liabilities, negatives, and unfavorable aspects of your character, actions, roles, acceptance, and affiliations. You might feel inferior, deflated, dispirited, or withdrawn. You might think, "I am nothing." As per the Mayo Clinic,[2] when you have a low or negative self-evaluation, "you put little value on your opinions and ideas. You focus on your perceived weaknesses and faults and give scant credit to your skills and assets. You believe that others are more capable or successful. You might be unable to accept compliments or positive feedback. You might fear failure, which can hold you back from succeeding at work or school."

Therefore, the appropriate intervention would be to increase self-subjective Importance. In Figure 7.2 we see this in two places:

Zone 1

The label that we have chosen for this force is "timid." In essence, it is an overly negative, significantly deflated sense of Importance. Force is way, way too low. This is an extreme state. Assuming a somewhat normal distribution,[3] two standard deviations to the left, approximately one in forty individuals would fall within this range. Dysfunctional timidity can be seen in those who very much depress their significant value. Therefore, when in this range, a large increase/boost in one's sense of Importance is appropriate.

Zone 2

The label that we have chosen for this force is "depreciating." In essence, it is a moderately negative and deflated sense of Importance. Force is substantially too low. This is a skewed state. Assuming a somewhat normal distribution, one standard deviation to the left, approximately one in eight individuals would fall within this range. Dysfunctional depreciation can be seen in those who somewhat depress their significant value. Therefore, when in this range, a small increase/boost in one's sense of Importance is appropriate.

When Force of Importance Is Healthy

If your force of Importance is *healthy*, you will most likely place a *balanced* (versus exceedingly negative or positive) and *grounded* (versus exceedingly deflated or inflated) emphasis on aspects of your character, actions, roles, acceptance, and affiliations. You might feel appropriately substantiated, simultaneously assured and cautious, reflectively appreciative and engaged. You might think, "I am not everything. I am not nothing. But I am definitely something."

Therefore, the appropriate action would be to maintain self-subjective Importance. In Figure 7.2 we see this in two places:

Zone 3

The label that we have chosen for this force is "humble." In essence, it is a balanced, perhaps slightly underestimated sense of Importance. Force is reasonably calibrated but with a restrained or reserved focus. This is a generally healthy state. Assuming a somewhat normal distribution, approximately one in three individuals would fall within this range. Functional humility can be seen in the unassuming and modest self-subjective successes. Therefore, when in this range, a maintenance (or in some cases a slight boost) in one's sense of Importance is appropriate.

Zone 4
The label that we have chosen for this force is "confident." In essence, it is a balanced, perhaps slightly overestimated sense of Importance. Force is reasonably calibrated but with an enthusiastic or emboldened focus. This is also a generally healthy state. Assuming a somewhat normal distribution, approximately one in three individuals would fall within this range. Functional confidence can be seen in the self-assured and poised self-subjective successes. Therefore, when in this range, a maintenance (or in some cases a slight temperance) in one's sense of Importance is also appropriate.

When Force of Importance Is Too High
If your force of Importance is *too high*, you will most likely overemphasize the assets, positives, and favorable aspects of your character, actions, roles, acceptance, and affiliations. You might feel overly superior, inflated, dominant, or aggressive. You might think, "I am everything." There are dangers in such an approach, which include but are not limited to a lack of learning and development.[4] As per the Mayo Clinic,[5] "If you regard yourself more highly than others do, you might have an unrealistically positive view of yourself. When you have an inflated sense of self . . . you often feel superior to those around you. Such feelings can lead you to become arrogant or self-indulgent and believe that you deserve special privileges."

Therefore, the appropriate intervention would be to scale back or reduce self-subjective Importance. In Figure 7.2 we see this in two places:

Zone 5
The label that we have chosen for this force is "indulgent." In essence, it is a moderately positive, inflated sense of Importance. Force is substantially too high. This is a skewed state. Assuming a somewhat normal distribution, one standard deviation to the right, approximately one in eight individuals would fall within this range. Dysfunctional arrogance can be seen in those who somewhat bias and exaggerate their significant value. Therefore, when in this range, a small reduction or reining in of one's sense of Importance is appropriate.

Zone 6
The label that we have chosen for this force is "arrogant." In essence, it is an overly positive, significantly inflated sense of Importance. Force is way, way too high. This is an extreme state. Assuming a somewhat normal distribution, two standard deviations to the right, approximately one in forty individuals would fall within this range. Dysfunctional indulgence can be seen in those who very much bias and exaggerate their significant value. Therefore, when in this range, a substantial reduction or reining in of one's sense of Importance is appropriate.

Taken Together
We can see these zones plotted at the bottom of Figure 7.2.

In the Green Zone—High Health

Utilizing a normal curve distribution,[6] we suggest that the force of Importance is largely *healthy* when it falls within one standard deviation of the center point. According to statistical norms, approximately two-thirds of the general population would fall within this area, with roughly 33 percent (or about one in three) generally humble and an equivalent 33 percent generally confident. This represents an enabling force and, as such, would suggest interventions (via personal choices and management strategies) oriented toward sustaining and reinforcing it for those in this zone to thrive and leverage/flourish.

In the Yellow Zone—Moderate Health

In addition, the force of Importance is *skewed* when it falls between one and two standard deviations of the center point. According to norms, a little over one quarter of the general population fall within this area with roughly 13.5 percent (or about one in eight) generally depreciating and an equivalent 13.5 percent generally indulgent. This represents a retarding force and, as such, would suggest incremental interventions (via personal choices and management strategies) for those in this zone to "unshackle" and adjust/fine-tune.

In the Red Zone—Low Health

Finally, the force of Importance is *extreme/pathological* when it falls beyond two standard deviations of the center point. According to statistical norms, about one in twenty people in the general population fall within this area with roughly 2.5 percent (or about one in forty) extremely timid and an equivalent 2.5 percent extremely arrogant. This represents a destructive force and, as such, would suggest radical interventions (via personal choices and management strategies) for those in this zone to "cleanse" and reimagine/reset.

So, all in all, the *force* of your Importance is, in general, most desirable when it strikes a healthy, grounded balance between over- and under-regard. In short: VIPs balance and ground the force of their Importance.

The Form of Importance

We will now discuss some of the key elements that define the form of your Importance.

The form of one's self-subjective value and significance can be examined at a given point in time or over a period of time. We focus on some of the most critical and interesting considerations of these two issues. For the sake of simplicity, form is discussed here in terms of:

- Level: Representing a question of in-time cross-sectional anchoring of self-subjective Importance, and considering whether it is attaching to relatively more independent/self or embedded/social identifications

- Stability: Representing a question of across-time longitudinal evolutions of self-subjective Importance, and considering whether it is shaping relatively more stable/firm or contingent/fragile trajectories

Each will now be discussed in turn.

Form Level

First, regarding form *level*, at a given point in time we can say that the anchoring of Importance can be (a) independent and rooted in one's self-identity, (b) embedded and rooted in one's social-identity, or (c) a hybrid of the two.

Independent Self-Identity

If the level of your self-subjective Importance is rooted in your *self-identity*, you have a more "independent" sense of Importance. In essence, you feel, *I have significant value because of the "me."* As an objectively agentic actor, and simultaneously as an intuitively reflective being, a person experiences a dynamic sense of selfhood.[7] When you define this selfhood as an independent self-construal, you are tying it to the distinct individualistic characteristics, actions, acceptances, roles, and affiliations that emerge from yourself as a discrete, unique entity. The unit of analysis is the "I." This is a typically Western-centric approach that tends to emphasize the player more than the play per se. Linking this with prior discussions, one might witness this form of selfhood embedded in more democratic, capitalistic systems. Similarly, one might also see its impact in consistent philosophical conceptualizations of the self-concept, scientific emphasis on the pragmatics of life, the efficient and effective (via and economic invisible hand of self-interests) utilization of human capital, and the accompanying alignment of personal values.

Thus, in a nutshell, an independent form of Importance emphasizes "differences" and the distinct, micro individualistic dynamic in constructing autonomous Importance.

Embedded Self-Identity

If the level of your self-subjective Importance is rooted in your *social identity*, you have a more "embedded" sense of Importance. In essence, you feel, *I have significant value because of the "we" that I belong to.* In contrast to the prior section, a person might define their selfhood as an interdependent actor rooted in, and as an intertwined contributing element of, collectivistic aggregations of characteristics, actions, acceptances, roles, and affiliations that relate to all interconnected entities. The unit of analysis is the "us." This is a typically Eastern-centric approach that tends to emphasize the play more than any particular player per se. Linking this with prior discussions, one might witness this form of selfhood embedded in more socialist and centrally planned systems, or those with exceedingly strong cultures, and the accompanying alignment of macro-focused societal and personal values. Moreover, as argued by Tajfel[8] and others, it supports the notion that identity can be driven by the larger social-, organizational-, or group-based reality that one associates oneself with and the corresponding shared norms, prototypes, stereotypes, and so on, that accompany them.

Thus, in a nutshell, an independent form of Importance emphasizes "similarities" and the aggregated, cohesive macro social dynamic in constructing collective Importance.

Form Stability

Second, regarding form *stability*, across successive points in time we can say that the trajectory of Importance can be (a) consistent—completely fixed and firm, (b) contingent—completely variable and fragile, or (c) a hybrid of the two.

Consistent, Fixed Importance

If the trajectory of your self-subjective Importance is firm and unchanging, you have a more consistent, fixed sense of Importance. It does not tend to vary with new information and feedback, evolving circumstances, fluxes in state, or other developmental/learning opportunities in the cinema of life. In a word: Your sense of significant value never or rarely changes.

This is akin to what some[9] term "true" or "global" self-conceptions that are not based in day-to-day accomplishments or failures but instead represent internal, overall estimations and their derivative conceptualizations. They tend to be trait based and, just like personality patterns, vary but slightly across situations and time. Kernis[10] suggests that these types of self-evaluations can be stable for several reasons; for example, because they are internally consistent, non-dependent on specific attainments and evaluative perspectives, and do not require continual validation. Moreover, Leary[11] suggests that it may represent a sort of natural "resting" or equilibrium state of self-evaluation.

Contingent, Variable Importance

If the trajectory of your self-subjective Importance is fragile and fluctuating, you have a more contingent, variable sense of Importance. It continually and drastically varies with seemingly each piece of new information and morsel of feedback, every evolving circumstance, and every event in the cinema of life. In a word: Your sense of significant value constantly or frequently changes.

This is akin to what some term "contingent" or "state" self-conceptions that are based on specific accomplishments or failures and represent external, explicit estimations and derivative conceptualizations. They tend to be assessed according to particular situations and events, and within particular points of time, and as such are more contextually and temporary bound. Kernis[12] suggests that these types of self-evaluations can be fragile or unstable for several reasons; for example, because they are contradictory, overly tied to specific attainments and evaluative perspectives (or, as per Leary,[13] a person's moment-to-moment relational evaluation), and require constant validation. They are in essence subject to globalized generalizations and overreactions spawning from isolated, limited instances. Deci and Ryan[14] add that their fluidity might also be catalyzed by the shifting expectations, standards, and approval of others.

$$Form = Level \times Stability$$

To reiterate, the form of your Importance is determined by the in-time anchoring of the level of your self-perceived significant value along with the across-time trajectory of the stability of your self-perceived significant value. Combining the two, we will make the argument that one's form of Importance can be (a) too narrow or broad, (b) too calcified or brittle, or (c) synergistically fused and cumulatively dynamic.

So you will be a true VIP if you realize a healthy (fused and dynamic) form of Importance. We plot this graphically, as a multidimensional target, in Figure 7.3 (see below).

When Form/Level of Importance Is Too Narrow, Too Broad . . . or Fused
First, in terms of level, the anchoring of one's Importance can be too narrow, too broad, or *fused*. If form is too self-focused, this manifests an overly narrow conceptualization, that is not inclusive enough, with little consideration for others, and ultimately exceedingly decontextualized. Alternatively, if it is too social focused, this manifests an overly generic conceptualization, that is not specific enough, with little consideration for oneself, and ultimately exceedingly depersonalized. Thus we need to honor both the independent and interdependent construals—that our Importance is inherently simultaneously

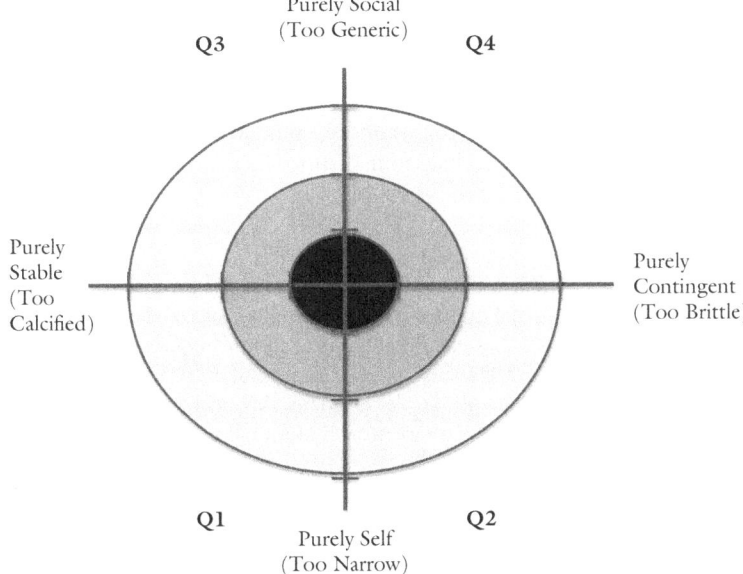

Figure 7.3   Form of Importance.

independent and interdependent. In general, all things being equal, we advance the argument that it is better to have a fused sense of Importance rather than being exclusively self or social centered about one's significance and/or value.

In this sense, and insofar as we are inexorably both "me" and "we," a fused sense of Importance transcends singularly micro or macro self-subjective considerations. As such, it is more internally representative and externally realistic.

When Form/Stability of Importance Is Too Calcified,
Too Brittle . . . or Dynamic
Second, in terms of stability, the trajectory of one's Importance can be too calcified, too brittle, or *dynamic*. If form is too stable, this manifests a calcified, overly fixating, inflexible conceptualization that is exceedingly insensitive and detached from events and feedback. There is no change, no learning, and no growing. Alternatively, if it is too fragile, this manifests an overly brittle, vacillating, inconsistent conceptualization that is exceedingly reliant and sensitive to discrete events and external feedback. There is no identity, no reliability, and no regularity. Thus we need to be synergistically cumulative and path dependent—simultaneously with fidelity and agility. In general, all things being equal, we advance the argument that it is better to have a cumulative, dynamic sense of Importance rather than holding an overly calcified or brittle conception about one's significance and/or value.

In this sense, and insofar as we are inexorably both "state" and "process" (perhaps logically akin to observations that matter is both particle and wave?), a dynamic sense of Importance transcends singularly short-term static or long-term dynamic self-subjective considerations. As such, it is also more internally representative and externally realistic.

Taken Together
We can see that, when these dimensions are plotted together, like those of a two-by-two matrix, they produce four distinct forms of Importance. These categories or quadrants are exhibited in Figure 7.3.

Quadrant 1: Stable Self-Importance
People who have a stable-self form of Importance adopt a predominantly *fixed* and *independent* construal. It is fixed insofar as one's sense of significant value never or rarely changes. For example, "I am always (un)important." It is independent insofar as this stable sense of significant value is based principally on personal measures and conditions. For example, "My unchanging (un)Importance is based on me and a micro-assessment of my paths."

Quadrant 2: Contingent Self-Importance
People who have a contingent-self form of Importance adopt a predominantly *variable* and *independent* construal. It is variable insofar as one's sense of significant value frequently or easily changes. For example, "I am sometimes (un)important depending on a variety of factors." It is independent insofar as this

contingent sense of significant value is based principally on personal measures and conditions. For example, "My constantly shifting (un)Importance is based on me and a micro-assessment of my paths."

Quadrant 3: Stable Social Importance

People who have a contingent-self form of Importance adopt a predominantly *fixed* and *interdependent* construal. It is fixed insofar as one's sense of significant value never or rarely changes. For example, "I am always (un)important." It is interdependent insofar as this stable sense of significant value is based principally on social, collective measures and conditions. For example, "My unchanging (un)Importance is based on us and a macro-assessment of our paths."

Quadrant 4: Contingent Social Importance

People who have a contingent-self form of Importance adopt a predominantly *variable* and *interdependent* construal. It is variable insofar as one's sense of significant value frequently or easily changes. For example, "I am sometimes (un) important depending on a variety of factors." It is interdependent insofar as this contingent sense of significant value is based principally on social, collective measures and conditions. For example, "My constantly shifting (un)Importance is based on us and a macro-assessment of our paths."

In general, all things being equal, it is better to have a fused, dynamic sense of Importance rather than enacting an overly calcified/brittle or overly narrow/generic conception about one's significance and value. That is to say, none of the four quadrants is inherently better than the other. What matters more is their deviation from the center of the "target" (some people that I have shown this graphic to have likened it to a sniper's scope or the bull's-eye of a dart board)—the degree to which they approximate cross-sectional *fusion* and longitudinal *dynamism*. The shaded areas of Figure 7.3 highlight this.

In the Green Zone (Inner Circle)—High Health

This area is the best place to be. It represents a *high* degree of health in one's form of Importance. Self-subjective significant value is (a) cross-sectionally fused and (b) longitudinally dynamic. It embodies an enabling form and, as such, would suggest interventions (via personal choices and management strategies) oriented toward sustaining and reinforcing it.

In the Yellow Zone (Middle Circle)—Moderate Health

This area is an OK place to be. It represents a *moderate* degree of health in one's form of Importance. Self-subjective significant value is somewhat (a) cross-sectionally disproportionate and (b) longitudinally skewed. It embodies a biased and potentially retarding form and, as such, would suggest incremental interventions (via personal choices and management strategies) oriented toward adjustment and fine-tuning.

In the Red Zone (Outer Circle)—Low Health

This area is the worst place to be. It represents a *low* degree of health in one's form of Importance. Self-subjective significant value is definitively (a) cross-sectionally hyperbolic and (b) longitudinally distorted. It embodies an extreme and potentially destructive form and, as such, would suggest radical interventions (via personal choices and management strategies) oriented toward significant overhaul and recalibration.

So, all in all, the *form* of your Importance is (in general) most desirable when it achieves a healthy balance of fused and dynamic regard. In short: VIPs fuse and make dynamic the form of their Importance.

Upshot of the Above

The nature of your Importance is (in general) most desirable (i.e., *healthy*) when it achieves (a) a balanced, grounded force and (b) a fused, dynamic form. In short:

- The force of my Importance is not too positive/negative or large/small.
  - Balanced: I do not cast my value in an overly affirmative or disconfirming light. Please repeat after me:
    I can make a positive, or negative, difference . . .
  - Grounded: I do not overly diminish or inflate the amount of my significance. Please continue to repeat after me:
    . . . in a measured but meaningful way.
- The form of my Importance is not too narrow/generic or calcified/brittle.
  - Fused: I do not overly depersonalize or decontextualize it. Please again repeat after me:
    My Importance is simultaneously within me and with my world . . .
  - Dynamic: I do not overly calcify or vacillate on it. Please once more repeat after me:
    . . . and evolves in a coherent, dynamic, and cumulative manner.

IDENTIFY . . .
The Nature of Importance

In examining the following cases, please utilize them in the following ways:

1. In general, can you overlay the template from this chapter onto the scenes below and see the impact of the characters' nature of Importance?
2. Now, as a *mirror* (looking specifically at *you*): Do any of these characters remind you of you and help to reveal the nature (force and form) of your Importance?
3. Finally, as a *window* (looking at specific *others*): Do any of these characters remind you of someone else that you know and help to reveal the nature (force and form) of their Importance?

Case Study (Personal)

Going through the Normans' Family Rites and Rituals

In the birthday party (*force valence*): When attending their twin nieces' birthday party, they discover that even sisters as close as these can have dramatically different views of their Importance. The older twin (by a full 20 seconds) Mandy revels in, and feels quite deserving of, all the regard. She is rightly the focus of the party and thrusts herself into the subject of each conversation so her comments can make them better. She is no doubt the star, the one who elevates everyone's day. More presents! More cake! The other twin, Randi, does not feel like others should be giving her such positive treatment. She feels largely undeserving, like an "imposter," and as such she feels like her presence detracts from an otherwise pleasant gathering. She does not want to bring everything down. As a result, Randi would rather hide in the corner and receive no attention lest she usurp the energy, diminish the fun, and ruin everyone's good time.

In the graduation ceremony (*force magnitude*): Two of the sisters' classmates could not have been more different with regard to their Importance. Strutting on stage to receive her degree, Leeza acted the proverbial queen. Receiving the piece of parchment elevated her to a larger-than-life superstar status. Wow, what a gigantic boost in her significance! The other classmate, Lana, acted more the pawn. She was confident in the power of her education (it represented some actual, hard-earned learning and this was symbolized in the diploma) but felt nothing special and at best only a negligible change in her significance. Truth be told, she felt altogether common in the sea of black caps and gowns and, more than this, as she slinked across the stage she did not see any real difference, for better or worse, about her specific accomplishments and their pending prospects.

At the wedding reception (*form level*): When the longtime family babysitter got married, she happily invited the entire Norman clan to the event. When the family arrived at the reception hall they noticed that the new bride never seemed to sit down and enjoy the moment, instead tirelessly "doing the rounds" making sure to express appreciation to everyone for coming and that she was there only because of them. She did not seem to ever relax or have much fun, and quite humorously almost missed the cake cutting and bouquet tossing ceremonies, but instead focused exclusively on fulfilling the obligation to support the shared communal rite. The babysitter's new spouse, however, was not as mobile. In fact he was the polar opposite. Instead of engaging the guests he preferred waiting for others to come to the dais and give the couple their due congratulations. He was very much emphasizing their unique individual life-stage and the personal focus that it should bring to them and only them.

In the unemployment center (*form stability*): After suffering the unexpected loss of his job, Mr. Norman was devastated. This really was a major blow to him. As he prepared to file an unemployment claim Mr. Norman had never felt so small, insignificant, and valueless—he used to be someone but was now a proverbial nothing. On the way home he was given a ride by Clifford, one of his fellow colleagues who was also laid off. When they chatted in the car the coworker expressed that he saw this development quite differently from Mr. Norman. To Cliff it was nothing to take much heed in or concern oneself about. It was merely a bump in a long road that should be taken as an opportunity for reflection but certainly not something that negated all the good qualities, deeds, and contributions that they had been so successful at over the range of their lives.

Can you see how self-subjective Importance might be more or less in balance? More or less grounded? How can you address valence (overly positive or negative) and magnitude (overly diminished or inflated) issues to make one's force of Importance healthier? Can you see how Importance might be more or less fused? More or less dynamic? How can you address level (overly narrow or generic) and stability (overly frail or calcified) issues to make one's form of Importance healthier?

Case Study (Professional)

Behind the Scenes at the Artists Den Gallery and Studio

In the theatre group (*force valence*): The play co-leads, and ironically also identical twins, have dramatically different views of their Importance. The older one revels in, and feels quite deserving of, all the attention. She is rightly the focus of the play and never wants to exit the center-stage position. She is awesome, the positive, driving force that makes the play as great as it is. More applause! More compliments! The other does not feel like others should be giving her such positive treatment. She feels like a hack or "imposter," and as such feels like her performance detracts from an otherwise pleasant production, the negative weakest link that can potentially ruin everything. She does not want to bring everything down so would rather sneak off stage-right behind the curtain and receive fewer lines and less of the spotlight.

In the singing troupe (*force magnitude*): The featured singers could not have been more different with regard to their Importance. One acted the prototypical diva. Her solo most definitely elevated her to larger-than-life superstar status. She was big-time. Significant. The real deal. The major mover who could make or break the production. As such she deserved to be on the cover of the playbill. The other acted more the pawn, less significant. She was somewhat confident in the pleasant nature of her voice but felt like she was about average in quality, tone, and strength. It was regularly lost and indistinguishable from the choir and did not elevate or detract from their overall sound. She really added nothing special, especially when comparing her abilities to others.

In the gallery showing (*form level*): When the local gallery hosted a showing for two of its more prominent contributors, the artists acted entirely differently at the event. One was completely deferent and made sure to express over-the-top appreciation to everyone for coming and that he was there only because of their common interest and support. He was very much focused on their interdependency and that the painting only had meaning within the inexorable interwoven relationship between artist and patron. It was not really about him at all. The other was not as mobile and perfectly content to wait for others to come to his front table and lavish their congratulations. In contrast to his colleague he was solely focused on the individual achievements that the paintings represented and the intended meaning of his personal masterpieces. It was and should be, all about him and his work.

In the film academy (*form stability*): After suffering a bad review of his new documentary, the director was devastated, completely crushed. He never felt so small, insignificant, and valueless. Whereas he used to be a "somebody" in the industry he was now a complete and utter failure. Later on when talking with the cast, he was given a particularly needed lift by one of his fellow producers. The colleague saw this as nothing to pay much attention to. Who were these critics anyway and what did they know? Instead it was merely a minor bump in a long road that did not change all the wonderful productions that the team had made and the accolades that they had received over the course of their careers.

Can your see how the characters' self-subjective Importance might be more or less in balance? More or less grounded? How can you help them address valence (overly positive or negative) and magnitude (overly diminished or inflated) issues to make their force of Importance healthier? Can your see how Importance might be more or less fused? More or less dynamic? How can you help them address level (overly narrow or generic) and stability (overly frail or calcified) issues to make their form of Importance healthier?

PERSONALIZE . . .
The Nature of Importance

This set of exercises gives you the opportunity to clarify the nature of your significant value. All together, the more balanced and grounded your force and the more fused and dynamic your form, the healthier your Importance. You can use this section to assess the nature of your significant value.

General

Come to grips with the force and form of your Importance.
    At the most basic level, please rate the degree to which the force and form of your Importance are less (low, say a "1") or more (high, say a "10") healthy.

1. Force valence: Is it balanced or too positive/negative?
2. Force magnitude: Is it grounded or too inflated/deflated?
3. Form level: Is it fused or too narrow/generic?
4. Form stability: Is it dynamic or too calcified/brittle?

Are you happy with your scores? What would you change? How could you change this? Does your ranking suggest a better or worse nature of Importance? Has the ranking changed as you have grown, experienced things, gone through life changes, or advanced in years? Is there any pattern to be found in these? Is there a sweet spot where everything fell into place? If so then how can you get (back) there?

Specific

Drill down further to isolate specific aspects of the form and force of your Importance.

Now please note the degree to which you agree with the following ways for completing this sentence, from most to least descriptive of you:

The nature of my Importance . . .

- Exhibits a healthy valence
  - Do not hold myself in unequivocally positive regard
  - Resist feeling wholly, always beneficial—automatically making things better
  - Do not hold myself in unequivocally neutral or indeterminate regard
  - Resist feeling wholly, always neutral—neither an agent of good nor bad
  - Do not hold myself in unequivocally negative regard
  - Resist feeling wholly, always detrimental—automatically making things worse
  - Instead . . . integrating the above to *balance* my sense of Importance
- Exhibits a healthy magnitude
  - Do not see myself as constantly having a large, meaningful impact
  - Resist feeling automatically extraordinary—always mattering greatly
  - Do not see myself as constantly having a moderate impact
  - Resist feeling automatically common
  - Do not see myself as constantly having a small, negligible impact
  - Resist feeling automatically trivial—never mattering at all
  - Instead . . . integrating the above to *ground* my sense of Importance
- Exhibits a healthy level
  - Am not wholly independent
  - Do not see myself as exclusively segregated in only the "me"
  - Resist locating my identity solely in the internal/distinct/unique/personal
  - Am not wholly interdependent
  - Do not see myself as exclusively embedded in only the "we"
  - Resist locating my identity solely in the external/common/shared/social
  - Instead . . . integrating the above to *fuse* my sense of Importance
- Exhibits a healthy stability
  - Resist a consistent, fixed, and firm Importance that never requires validation
  - Do not avoid adjusting or ever changing my sense of significant value

- ○ Am not always immune to day-to-day feedback or successes/failures
- ○ Resist a contingent, variable, and fragile Importance that always requires validation
- ○ Do not constantly adjust or easily change my sense of significant value
- ○ Am not always hyper-sensitive to day-to-day feedback or successes/failures
- ○ Instead . . . integrating the above to make *dynamic* my sense of Importance

APPLY . . .
The Nature of Importance

From a personal perspective, the nature of your Importance is partly determined by the choices that you make about its force and form. From a professional perspective, your people's Importance is partly determined by the management strategies that you employ to help them shape their force and form.

Please take a moment to apply the material from this chapter to make better choices and craft better strategies about the nature of Importance.

Making Personal Choices

Choice 5: You are, to varying degrees, in control of shaping the nature of your Importance. That is to say, you can influence both its force and form.

Choice 5a. You can choose to better balance the force *valence* of your Importance.

Is my force of Importance appropriately positive, neutral, or negative? If not, how can I better balance it? Does it need to be better reinforced/supported? Moderated/subdued?

Choice 5b. You can choose to better ground the force *magnitude* of your Importance.

Is my force of Importance appropriately small, moderate, or high? If not, how can I better ground it? Does it need to be better increased/boosted? Or perhaps decreased/lessened?

Choice 5c. You can choose to better fuse the form *level* of your Importance.

Is my form of Importance appropriately self- or socially based? If not, how can I better fuse it? Does it need to be more distinctive/individual? Or perhaps more contextualized/shared?

Choice 5d. You can choose to make more dynamic and cumulative the form *stability* of your Importance.

Is my form of Importance appropriately fixed or fluid? If not, how can I better make it dynamic? Does it need to be more stable/coherent? Or perhaps more flexible/adaptive?

Crafting Management Strategies

Management Strategy 5: You can, to varying degrees, help others shape the nature of their Importance. That is to say, you can influence their forces and forms of Importance. Again, your efforts might facilitate or impede the degree to which their choices achieve a healthy balanced-grounded force and a fused-dynamic form.

This can happen at work, at home, or anywhere.

Strategy 5a. You can help them achieve a balanced Importance *valence*. Appropriately emphasize the positive and negative. For example:

Help them to recognize their positive, neutral, or negative self-subjective valuation. If too optimistic, explore ways of reining it in. If too pessimistic, explore ways of enhancing it. Match the level of intervention (radical or incremental) with their deviation (extreme or minor) in force valence.

Strategy 5b. You can help them achieve a grounded Importance *magnitude*. Boost or reduce reasonably, but do not go crazy. For example:

Help them to recognize their high, moderate, or low self-subjective significance. If overstated, explore ways of decreasing it. If understated, explore ways of increasing it. Match the level of intervention (radical or incremental) with their deviation (extreme or minor) of force magnitude.

Strategy 5c. You can help them achieve a fused Importance *level*. Simultaneously honor the independent and interdependent. For example:

Help them to recognize the self- or socially based anchors of their Importance. If too distinct/individual, explore ways for better integrating the shared "we." If too amalgamated/social, explore ways for better integrating the personal "me." Match the level of intervention (radical or incremental) with the deviation (extreme or minor) in form level.

Strategy 5d. You can help them achieve a dynamic, cumulative Importance *stability*. Take into account that the dynamic cinema is both path dependent and cumulative. For example:

Help them to recognize their fixed or fluid trajectories of their Importance. If too calcified, explore ways for making it more flexible and adaptive. If too fragile, explore ways for making it more stable and coherent. Match the level of intervention (radical or incremental) with their deviation (extreme or minor) in form stability.

Checkpoint

Now that we have concluded this chapter, it is appropriate to pause for a moment at this checkpoint and answer the following questions:

- Do you UNDERSTAND the forces and forms of Importance? Can you see how Importance can be healthier: Grounded and balanced? Fused and dynamic?
- Can you IDENTIFY the forces and forms in personal and professional settings?
- Have you PERSONALIZED the forces and forms by relating them to your own Importance journey?
- Will you APPLY the above to (a) develop your forces and forms to make better choices and (b) facilitate others' forces and forms to craft better strategies?

If not, circle back.

If so, let's move on to the next part of the model: *use* . . . and the engagement of Importance.

8

Use—The Engagements
of Importance

Utilize your Importance in integrated, constructive ways.

Chapter 8 presents the *use* of Importance. In this chapter we will consider its different methods or alternative strategies of engagement. First, we will seek to UNDERSTAND the engagement of Importance, in particular:

- Its *direction*, or whether it is used in an end-oriented (target) or means-oriented (tool) manner
- Its *function*, or whether it is used in an open (genuine) or closed (defensive) manner
- Its *expression*, or whether it is used in an implicit (dispersing) or explicit (absorbing) manner

The upshot of these choices will be reconciled in terms of how they can strengthen/help or weaken/harm the links between nature and outcome. Second, we will seek to IDENTIFY the engagements of Importance by sketching personal and professional case study illustrations. You might use them to see yourself (mirror) or others (window) more accurately. Third, we will seek to PERSONALIZE the engagements of Importance by presenting reflective exercises that you can use to relate them to your particular Importance journey. Fourth, we will seek to APPLY the above by deriving guided checklists that can help you make better personal choices and craft better management strategies.

UNDERSTAND . . .
The Use of Importance

Is there a single, universally applicable, completely predictable way that people employ their Importance? If not, what are the various ways that you can use it? Why do people use their Importance in different manners? Are some of these better or worse than others? If so, how could you use it more constructively?

This chapter will address these issues by taking up the underlying question "What are the different ways of engaging your Importance?" Stated plainly, "What are some of the key factors influencing the uses of Importance?" Stated colloquially, "Why do certain ways of using Importance make people feel more or less like a VIP?"

Or, in terms of our model, "How does the way that you use Importance mediate its outcomes?"

Here we will advance the proposition that the power of our Importance to impact our outcomes is filtered through its *engagements*. Therefore, the nature of our Importance will vary in impact depending on how it is used. Lesson: Make sure that your Importance is employed in constructive and integrated ways.

Before we get started, a few points of clarification:

- POINT A: Importance can be used in a variety of ways. We can orient its *direction* inwardly (as an end—a target) or outwardly (as a means—a tool). We can employ its *function* genuinely (to enhance growth—improve and be better) or defensively (enhance image—project and look better). We can manifest its *expression* implicitly (in the background—as a checkpoint to regulate) or explicitly (front and center—as our primary focus and consuming objective).
- POINT B: These different types of directions, functions, and expressions are key. They affect the way in which your Importance will translate into different outcomes.
- POINT C: The uses of Importance are complex and can include a large variety of dimensions. However, there are some factors that are particularly potent and, at a given point in time, must be oriented properly to produce desired outcomes. That is to say, there are better and worse uses of Importance.

Now for a discussion of some of the different ways that Importance can be used.

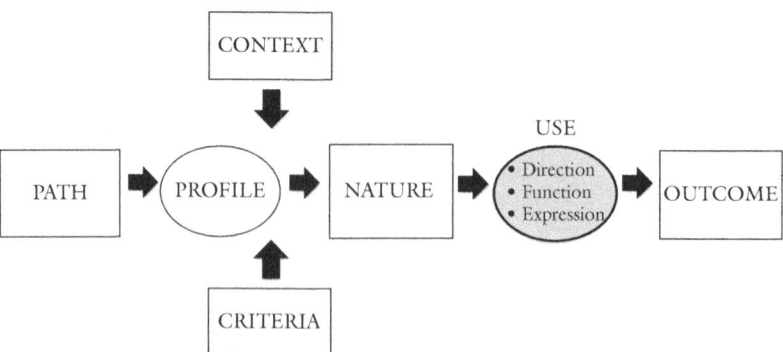

Figure 8.1   Uses of Importance.

The Direction of Importance

Importance can be used in varying directions—as an end (terminal direction-ality) or as a means (instrumental directionality).

A means implies that Importance is oriented toward the instrumental—it is pursued as a tool so that it can enable a higher-order goal or held principle. An end implies that Importance is oriented toward the terminal—it is pursued as a goal or principle target unto itself. The ends-means dichotomy is, in general, a subject of much moral debate as it relates to the ideal and practical treatment of people. On the one hand this applies to the notion, attributed to Machiavelli's[1] self-ascribed pragmatic stance, that "the ends justify the means." On the other hand this is countered by the Kantian[2] categorical imperative, or normative claim that one should "act in such a way that you always treat humanity, whether in your own person or in the person of any other, never simply as a means, but always at the same time as an end . . . [to achieve] a possible kingdom of ends." Notwithstanding, the issue might be interpreted slightly differently when applied to more abstract qualities and perceptions. If something is the *end*, things are aimed at it—it is the primary targeted goal. If something is a *means*, it is a tool aimed at things—it is merely contributory in achieving another goal.

As an End, Inward, a Target
Importance can be oriented or aimed inward, toward itself. It can thus represent an end in and of itself. That is to say, it can take the form of a dependent variable. Here your focus would be on the first part of our book's model—getting Importance for the sake of getting it. The story ends when you traverse your mediated, moderated path. Importance realized; game over.

In short, Importance may be used as a target. It can be your sole ambition. Here, you want to be important . . . because Importance is seen as just plain desirable (inherently good, fun, etc.).

As discussed in the opening chapter, and consistent with the above, sometimes Importance can be selfishly pursued. This is akin to the concept of "personalized power"[3] where people build their potential to influence (i.e., orient their power-seeking behavior) as their goal for narrow, individualized benefit. Or if you prefer a different analogy, this type of orientation—inwardly seeking Importance as a targeted end—is akin to accumulating money and wealth simply because money is cool; it is seen as good in and of itself and provides immediate, selfish pleasures.

As a Means, Outward, a Tool
Importance can also be oriented or aimed outward, toward other things. It can thus represent a means toward a larger, subsequent end. That is to say, it can take the form of an independent variable. Here your focus would be on the second part of our book's model—using Importance in the service of a (greater) higher-priority set of objectives. The story just begins after you traverse your mediated, moderated path. Importance realized; now do something good with it.

In short, Importance may be used as a tool to hit a target. It can enable your goal. Here, you want to be important . . . because Importance empowers/ advances a larger priority or objective. It helps attain something bigger/more desirable.

Also as discussed in the opening chapter, and consistent with the above, sometimes Importance can be benevolently pursued. This is akin to the concept of "socialized power"[4] where people build their potential to influence as a resource for wider group, organizational, or even societal benefit. Or if you prefer a different analogy, this type of orientation—outwardly seeking Importance as a means or tool—is akin to accumulating money and wealth because money increases your potential for doing good; it is seen as enabling greater potential for doing well and larger, broader need enhancement. It is focused on service and contribution.

Taken Together

In general, all things being equal, it is our contention that Importance is better used in a constructive manner—*as a means rather than an end.*

When Importance is used as an end in itself, it disorients us. It distorts our conceptions. It distracts our actions. It hinders our long term success. It diminishes our well-being. If Importance is used as your primary objective, something is probably wrong. Rather, we put forth that it should instead be used as a tool to increase your power to do good, not as a targeted good in itself. Thus one would be advised to reorient the Importance path, recalibrate the Importance mechanism, re-aim the Importance trajectory, and readjust the Importance journey (i.e., change its direction).

So you will be a true VIP if your Importance is well integrated with your development and success as you progress along your path—utilized in its service as an enabling means, not as a tangential end.

The Function of Importance

Importance can be used in varying ways—genuinely or defensively.

Genuineness implies that Importance is tasked with a true, honest, and authentic role. It is pursued as an open-loop mechanism for enlightenment and discovery. Its job is to reveal and enable. Alternatively, defensiveness implies that Importance is tasked with a slanted, skewed, and self-serving role. It is pursued as a closed-loop mechanism to protect, reinforce, and manipulate. Its job is to distort and bias. This contrast is related to the different motives of self-evaluative processes: Self-knowledge, self-verification, and real improvement, or alternatively self-image, self-promotion, and manipulated enhancement.[5]

Genuinely and Open

Importance can be intended genuinely—as an instrument for learning, enriching, and growing. It can thus represent a proverbial "open door," opportunity as a mechanism to better understand and to improve. Said another way, it can take the form of an organic development process. For example, in terms of learning theory,[6] Importance could act to gauge the degree to which "I am doing things right" (our efficiency, posing the single-loop question of whether we are traversing our path well) as well as "I am doing the right things" (our effectively, posing instead the double-loop question of whether we are selecting the correct path in the first place). As an additional example, in terms of change theory,[7] the genuine use of Importance might serve as a *force* for change insofar as it identifies gaps—between where one is and wants to be—and impels specific, appropriate actions to bridge them.

If someone used Importance genuinely, their focus would be on amassing, interpreting, and utilizing information to address "real" issues, such as enhancing advantages and assets and/or mitigating shortcomings and liabilities. As discussed in the opening chapter, and consistent with the above, sometimes Importance can be used as a driver to honestly, actively increase our impact and outcomes. In short, it may be used as an authentic assessment of one's significant value. This implies an *honest* Importance. Real Importance. Here, you want to become better and be more important—be more significant, be more valuable—in a deep, sincere sense.

Defensively and Closed

Importance can also be intended genuinely—as an instrument for projecting, protecting, and managing one's appearance and ego. It can thus represent a proverbial "closed door," obstacle acting as an impediment or constraint to limit honest understanding and real growth. Said another way, it can take the form of an artificial ego-padding process. For example, in terms of political theory,[8] the defensive use of Importance is more concerned with impression management than actual management. As an additional example, in terms of change theory,[9] the defensive use of Importance serves as a *barrier* for change insofar as it reduces the urge to change and instead refocuses issues and energies toward protection, the maintenance of the status quo, and the propagation of inertial tendencies.

If someone used Importance defensively, their focus would be on filtering, spinning, and manipulating information to address perceived issues, such as enhancing positive image and brand perceptions and/or mitigating negative image and brand perceptions. As discussed in the opening chapter, and consistent with the above, sometimes Importance can be used calculatingly and protectively to slant public relations. In short, it may be used as an inauthentic gauge of one's stature or impact. This implies a *synthetic* Importance. Fake Importance. Here, you want to come across as better and be more important—merely seem more significant, seem more valuable—in a surface, superficial sense.

Taken Together

In general, all things being equal, it is our contention that Importance is better used in a constructive manner—*genuinely rather than defensively*.

If Importance is used purely, or primarily, as an image-enhancement strategy, something is probably wrong. Rather, we put forth that it should be used to learn and grow, not just to stroke one's ego. Thus one would be advised to open the door, reprogram the process, redefine its role, and recast its job (i.e., change its function).

So you will be a true VIP if your Importance is well integrated with your development and success as you progress along your path—genuinely, not defensively, utilized in its service.

The Expression of Importance

Importance can be used in varying modes—implicitly or explicitly.

Implicitness implies that Importance resides in the background and manifests as an energy-dispersing activity. It gives. It provides. It adds to you and makes you stronger. Explicitness implies that Importance resides in the foreground and manifests as an energy-absorbing activity. It takes. It absorbs. It withdraws from you and makes you weaker.

Implicitly

Importance can be manifested implicitly—in the background—as a regulatory mechanism. Said another way, it can be pushed down lower in our awareness and understanding so that we are barely conscious of it. It would not be a matter for preoccupation or constant anxiety. We do not invest time and effort into it per se. Here it serves as a check to make sure that our time and effort is going into the right places. Once well constructed (i.e., healthy—balanced, grounded force, and fused, dynamic form) we look at Importance when the figurative alarms go off.

That is, in this case, Importance would be engaged in an as-needed capacity to warn, and adjust, temporary deficiencies or strategic shortcomings in your path to significant value. In many ways this is not altogether dissimilar to the workings of a stock index fund. In short, it might be used as an unconscious, automatic, programmed, troubleshooting and reorientation management mechanism to align drivers with profiles, contexts, and criteria. Here, you use your Importance to supply, rather than consume, energy. That it accentuates you, and frees up your focus, makes more likely the productive achievement of positive outcomes.

Explicitly

Importance can also be manifested explicitly—in the foreground—as an absorptive mechanism. Said another way, it can be pushed higher in our awareness and understanding so that we are keenly, constantly aware of it. It would be a matter for preoccupation or perpetual anxiety. That is to say, just like a harmful narcotic, Importance can become "addictive."[10] Here we pour time and effort into it within a vicious self-perpetuating cycle of dependency. We then look at Importance always, obsessively and fanatically.

That is, in this case, Importance would be engaged in an always-on capacity to preoccupy, engross, and magnify worry about your path to significant value. In short, it might be used as a conscious, voluntary, manual, active engagement mechanism. In contrast to a prior example, this is more akin to the patterns of a hyperactive stock day trader. Here, you use your Importance in a way that consumes, rather than supplies, energy. It drains you and encumbers your focus, makes less likely the productive achievement of positive outcomes.

Taken Together

In general, all things being equal, it is our contention that Importance is better used in a constructive manner—*implicitly rather than explicitly.*

If you use your Importance in an all-encompassing, obsessive manner, something is probably wrong. Rather, we put forth that it should be used to positively affect one's objective, not to divert from it. Thus one would be advised to channel it within the background, automate its processes, and use it in a way that it gives more energy/awareness than it takes (i.e., change its expression).

So you will be a true VIP if your Importance is well integrated with your development and success as you progress along your path—implicitly, not explicitly, utilized in its service.

Upshot of the Above

Your Importance can be used in a more or less desirable manner. The use of your proverbial "shine" can be directed, exploited, and manifested in a way that impacts the translation of its nature into real, concrete consequences (see Chapter 9). Specifically, it is suggested here that Importance is *well* used as a means or tool for open-loop, genuine growth and development in an implicit, regulating, energy-giving manner.

Conversely, Importance is *poorly* used as an end or ambition for closed-loop, skewed image aggrandizement in an obsessive, engulfing, energy-draining manner.

Thus true VIPs use their Importance to actually help others and enable greater objectives (versus promote their own indulgences); to authentically improve and grow stronger (versus pad their own egos); and to tacitly infuse their efforts (versus preoccupy their own agendas).

This is illustrated in the following table.

Table 8.1   Key Dimensions in the Use of Importance

USE	IMPACT	
	HARMS	*HELPS*
Direction	As an End [Ambition/Disorienting]	As a Means [Tool/Enabling]
Function	Defensive [Closed/Skewed]	Genuine [Open/Authentic]
Expression	Explicit [Obsessive/Draining]	Implicit [Regulating/Empowering]

IDENTIFY . . .
The Use of Importance

In examining the following cases, please utilize them in the following ways:

1. In *general,* can you overlay the template from this chapter onto the scenes below and see the impact of the characters' engagement of Importance?
2. Now, as a *mirror* (looking specifically at *you*): Do any of these characters remind you of you and help to reveal the engagement (direction, function, expression) of your Importance?
3. Finally, as a *window* (looking at specific *others*): Do any of these characters remind you of someone else that you know and help to reveal engagement (direction, function, expression) of their Importance?

Case Study (Personal)

In the Dance Hall—Saturday Night Out with the Normans

At the bar (*direction*): The Norman cousins Sandy and Brad are local stars. They are the proverbial "big men on campus." Their high school athletic exploits are legendary. They worked together on the football field in incredible harmony to lead the school to its first-ever state championship. However, this is where the similarities end. When Sandy rolls back into town, he does so with much fanfare, announcing his arrival, clad in his old, now way-too-tight jersey, and being escorted in the front door where the crowd welcomes him like a returning hero. He takes advantage of the throngs to buy him his drinks, and he holds court as they listen enraptured to stories of the glory days. In contrast, Brad comes back in a much more low-key manner. He has moved on from this and has used his popularity to focus attention on things that he cares about that touch his heart, such as investing in the local homeless shelter and providing more support to children with special needs. Others' offers of free drinks are deflected as he encourages patrons to instead fill the charities' collection jars on the bar, and he even uses his own book-advance money to treat his friends to a round on him.

On the dance floor (*function*): The Norman cousins Millie and Desire are, and have been for as long as they can remember, in love with dancing. As youngsters they took ballet classes, they practiced their moves to the popular television dance shows, and they constantly listened to popular club music. However, this is where the similarities end. Now when Millie gets on the floor she breaks out only her best moves, the ones that she rehearsed relentlessly even though she has long lost the fun of doing them, solely to impress the cheering fans that encircle her. As a result she never learns anything new and never gets any better. Basically her stature stymies her growth. When a partner deviates from the script, he is coldly rebuffed. Everything about her screams "Look at me," "See how cool I am." This goes on night after night just like a proverbial broken record. In contrast, Desire is not afraid to try new things. She is often seen on the floor studying new steps, trying new moves, and thoroughly relishing in the process. Rarely does she engage her "autopilot" or play it safe. Instead, when a partner starts an unfamiliar move, she enthusiastically engages, even if it pushes her out of her comfort area to potentially look the fool. She is using her stature to provide a platform for constantly learning and growing as a dancer.

In the table area (*expression*): The Norman cousins Nancy and Larry mingle with the people who are sitting down and grabbing a bite. Nancy is a relentless and obsessive name-dropper, focusing all of her energy on looking cool, networking and working the room, and redirecting every conversation toward her perpetual goal of feeling highly significant and valuable. Her eyes noticeably glaze over and her ears definitely tune out when anyone else speaks about themselves. She just bides her time until it is her turn to again impress. To her the Nancy "image" is a full-time job. She even spends much of her free time practicing famous politicians' techniques and mirroring them to appear more important. In contrast, Larry looks even cooler but, ironically, this is precisely because he doesn't really obsess about how impressive he comes across. He has a healthy sense of self so has no problem really listening to others, staying true to his nature, as a result becoming energized by the freedom the experience provides, and genuinely enjoying the evening way more than Nancy. Nary a thought of personal significance or value crosses his mind . . . until something said by a friend makes him question his filtered path; he then uses this as an opportunity to consider the point and reflect back on how it relates to his choices and how he might improve them.

Can you see how self-subjective Importance might be used differently? In different directions? Toward different functions? With different expressions? How can you make more constructive uses of your Importance to be means (versus ends) focused to better orient? Genuine (versus defensive) to better grow? Implicit (versus explicit) to better regulate?

Case Study (Professional)

At the Law Firm—Behind the Scenes at Samuels, Jacobs, Daniels, Hoyer, and Bergen, LLP

In the C Suite (*direction*): Some 40 years after Nathan Samuels founded the law firm, he eventually retired from it, passing on his interest to the remaining four partners. They quickly formed two camps based on their competing view of how they should use their newly consolidated potential. Charlie Hoyer and Kendrick Bergen were keen on using the revenues to pay themselves big bonuses. They quickly staked out the best office space on the top floor of a new building and chartered a company helicopter to ferry them back and forth from work. They were important . . . so they deserved it. Alternatively, Franklin Jacobs and Alexander Daniels shared a different view—that they should use the surprisingly substantial supplemental revenue stream to pay out greater dividends and donate to needy causes that the office voted on. They also campaigned for the premier upper-floor space to be converted into a community lounge and common meeting area that everyone could enjoy. In addition, they wanted to invest more resources in staff to better serve their clients. They were important . . . so they were responsible for using it well.

In the research library (*function*): Hoyer and Bergen ordered volumes of impressive-sounding, meticulously bound books and housed them on rich mahogany shelving. The chairs, clever but fake designer replicas, were also meant to impress. In addition, the organizational chart remained very tall and narrow, placing them on the top and giving very little discretion or enrichment to the new crop of recruits they were employing. Nothing, not even dramatic changes in the way that law was being prepared and practiced, made them diverge from the traditional way in which the firm designed and presented itself. It was obvious to even the casual observer that they cared more about looking good than being good. Alternatively, Jacobs and Daniels wanted to use their newfound discretion to modernize the space, empower others, flatten the hierarchy, and make real changes in their sometimes overly traditional practices to honestly and accurately account for the changing legal landscape (even if it meant a slight reduction of their personal status and power).

In the courthouse (*expression*): The schism between the partner groups extended beyond their formal boundaries and into the very arena of their outside courtroom engagements. Hoyer and Bergen were preoccupied, to the point of obsession, with how they were reviewed by the attending press and designed each motion and process to come across well . . . even if it was at the detriment of their case or client. Importance consumed them. It was always on their mind. Its attribution made them discernably giddy whereas its absence made them noticeably anxious and pushed them to near despondence. And this not-so-hidden agenda drained their attention and distracted their efforts from many a case. The attorneys, after all, deserve their due credit. If they didn't get their share, things should change. Alternatively, Jacobs and Daniels did not usually give much thought to these personal matters of Importance or others' reviews of it. Instead they focused entirely on the court proceedings at hand without exception . . . until one day when the assistant council questioned whether they were adding enough service to warrant their standard fees. They then reflectively considered the matter to ensure that requisite significant value was indeed being marshaled and imparted. The client, after all, deserves their money's worth. If they don't get their best efforts, things should change.

Can you see how the characters use their self-subjective significant value differently? In different directions? Toward different functions? With different expressions? How can you help them make more constructive uses of their Importance to be means (versus ends) focused to better orient? Genuine (versus defensive) to better grow? Implicit (versus explicit) to better regulate?

PERSONALIZE . . .
The Use of Importance

This set of exercises gives you the opportunity to clarify the engagement of your significant value. All together, the better the direction (means versus end), function (open versus closed), an expression (implicit versus explicit) of your Importance the more positive the use your Importance. You can use this section to assess the use of your significant value

General

Come to grips with the use of your Importance.

At the most basic level, please rate the degree to which the engagement of your Importance is less (low, say a "1") or more (high, say a "10") positive.

1. In its direction: Is it a means or more of an end?
2. In its function: Is it genuine or more defensive?
3. In its expression: Is it implicit or more explicit?

Are you happy with your scores? What would you change? How could you change this? Does your ranking suggest better or worse uses of Importance? Has the ranking changed as you have grown, experienced things, gone through life changes, or advanced in years? Is there any pattern to be found in these? Is there a sweet spot where everything fell into place? If so then how can you get (back) there?

Specific

Drill down further to isolate specific aspects of the use of your Importance.

Now please note the degree to which you agree with the following ways for completing this sentence, from most to least descriptive of you:

I use my Importance . . .

- Direction: In a means-oriented (versus ends-oriented) manner
  - Care about using my significance and value well more so than merely the realizing or accumulating of it
  - See it as an instrumental implement, not a terminal objective
  - Focus it outward, for others, versus inward to only myself
  - Employ it as a small piece to the puzzle, not the end-all, be-all
  - Leverage it to orient, versus disorient, my better efforts
  - Try to do good with it, versus use it to further narrow personal interests
  - Use it to increase my power to do good things, not as a good in and of itself
- Function: In a genuine (versus defensive) manner
  - Care about authentically evolving my significance and value more so than merely looking the part
  - See it as a genuine gradient, not a manipulated surface image enhancer
  - Focus it sincerely, for growth, versus defensively, for skewing perceptions
  - Employ it to learn deeply and develop, not slant and superficially manipulate
  - Leverage it openly to clarify and change, versus calculatingly distort and protect

- ○ Try to faithfully appraise it, versus aggressively promote it
- ○ Use it to improve my honest introspective insight, not an artificial/fake persona
- Expression: In an implicit (versus explicit) manner
  - ○ Care about drawing from my significance and value more so than merely dwelling on or obsessing over it
  - ○ See it as a troubleshooting check, not as a constant concern
  - ○ Focus it in the background, not make it a point of primary emphasis
  - ○ Employ it to center myself, not to distract myself
  - ○ Leverage it to increase versus deplete my energy and focus
  - ○ Try to address it when needed, not in an addictive or compulsive manner
  - ○ Use it to regulate my life, not consume it

APPLY . . .
The Use of Importance

From a personal perspective, the consequences of your Importance are partly determined by the choices you make about how to use it. From a professional perspective, the consequences of your people's Importance are partly determined by the management strategies you employ to help them use it.

Please take a moment to apply the material from this chapter to make better choices and craft better strategies about the uses of Importance.

Making Personal Choices

Choice 6: You are, to varying degrees, in control of using your Importance in better and worse ways. That is to say, you can influence its direction, function, and expression.

Choice 6a. You can choose to enhance the direction—using it more as a means than an end—of your Importance.

> Do I use my Importance in the best direction? If not, how can I use it more as a means, or tool, to further bigger objectives and advance better outcomes? Less as an end, or target, not as my ultimate goal or to pad trivial ambitions?

Choice 6b. You can choose to enhance the function—using it more genuinely (open) than defensively (closed)—of your Importance.

> Do I use my Importance through the best function? If not, how can I use it more in an open manner as an authentic calibration and facilitator of learning and growth? Less in a closed manner, not as an artificial, skewed projection to pad my ego?

Choice 6c. You can choose to enhance the expression—using it more implicitly than explicitly—of your Importance.

Do I use my Importance with the best expression? If not, how can I use it more implicitly as a regulating mechanism to center and empower me? Less explicitly, not as an obsessive, addictive compulsion to occupy my time and drain my energy?

Crafting Management Strategies

Management Strategy 6: You can, to varying degrees, help others use their Importance in better versus worse ways.

This can happen at work, at home, or anywhere.

Strategy 6a. You can help them use their Importance more as a *means*. For example:

> Help them to recognize the direction of how they use their Importance. If misused, reorient by emphasizing that Importance is best engaged as a way of assessing and increasing one's capacity to do well and do good. Reinforce that Importance is not an end that is good in and of itself; it is constructive insofar as it better enables good things.

Strategy 6b. You can help them use their Importance more *genuinely*. For example:

> Help them to recognize the function of how they use their Importance. If misused, reconceptualize by emphasizing that Importance is best engaged as a way for openly discovering/leveraging strengths and uncovering/mitigating weaknesses. Reinforce that Importance is not something to be defended or manipulated; it is good insofar as it reveals and remedies.

Strategy 6c. You can help them use their Importance more *implicitly*. For example:

> Help them to recognize the expression of how they use their Importance. If misused, recast by emphasizing that Importance is best engaged as a background/regulating mechanism versus an obsessive aspiration. Reinforce that Importance is not something to be preoccupied or consumed with; it is good insofar as it synchronizes and centers.

Checkpoint

Now that we have concluded this chapter, it is appropriate to pause for a moment at this checkpoint and answer the following questions:

- Do you UNDERSTAND the engagements of Importance? Can you see how Importance can be used as a means or tool for advancing subsequent objectives versus an end in and of oneself? Openly for growth versus closed for protection? Implicitly to energize versus explicitly to drain?

- Can you IDENTIFY its use in personal and professional settings?
- Have you PERSONALIZED its use by relating it to your own Importance journey?
- Will you APPLY the above to a) use it to make better choices and b) facilitate others' use of it to craft better strategies?

If not, circle back.

If so, let's move on to the next part of the model: *outcomes* . . . and the consequences of Importance.

Outcome—The Consequences of Importance

Monitor and manage your Importance for optimal results.

Chapter 9 presents the *outcome* or consequences of Importance. In this chapter we will consider the model's proverbial "bottom line." First, we will seek to UNDERSTAND the various implications of Importance, in particular its:

- Cognitive consequences or how you think (i.e., "see" better)
- Affective consequences or how you feel (i.e., "be" better)
- Behavioral consequences or how you act (i.e., "do" better)

The upshot of these choices will be reconciled in terms of how they relate to your ultimate success, broadly conceived. Second, we will seek to IDENTIFY the consequences of Importance by sketching personal and professional case study illustrations. You might use them to see yourself (mirror) or others (window) more accurately. Third, we will seek to PERSONALIZE the consequences of Importance by presenting reflective exercises that you can use to relate them to your particular Importance journey. Fourth, we will seek to APPLY the above by deriving guided checklists that can help you make better personal choices and craft better management strategies.

UNDERSTAND . . .
The Consequences of Importance

Does your sense of Importance impact how you think? Feel? Act? Is Importance always good or always bad? If not, what are its different possible conclusions?

This chapter will address these issues by taking up the underlying question "What are the different effects of Importance?" Stated plainly, "What are some of the key consequences of Importance?" Stated colloquially, "What are the bottom-line results of feeling like a VIP?"

Or, in terms of our model, "What is the outcome of Importance?"

Here we will advance the proposition that our Importance impacts our cognitive, affective, and behavioral *consequences*. Therefore, the outcomes of our Importance have the potential to influence us in a variety of ways. Lesson: Make sure that you monitor and manage your Importance for optimal results.

Before we get started, a few points of clarification:

- POINT A: There is a cognitive or intellectually oriented "thinking" dimension to Importance. There is an affective or emotionally oriented "feeling" dimension to Importance. There is also a conative or behaviorally oriented "action" dimension to Importance. Net net: our Importance impacts our and our organization's bottom line.
- POINT B: These different consequences can be managed better or worse. On the downside, we can mismanage (the conditions, nature, and use of) our Importance to become more oblivious, dissatisfied, and unproductive. On the upside, we can manage our Importance well to become more mindful, happy, and effective.
- POINT C: The research surrounding these outcomes is far from conclusive. And there are many variables that bear upon these outcomes. However, the relationships are compelling enough in their logic and insight to suggest that Importance is indeed important, not just in and of itself, but also because it can influence a variety of desired outcomes. That is to say, there are significant consequences of Importance.

Now for a discussion of some of the different outcomes of Importance.

We will consider these outcomes in the following manner.

First, we will discuss some of the *cognitive*—cerebral, intellectual, mental—consequences of one's Importance. In doing so, we will make the argument

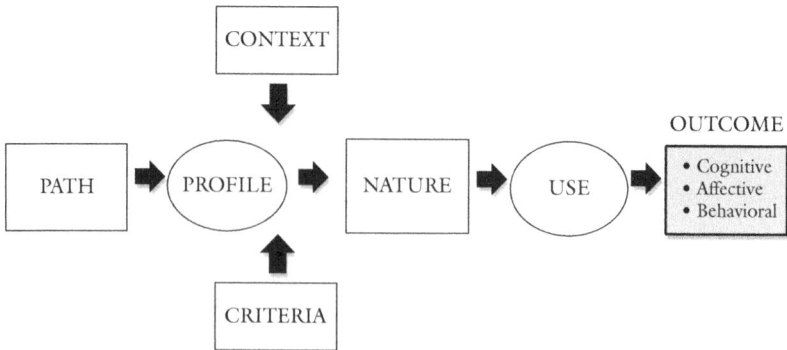

Figure 9.1   Outcomes of Importance.

that Importance influences to some degree how you think. We will then relate this to the idea of *mindfulness*:

> Mindfulness is a complex construct. It is no doubt partly about feeling in the moment—the heart is passionately present. It is no doubt partly about acting in the moment—the body is physically present. And there are many factors that have the potential to act on and influence it. However, the focus here will be on the thinking dimension of mindfulness. How you see. And it will concentrate on realizing an intellectual, reflective awareness of one's Importance.

Second, we will discuss some of the *affective*—or emotional—consequences of one's Importance. In doing so, we will make the argument that Importance influences to some degree how you feel. We will then relate this to the idea of *happiness*.

> Happiness is a complex construct. It is no doubt partly about thinking in positive ways—a function of one's judgment of circumstances, objectives, and assessment of progress toward them. It is no doubt partly about acting in positive ways—a manifest pattern or habit of interacting with the environment and conducting one's affairs. And there are many factors that have the potential to act on and influence it. However, the focus here will be on the feeling dimension of happiness. Being happy. And it will concentrate on approximating an emotional satisfaction of one's Importance.

Third, we will discuss some of the *behavioral*—or conative—consequences of one's Importance. In doing so, we will make the argument that Importance influences to some degree how you act. We will then relate this to the ideas of *effectiveness* in terms of synergy, excellence, and innovativeness.

> Effectiveness is a complex construct. It is no doubt partly about channeling your thinking about things in productive streams—how you perceive, make decisions, and so on—perhaps related to intellectual quotients such as IQ. It is no doubt partly about channeling your feeling about things in productive streams— how you master and manage your sentiments—perhaps related to emotional quotients such as EQ. And there are many factors that have the potential to act on and influence it. However, the focus here will be on the behavioral or action-oriented dimension of effectiveness. Doing well. And it will concentrate on achieving measurable, quantifiable returns from leveraging one's Importance.

The following table captures some of the interrelated dimensions of Importance's potential consequences as well as the focal outcomes (darker shades) of our present discussion.

Table 9.1   Key Outcome Dimensions of Importance

	Mindfulness	*Happiness*	*Effectiveness*
Cognitive	**SEE**	See	See
Affective	Be	**BE**	Be
Conative	Do	Do	**DO**

Interestingly enough, these outcome dimensions intersect with recent research on human well-being and the notion that modern socioeconomic transformations are challenging people's sense of coherence in at least three core ways.[1] First, within the ever-increasing uncertainty and complexity of life, people seek a sense of *comprehensibility*—this is addressed in our model via the cognitive dimension of Importance and by being mindful of one's unique significant value. Second, within the expanding individualistic, materialistic, and instrumental streams of life, people seek a sense of *meaningfulness*—this is addressed in our model via the affective dimension of Importance and by being satisfied with one's inherent significant value. Third, within the enlarging scope of choices and decision points in life, people seek a sense of *manageability*—this is addressed in our model via the conative dimension of Importance and by effectively integrating, optimizing, and sustaining one's pragmatic significant value.

Taken together, we will continue the argument that threads through the book . . . that there are better and worse ways of managing our, and others', Importance. Simply put, if we do this well then good things can happen. Depending on our choices (of paths, filters, context, criteria, nature, and use) we can be relatively more oblivious or mindful of our Importance, dissatisfied or happy about our Importance, and unproductive or effective with our Importance.

We will now consider these in turn.

Cognitive Consequences—How You Think (See Better)

There is a cognitive component to Importance. It influences how you think.

Of course, many factors well beyond the scope of this book influence your thoughts. And there are no guarantees that intellectually connecting with your Importance will somehow, like a panacea, cure your entire range of intellectual ails. However, better shaping, realizing, and using your self-subjective value can serve as a positive factor or catalysis toward its end. Said another way: If your "brain" sees the nature of your Importance . . . if you can intellectually grasp the aspects of its paths and contingencies . . . and if you can logically manage their consequences . . . then some nice things can happen, including positive impacts on your cognitive awareness, understanding, security, control, and expansion.

Cognitive Awareness
STEP 1. You can become more *cognizant* to be better mentally aware of your Importance. That is to say, you would be able to intellectually *identify* or detect your significant value better. Identify the logic of your drivers and its paths. Identify the logic of your profile and its filters. Identify the logic of its external and internal contexts. Identify the logic of its nature—force and form. Identify the logic of its use. In this sense, you can become more mentally self-conscious of your significant value and the process in which it is

determined. The dynamic here is essentially a sharpening of one's cognitive discovery capabilities. More data is detected by our sensors and makes it onto our radar screen. As a result, we are better able to incorporate these into our thought processes. Upshot: We can be more or less cognizant of and through our Importance.

More data and better awareness is a good first step in cognitively connecting with our Importance. However, it is not the only step . . .

Cognitive Understanding
STEP 2. You can become more *knowledgeable* to better comprehend and grasp your Importance. You would be able to intellectually *understand* your significant value better. Understand the logic of your drivers and its paths. Understand the logic of your profile and its filters. Understand the logic of its external and internal contexts. Understand the logic of its nature—force and form. Understand the logic of its usage. In this sense, you can become more mentally self-knowledgeable about your significant value and the process in which it is determined. This process is essentially a sharpening of one's reflective, introspective capacities. As a result, we are better able to understand the above data and translate it into greater information and knowledge. Upshot: We can be more or less knowledgeable of and through our Importance.

More information/knowledge and better understanding can be a good thing. It is generally necessary, but not always sufficient, for an intellectually fruitful life and might then be supplemented with . . .

Cognitive Security
STEP 3. You can become more *confident* to be more centered or coupled in your Importance. You would be able to intellectually *embrace* your significant value better. Embrace the logic of your drivers and its paths. Embrace the logic of your profile and its filters. Embrace the logic of its external and internal contexts. Embrace the logic of its nature—force and form. Embrace the logic of its usage. In this sense, you can become more mentally self-secure in your significant value and the process in which it is determined. Confidence can enable virtuous cycles that have been argued to increase efficacy,[2] integrity,[3] and put you on a "winning path"[4] in life. As a result, we are better able to engage our resources in the pursuit of our goals. Upshot: We can be more or less confident of and through our Importance.

More confidence and better security can be quite beneficial. When it is combined with awareness and understanding, it can take us to another level that enables . . .

Cognitive Control
STEP 4. You can become more *focused* to be short-term capable of processing and optimizing your Importance. You would be able to intellectually *influence and emphasize* your significant value better. Influence and emphasize the logic of your drivers and its paths. Influence and emphasize the logic of your profile

and its filters. Influence and emphasize the logic of its external and internal contexts. Influence and emphasize the logic of its nature—force and form. Influence and emphasize the logic of its usage. In this sense, you can become more mentally concentrated and in command of your significant value. As a result, we are better able to highlight or accentuate our leveraged knowledge. Our judgment and decision making are thereby sharpened. Upshot: We can be more or less in immediate control of and through our Importance.

Focus helps us concentrate our mental faculties in an intentional manner. When plotted in a cumulative, mutually reinforcing trajectory over time it can lead to . . .

Cognitive Expansion

STEP 5. You can utilize the preceding over time to inspire *development* to become more long-term capable of progressing and optimizing on your Importance. You would be able to intellectually *expand* your significant value better. Expand the logic of your drivers and its paths. Expand the logic of your profile and its filters. Expand the logic of its external and internal contexts. Expand the logic of its nature—force and form. Expand the logic of its usage. In this sense, you can become more mentally progressive in your significant value. As a result, we are able to build it cumulatively, with agility, and with purpose. Upshot: We can be more or less longitudinally developmental of and through our Importance.

All Together

All in all, if Importance is well fit, well manifest, and well used, it can (via a cognizant, knowledgeable, confident, focused, and expanded cognitive process) facilitate *mindfulness*.

Mindfulness is an in-vogue but complex construct. It can generally be understood as the quality or state of being fully conscious or aware of something. It is, in a sense, a mental state achieved by focusing one's awareness on the present moment while simultaneously acknowledging and accepting the cumulative implications of that moment.[5] The research on mindfulness is very fluid, some might say in its infancy; nonetheless, we can surmise several important relationships related to our model, namely that it has the potential to help you boost and be boosted by your cognitive competencies[6].

With regard to cognitive awareness: Mindfulness helps us become more conscious and attentive, more open to a given moment or able to better "listen to life." With improved mindfulness, one might discover that "the notes and rhythms were always there, of course. But these days they seem richer and more important."[7] Thus a mindful approach to Importance allows one to be more cognizant of one's self-subjective significance and value—to better see your (and others') Importance.

With regard to cognitive understanding: Mindfulness helps us give meaning to what we are doing. Another quote from the above referenced article: "The mind is like a muscle, and as such we must exercise and strengthen it." When we increase our processing capacity, we increase our ability to understand and the cumulative reservoir of accumulated insights that we can focus this capacity on. Thus a mindful approach to Importance allows one to be more informed of and knowledgeable about one's self-subjective significance and value—to better understand your (and others') Importance.

With regard to cognitive security: Mindfulness helps us achieve harmony with oneself in the here and now as well as across the life span, to better cope with anxiety and stress and in doing so handle a complicated life and world. Thus a mindful approach to Importance allows one to be more centered and secure in one's self-subjective significance and value—to better appreciate your (and others') Importance.

With regard to cognitive control: Mindfulness helps us increase flexibility and adaptability to situations. This relates to research on neuroplasticity:[8] the brain's ability to reorganize itself by forming new neural connections throughout life. Neuroplasticity allows the neurons (nerve cells) in the brain to adjust their activities in response to new situations or to changes in their environment. Thus in a similar sense a mindful approach to Importance allows one to be more focused, agile, and in control of their self-subjective significance and value—to better influence your (and others') Importance.

With regard to cognitive expansion: Mindfulness helps us quiet our busy minds and free up space for original, strategic, big-picture thinking. It enables creativity, learning, and growth. It puts us on a dynamic path-dependent trajectory. Thus a mindful approach to Importance allows one to be more developmental in their self-subjective significance and value—to better learn about and cumulatively, iteratively enhance your (and others') Importance.

So optimizing your Importance can facilitate positive cognitive outcomes—it can help you *see better* (i.e., more mindful). Thus you will be a more mindful VIP if you can cognitively identify, understand, embrace, emphasize, and develop the conditions, nature, and consequences of your and others' Importance. In short: VIPs are more mindful of and in their significant value.

Affective Consequences—How You Feel (Be Better)

There is an affective component to Importance. It influences how you feel.

Of course, many factors well beyond the scope of this book influence your emotions. And there are no guarantees that affectively connecting with your Importance will somehow, like a panacea, cure your entire range of emotional ails. However better shaping, realizing, and using your self-subjective value can serve as a positive factor or catalysis toward its end. Said another way, if your "heart" experiences the nature of your Importance . . . if you can connect to the emotional aspects of its paths and contingencies . . . and if you can emotionally manage their consequences well . . . then some nice things can happen, including positive impacts on your emotional attentiveness, appreciation, hardiness, affirmation, inspiration

Emotional Attentiveness

STEP 1. You can become more *attuned*—to be better emotionally attentive to your Importance. You would be able to emotionally *sense* your significant value better. Sense the emotions of your drivers and its paths. Sense the emotions of your profile and its filters. Sense the emotions of its external and internal contexts. Sense the emotions emerging from its nature—force and form. Sense the emotions of its usage. In this sense you can become emotionally attentive or sensitive. This is consistent with research on what has become known as emotional intelligence,[9] particularly its self-awareness competency of understanding one's feelings and gaining insight into how they can impact oneself in an organic, holistic manner. Upshot: We can be more or less attuned with and through our Importance.

More attuned and better attentiveness is a good first step in emotionally connecting with our Importance. However it is not the only step . . .

Emotional Appreciation

STEP 2. You can become more *content*—to be at peace with your Importance. You would be able to emotionally *appreciate* your significant value better. Appreciate the emotions invoked by your drivers and its paths. Appreciate the emotions embedded in your profile and its filters. Appreciate the emotions that stem from its external and internal contexts. Appreciate the emotions manifest in its nature—force and form. Appreciate the emotions that are derivative of its usage. In this sense you can become emotionally assured. This insight is related to research about how generally appreciative assessments of self-liking positively correlate with psychological well-being and self-belief and negatively correlate with anxiety and depression.[10] Upshot: We can be more or less at peace with and through our Importance.

A sense of peace/contentment and better appreciation can be a good thing. It is generally necessary, but not always sufficient, for an emotionally fruitful life and might then be supplemented with . . .

Emotional Hardiness

STEP 3. You can become more *resilient*—to be more energized/nourished (versus drained) by your Importance. You would be able to eliminate or buffer against negative emotional forces to *de-stress* your significant value better. De-stress the emotions of your drivers and its paths. De-stress the emotions of your profile and its filters. De-stress the emotions of its external and internal contexts. De-stress the emotions of its nature—force and form. De-stress the emotions of its usage. In this sense you can become emotionally self-regulated. This relates to an additional dimension of the aforementioned emotional intelligence construct, namely what researchers term self-management or the stress-regulatory competency of psychological resiliency.[11] Here we are better able to mitigate and withstand the negative emotions in our lives, and as such limit the negative threats to our emotional wellness by alerting our inclinations and directing them to channel these feelings in a controlled, committed manner. As per the Mayo Clinic, hardiness helps us weather stress and setbacks and makes us less likely to experience feelings such as hopelessness and worthlessness.[12] Upshot: We can be more or less hardy with and through our Importance.

Hardiness can be quite beneficial. When it is combined with enhanced attunement and contentment it can take us to another level that enables . . .

Emotional Affirmation

STEP 4. You can become more *positive*—to be short-term capable of shaping your Importance. You would be able to emotionally *affirm* your significant value better. Affirm the emotions of your drivers and its paths. Affirm the emotions of your profile and its filters. Affirm the emotions of its external and internal contexts. Affirm the emotions of its nature—force and form. Affirm the emotions of its usage. In this sense you can become emotionally more positive. This relates to several growing streams of research around the themes of Positive Psychology (PP) and Positive Organizational Scholarship (POS) that connect to an affirmative outlook in how people feel about themselves.[13] In the former (PP), scholars such as Martin Seligman and Mihaly Csikszentmihalyi advocate for an emphasis on the aspects of our existence that allow us to immerse and energize, to excel and flourish, to experience joy and fulfillment, and live "the pleasant life." Regarding the latter (POS), the application of a positive perspective on our lives and engagements, particularly at work, is agued to help people to better identify their virtues, tap their resources, grow their competencies, and be their very best selves. Embedded, or implied, in each of these streams are mechanisms for affirming one's significance (of their contribution) and value (toward a meaningful purpose) in constructing and experiencing a life that is truly worth living. Upshot: We can be more or less affirming with and through our Importance.

Positivity helps us concentrate our emotional faculties in an uplifting progressive manner. When plotted in a cumulative, mutually reinforcing trajectory over time it can lead to . . .

Emotional Inspiration

STEP 5. You can utilize the preceding over time to become more (intrinsically) *motivated*—to be long-term inspired and internally satisfied by enhancing and growing your Importance. Through this you would be able to emotionally *internalize*, in a deep and internalized way, your significant value better. Internalize the emotional joy of your drivers and its paths. Internalize the emotional joy of your profile and its filters. Internalize the emotional joy of its external and internal contexts. Internalize the emotional joy of its nature—force and form. Internalize the emotional joy of its usage. In this sense you can become more emotionally inspired. This relates to much research that touts the benefits of intrinsic motivation. For example, Hackman and Oldham[14] tell us that we can work to heighten our psychological states of—and design jobs so they are better able to provide—experienced meaningfulness and value, responsibility and accountability, and feedback and support. We also know from Deci and Ryan[15] that people are ignited (i.e., their deepest, most fundamental needs are satisfied and their higher-order autonomous motivations are advanced) when they are able to act with an intrinsic sense of volition, choice, and congruence. All in all, the evidence suggests that over time we can, in our best moments, indeed develop upward patterns of internalized enthusiasm. Upshot: We can be more or less intrinsically inspired with and through our Importance.

All Together
All in all, if Importance is well fit, well manifest, and well used, it can (via an attuned, content, positive, resilient, and intrinsically inspired emotional process) facilitate true, deep-seated *happiness*.

Happiness can be conceptualized in many ways, and we must appreciate its nuanced complexity if we are to uncover and unpack the connection. For the purposes of this book, we attempt to make at least precursory sense of the vast literature on the subject to embrace the notions that happiness can be realized:

- Within a (a) cross-sectional "state" and/or across a (b) longitudinal process
- As calibrated by a (c) defined "contextual" function and/or a (d) broad "collective" experience

Happiness can be seen (a) as a temporal state, akin to how positive psychologists such as Seligman[16] focus on its different parts or components (e.g., pleasure, engagement, and meaning). Here the happiness concept is essentially a multidimensional phenomenon subject to a complex optimization assessment. Thus in this sense, and in terms of our model—insofar as one gains an emotional understanding, appreciation, hardiness, affirmation, and inspiration of and from one's significance and value—one can potentially enhance each of these dimensions and reinforce positive states of felt Importance. Bottom line: True VIPs are able to check off more of the proverbial happiness boxes.

Happiness can also be seen (b) as an unfolding process, akin to what utilitarian economists such as Bentham and Mill as well as numerous behavioral psychologists conceptualize as the accumulating experiences of utility (pleasure or pain) over a defined or discrete period of time. To this end Nobel Laureate Daniel Kahneman[17] actually builds a "U-Index" to measure the dynamic integration of momentary state utilities by assessing the proportion of time a person experiences unpleasant verses pleasant feelings. Others have also proposed similar metrics. For example, Ben-Shahar[18] talks about ways of "getting happy" through both short-term and long-term mechanisms. Thus in this sense, and in terms of our model—insofar as one gains an emotional understanding, appreciation, hardiness, affirmation, and inspiration of and from one's significance and value—one can potentially shape these progressions, facilitate their "process benefits," and support their overall cumulative development of felt Importance. Bottom line: True VIPs are able to amass more proverbial happiness points.

In addition, happiness can be seen (c) as a contextualized, defined goal-oriented function. This intersects with some of the arguments advanced by Diener[19] and his much-championed concept of "subjective well-being." Here happiness is conceptualized as an evaluation made by a person of one's life and the degree to which they have achieved their goals. A "worthwhile" life is one where one is content with how one has performed, in total as well as specifically, within discrete differentiated domains of their life that are of consequence to them (e.g., work, school, home, social, marriage, etc.). The key here, says Diener, is that "the person himself/herself is making the evaluation of life . . . the person herself or himself is the expert here: Is my life going well, according to the standards that I choose to use?"[20] This is consistent with recent research that studied people's happiness using brain scans; it found that people were happiest when they "performed better than they expected during a risk-reward task" and that overall someone's "sense of happiness depends on the size of the gap between what you achieve and what you expect."[21] Further, it is of interest to note that this type of happiness assessment was highly correlated with income-level (money as a metric of successful goal attainment) and a society's cultural individualism (goal attainment on a personal level).[22] Thus in this sense, and in terms of our model—insofar as one gains an emotional understanding, appreciation, hardiness, affirmation, and inspiration of and from one's significance and value—one can potentially frame their goals and their approximations thereof in ways that would reinforce versus detract from their felt Importance. Bottom line: True VIPs are able to achieve more of their prototypical happiness objectives.

Finally, happiness can also be seen (d) as a broad-based, globally oriented, collective experience. To this end several collective measures approximating real or potential aspects of happiness have been developed. For example, as per the Human Development Index derived from the work of Nobel Laureate Amartya Sen,[23] it is to an extent derived from a summary aggregated measure—specifically the composite of various indicators and the geometric mean of multiple normalized indexes over time—of a country's (or region's) average indexes in key aspects of life, such as opportunities for a long and healthy existence, being knowledgeable and educated, and having a decent standard of living. A multitude of other measures can also be found, such as The Happy Planet Index (HPI),[24] which calculates countries' ability to enable sustainably happy lives via multiple measures such as life expectancy, ecological footprint, and where their people feel that they stand on the "ladder of life"; and the Legatum Prosperity Index, which aggregates factors worldwide to compare countries via such indicators as wealth, economic growth, and quality of life. Thus in this sense, and in terms of our model—insofar as one gains an emotional understanding, appreciation, hardiness, affirmation, and inspiration of and from one's significance and value—one can potentially make more or less likely the collective experience of felt Importance. Bottom line: True VIPs are able to advance more prototypical happiness potencies.

The research on happiness is clearly complex and evolving, nonetheless we can surmise several important relationships related to our model, namely that a healthy sense of Importance has the potential to help you with:

1. Being sensitive to and becoming more attuned with your happiness . . . and as such to be more emotionally attentive of and in your significance and value (i.e., to accept/welcome it)
2. Being at peace with and becoming more content with our happiness . . . and as such to be more emotionally appreciative of and in your significance and value (i.e., to be comfortable with it)
3. Being nourished by and becoming resilient within our happiness . . . and as such to be more emotionally hardy within life's impact on and in your significance and value (i.e., to sustain it)
4. Being in control of and becoming positive about our happiness . . . and as such to be more proactively affirmative of and in your significance and value (i.e., to shape it)
5. Being in sync with and becoming intrinsically motivated by our happiness . . . and as such to be more deeply inspired by and in your significance and value (i.e., to thrive within it)

So optimizing your Importance can facilitate positive affective outcomes—it can help you *be better* (i.e., happier). Thus you will be a happier VIP if you can emotionally attune, appreciate, nourish, affirm, and be inspired by the conditions, nature, and consequences of your and others' Importance. In short: VIPs feel happier with and in their significant value.

Conative Consequences—How You Act (Do Better)

There is a behavioral component to Importance. It influences how you act.

Of course, many factors well beyond the scope of this book influence your behaviors. And there are no guarantees that conatively connecting with your Importance will somehow, like a panacea, cure your entire range of behavioral ails. However, better shaping, realizing, and using your self-subjective value can serve as a positive factor or catalysis toward its end. Said another way, if your act on the nature of your Importance . . . if you can activate and implement the aspects of its paths and contingencies . . . and if you can proactively as well as reactively manage their consequences well . . . the some nice things can happen, including positive impacts on your behavioral/conative synergy, excellence, and innovation.

Behavioral/Conative Synergy—Inward
STEP 1. You can develop better *relationship* dynamics to pull things together, to become whole, to synergistically enhance significant value.

Conative synergy involves behaviors directed *inward* toward becoming a whole (significant, valuable) person. Consistent with this, personal choices strive for our elements/aspects/dimensions to work together in harmony for a resonant, contextualized, congruent, balanced and grounded, fused and dynamic, well-used Importance. Our essential argument here is this: When the Importance model is humming, you are a more complete, synergistic person in terms of coalescing significant value. Upshot: We can be more or less whole with and through our Importance.

Extending this to the management of others, conative synergy strives to develop behaviors oriented toward becoming a whole group, team, or organization—a significant, valuable entity. As a consequence, management strategies strive for you and others to work together in harmony for a resonant, contextualized, congruent, balanced and grounded, fused and dynamic, well-used Importance. Thus when the Importance model is humming, you are a more complete, mutually reinforcing collective in terms of amalgamating and conjoining significant value.

Digging deeper, the roots for conative synergy can be found in the philosophical branch of epistemology where issues are surfaced about how common language and meaning can be harvested to unite disparate entities.[25] Using the tools of this domain, you would be able to advance your significant value better by optimizing the composition and alignment of your multifarious elements to achieve complementarity. A healthy sense of Importance enables the enhancement of complementary drivers—regarding characteristics, actions, acceptances, roles, and affiliations—their purposeful differentiation within a system, and their strategic integration toward the enhancement of that larger system—you! For example, rather than experience conflict between oneself and one's roles (e.g., being overwhelmed or ill cast for a particular engagement), or conflict between the roles themselves (e.g., tension between one's personal and professional responsibilities), conative synergy aligns the person with the role and the roles with themselves so that they work with one another rather than against one another. To this point, the Mayo Clinic reports that people with a healthy sense of value generally have (a) more positive relationships with others and are able to form secure and honest relationships and are less likely to stay in unhealthy ones, and (b) are less likely to experience internal conflict and be at "war" with themselves, such as being more realistic in their expectations and less hyper-critical or demeaning of their significance and value.[26]

In addition, conative synergy involves communication and coordination, within and between oneself, so that a consistent versus fragmented whole is achieved. For example, this happens when our paths all flow in the same directions and our subsequent progress along them is reinforcing rather than disjunctive. This happens when we seek win-win integrative solutions to our challenges rather than boosting one aspect of our path at the expense of another. This happens when we structure our engagements, and establish a cohesive culture, within us and between others so that our micro logics do not lead to macro nonsense.

Applying this across our Importance model, we are charged with advancing and facilitating synergistic, collaborative paths to pursue Importance, filters to customize Importance, external (context) fit to embed Importance, internal (criteria) fit to assess Importance, force and form to realize Importance, and engagements to use Importance.

The bottom line: A conatively synergistic VIP is whole. They exhibit extraordinary collaboration to pull things together—internally (within themselves, "have it together") and externally (with other people, comprise a cohesive entity)—to create synergistic significant value. In short: True VIPs enable a personal and professional Importance infused with unity.

Behavioral/Conative Excellence—Outward
STEP 2. You can develop better *performance* dynamics to "push" things forward, to become strategic and productive, to apply significant value well. This is complementary to (and enabled by) the synergistic "pull" function described earlier.

Conative excellence also involves behaviors directed *outward* toward becoming a contributing and achieving person. Consistent with this, personal choices strive for our elements/aspects/dimensions to attain outcomes, realize goals, and actually add significant value for an operationally and strategically resonant, contextualized, congruent, balanced and grounded, fused and dynamic, well-used Importance. Our essential argument here is this: When the Importance model is humming, you are a more high-performing person in terms of doing (versus just seeing or being) things and producing real, practical significant value. Upshot: We can be more or less productive with and through our Importance.

Extending this to the management of others, conative excellence strives to develop behaviors oriented toward becoming a successful group, team, organization—a significant, valuable entity. As a consequence, management strategies strive for you and others to propel each other forward and achieve objectives for an operationally and strategically resonant, contextualized, congruent, balanced and grounded, fused and dynamic, well-used Importance. Thus when the Importance model is humming, you are a more prolific and high-performing collective in terms of creating, generating, and contributing accumulated, shared significant value.

Digging deeper, the roots for conative excellence are found in many places, including the philosophical conceptions of Aristotelian phronesis and Jamesian pragmatism where practical thought and workable knowledge are leveraged and applied for "real-world" results.[27] Within this perspective, you would be able to advance your significant value better by optimizing your efforts in a manner consistent with your personal "mission statement." That is, to channel your synergistic potential and deploy your capacities to do the right things. You would also be able to advance your significant value better by being more efficient in its pursuit; by optimizing your structures and processes to maximize high-value activities and minimize unproductive efforts. That is, to channel your synergistic potential and align resources to do things the right way.

At its best, Importance enables a more coherent, impelling, well-articulated vision—regarding the construction of characteristics, actions, acceptances, roles, and affiliations—their purposeful deployment within a system, and their well-organized, cost- and time-effective application toward accomplishing your specific goals and objectives. For example, rather than waste time with peripheral or lesser endeavors, conative excellence enables one to optimize their potential to the most central and critical issues so that they "put first things first"[28] and achieve the most "bang for the buck." Rather than execute within bloated, flawed, constrained, chaotic, compromised, and ill-conceived frameworks, conative excellence enables one to act as a more lean, optimized, natural, controlled, high-quality, and well-intentioned manner.

To these points, the Mayo Clinic reports that people with a healthy sense of self-significance and value generally construct better skill sets, make higher-quality decisions, and achieve greater work-level performance. These arguments are also consistent with research connecting conative aspects related to Importance with specific performance dimensions, for example, Rosenberg's ideas on task-specific esteem and level of functioning, Fishbein and Azjen's ideas on task-specific attitudes and connected actions, Bandura's ideas on self-efficacy and behavioral outcomes, and Brockner's ideas on the link between these types of properties and positive (content-related) work motivation, performance, and job satisfaction as well as (process-related) socialization, decision making, goal setting, occupational interactions, and job design.[29]

In addition, conative excellence indirectly involves (as per the discussion in Chapter 2) an overall orientation, within and between oneself, so that we create and execute our best possible contexts and strategies. For example, and in terms of our model, this happens in organizations when our paths are reinforced and propagated by the micro-individual dynamic of human resources and human capital management; our profile resonance is customized and supported by the meso-dynamic of management functionality; our contextual and evaluative fit is established and extended by the macro-dynamic of (visible) structural and (invisible) cultural design; and our nature, and its engagement, are guided and optimized by internally leveraged core competencies and capabilities, tacit and explicit knowledge, product and service portfolios, and externally exploited niches, networks, interdependencies, advantages, and positions.

Taken together, and as per the above points, we are charged with creating effective paths to pursue Importance, effective filters to customize Importance, effective external/context fit to embed Importance, effective internal/criteria fit to assess Importance, effective force and form to realize Importance, and effective engagements to use Importance.

The bottom line: A conatively excellent VIP is productive. They exhibit extraordinary application to push things along internally (within themselves, "get it going") and externally (with other people, "move us forward") to realize both quality and quantity of significant value. In short: True VIPs enable a personal and professional Importance infused with a high level of performance.

Behavioral/Conative Innovation—Upward

STEP 3. You can develop better *improvement* dynamics to change and "grow" things, to become a perpetual learner, to sustainably cultivate and dynamically propagate significant value. This is complementary to (and enabled by) the "pull" and "push" functions described earlier.

Conative innovation adds to the conversation behaviors directed not necessarily inward or outward but instead *upward* toward becoming innovative—a more agile, progressive, and sustainable person. Consistent with this, personal choices strive for our elements/aspects/dimensions to constantly nurture and evolve so to relentlessly and perpetually (re)create significant value. As such it facilitates a cybernetically adjusting and continuously expanding resonant, contextualized, congruent, balanced and grounded, fused and dynamic, well-used Importance. Our essential argument here is this: When the Importance model is humming, you are a more dynamic person in terms of continually enriching (versus just seeing, being, or short-term doing) things and re-imagining significant value. Upshot: We can be more or less innovative with and through our Importance.

Extending this to the management of others, conative innovation strives to develop behaviors oriented toward becoming a continuously improving group/team/organization—an ever-increasing and sustainably significant, valuable entity. As a consequence, management strategies strive for you and others to propel each other upward, expanding and reimaging possibilities, for perpetually adjusting and enhancing your mutually resonant, contextualized, congruent, balanced and grounded, fused and dynamic, well-used Importance. Thus when the Importance model is humming, you are a more sustainable collective in terms of evolving and growing shared significant value.

Importance at its best enables a type of personal or organizational intra- or entrepreneurial process —regarding the expansion of characteristics, actions, acceptances, roles, and affiliations —that serves as a platform for their institutionalized invention and innovation as well as their sustainable progression across arenas (cross-sectional agility) and time (longitudinal agility). For example, building upon the synergistic and productive outcomes discussed in the prior sections, one can also draw from these to foster an: (a) innovative orientation to one's Importance, to confront new challenges, seek new opportunities, and address outstanding issues rather than hide or run away from them; (b) an innovative mind-set about one's Importance, to perpetually discover and proactively engage in "pushing the envelope" for oneself and one's charges rather than playing it too safe; (c) an innovative drive toward one's Importance, to intrinsically embrace the dynamic and through this thrive in uncertain, complex, and fluctuating conditions rather than remain overly conservative, artificially create false certainties, and fear inevitable change; and (d) an innovative arc with one's Importance, to learn from mistakes and continuously, incrementally, and radically challenge the status quo within and across domains rather than simply keep on keeping on.

In addition, conative innovation has the potential to propagate innovative ways of approaching the Importance issue in general, such as via: more balanced success practices and metrics, emphasizing different indicators (versus selective definitions of significance and value); broader success practices and metrics, emphasizing different stakeholder concerns and perspectives (versus narrow definitions of significance and value); faster evolving success practices and metrics, emphasizing cumulative and disjunctive trajectories (versus static targets for significance and value); deeper success practices and metrics, emphasizing fundamental education and edification as to underlying realities as well as task-specific training (versus superficial, ill-understood fixes, policies, tools, or templates for significance and value); and ultimately more sustainable success practices and metrics, for viable and integrative problem solving (versus myopic and temporary definitions of significance and value). When your entire personal/professional Importance system is subject to these types of innovations it can supersede transient or idiosyncratic conceptualizations of significance and value and instead, through this process, provide a simultaneously solid yet flexible foundation to constantly crystalize, move, and flourish.

Taken together, we thus are charged with persistently learning, improving, and sustaining paths to pursue Importance, filters to customize Importance, external/context fit to embed Importance, internal/criteria fit to assess Importance, force and form to realize Importance, and engagements to use Importance.

The bottom line: A conatively innovative VIP is progressive. They exhibit extraordinary innovation and agility to grow things upward internally (within themselves, e.g., never stop learning) and externally (with other people) to evolve sustainably significant value. In short: True VIPs enable a personal and professional Importance infused with resourceful, prescient, creative, and continuous improvement.

All Together

All in all, if Importance is well fit, well manifest, and well used, it can (via a synergistic, excellent, and innovative conative process) facilitate behavioral effectiveness. More specifically, with regard to synergy, pulling the elements of the Importance process together helps us to become whole. As a result, it guides and propels efforts inward to coalesce, and thereby unify, our significant value. With regard to excellence, pushing the Importance process forward helps us to become productive. As a result, it guides and propels efforts outward to apply, and thereby achieve, quality and quantity with our significant value. With regard to innovation, growing the Importance process upward helps us to become dynamic and agile. As a result, it guides and propels efforts to innovate and enhance, and thereby sustain, our significant value.

So optimizing your Importance can facilitate positive conative outcomes; it can help you *do better* (i.e., effectiveness). Thus you will be a more effective VIP if you can behaviorally integrate, leverage, and transform the conditions, nature, and consequences of your and others' Importance. In short: VIPs are more effective with and in their significant value.

Upshot of the Above

A healthy (see Chapter 7) and positively engaged (see Chapter 8) sense of significant value can enlighten our self-conception and how we see ourselves, enhance our emotional well-being and how we feel about ourselves, and impel our performance and how we behave in personal as well as professional settings. More specifically, it can facilitate one's:

1. Cognitive, intellectual success: Seeing one's significant value better; becoming a more mindful VIP
2. Affective, emotional success: Feeling better about one's significant value; becoming a happier VIP
3. Conative, behavioral success: Doing better with one's significant value; becoming a more effective VIP

Optimizing your Importance can facilitate positive outcomes. And you will be a true VIP if you are able to see, feel, and do better (for yourself, through personal choices, and for others, through management strategies) with your significant value. Of course, there are no guarantees that one will become more mindful, happier, and more effective. We are not selling any "magic bullets" or promising any panaceas. Notwithstanding, a better cognitive, affective, and conative sense of Importance can go a long way in making it happen.

The following table illustrates some of these major outcomes of Importance.

Table 9.2   Managing the Outcomes of Importance

OUTCOMES	If Managed Well . . .	
COGNITIVE Intellectual How You Think	MINDFULNESS Cognizant Informed Confident Focused Developed = SEE BETTER	S U
AFFECTIVE Emotional How You Feel	HAPPINESS Attuned Content Resilient Positive Inspired = BE BETTER	C C E S
CONATIVE Behavioral How You Act	EFFECTIVENESS Synergistic Excellent Innovative = DO BETTER	S

IDENTIFY . . .
The Consequences of Importance

In examining the following cases, please utilize them in the following ways:

1. In *general*, can you overlay the template from this chapter onto the scenes below and see the characters' consequences of their Importance?
2. Now, as a *mirror* (looking specifically at *you*): Do any of these characters remind you of you and help to reveal the (cognitive, affective, conative) consequences of your Importance?
3. Finally, as a *window* (looking at specific *others*): Do any of these characters remind you of someone else that you know and help to reveal the (cognitive, affective, conative) consequences of their Importance?

Case Study (Personal)

In the Office—Shadowing Mr. Norman at His Nine-to-Five Job

In the virtual meeting (*mindfulness*): Mr. Norman has come a long way from his initial days as a budding professional. Take for instance Monday morning's planning meeting that was conducted via video conference technology with corporate headquarters. Before becoming more mindful of his significant value, and how it related to his firm, he was not a very useful member of the team. In fact, he would frequently daydream and mentally check out of these types of activities. If he could not identify with the meeting's purpose, understand its thrust, embrace its objectives, influence its direction, or develop its points, why bother paying attention. He would instead embody the very disconnected, marginalized "space cadet" that he tells his kids not to be and put the conference on mute as he checked his messages or played solitaire on his laptop. Now everything has changed. He is now decidedly more cognizant, better informed, more confident, better focused, and growth oriented about the intersection of his job, the company, and this meeting. He is now the prototypically immersed, committed contributor—at last practicing himself what he so often preaches to others. Basically, he has advanced his cognitive capacity for greater comprehension and, as such, leverages his Importance to become fully intellectually engaged.

On the commute (*happiness*): If you will excuse the pun, Mr. Norman has also come a long way on his daily train commute. When he was younger and less secure in his significance and value, he used to be the classic grumpy passenger. The train and he were alien combatants locked in a zero-sum battle. There was little to no sensitivity to his feelings or how they affected others, appreciation for his surroundings and the dedicated effort it took to build and maintain it, relaxation among the potential stressors such as time delays and close-quarters contact, affirmation of the good things that could be as opposed to the potential problems and detractors that loomed, or motivational internalization of the experiences to enrich and vitalize his spirit. What a miserable, tormented, raging grouch he was! Now he has learned how to more favorably connect the self with the situation. Now he works to emotionally attune to the experience, find contentment in the journey, build resilience to potential stressors, adopt a positive outlook, and become intrinsically inspired by all that he has. The grouch has turned into a downright cheery, appreciative, peaceful "traveler." Basically, he has advanced his affective well-being for greater meaningfulness and, as such, leverages his Importance to become fully emotionally engaged.

At the client site (*effectiveness*): Perhaps the most tangible indicator of Mr. Norman's progress has been in the observable way in which he manages his team. At one time his unproductiveness was in danger of getting him fired. For example, last February when working at one client's remote site, he recalls a complete inability to connect himself or his colleagues to the task at hand. He could not synthesize people to pull the team together; they were a fractured interaction of self-absorbed individuals. He could not tap into complementary capabilities and resources to push them forward; they were a dysfunctional set of factions that moved in different directions. He could not invent new solutions to grow their options; they were a stagnant unit that was encased in tradition and shackled to the past. Even though he was being paid to get results, the fact of the matter was that his failure to generate meaningful collaborations, productive applications, or progressive improvements made him more of an obstacle to their success. Now he is much different. Now he has put rubber to road and applies what he learned in grad school about turning groups into teams. Now he taps into people's sense of significance and value to unify them, to get things done, and to creatively expand their horizons and potential. Basically, he has advanced his conative competency for greater performance and, as such, leverages his Importance to become fully behaviorally engaged.

Can you appreciate that it is also critical to manage the back end of the Importance model and achieve positive results through your self-subjective significant value? By leveraging it to become more cognitively engaged? By leveraging it to become more emotionally engaged? By leveraging it to become more behaviorally engaged? How can you emulate Mr. Norman to use your head to see better, use your heart to feel better, and use your actions to do better . . . and via the process be more successful?

Case Study (Professional)

Behind the Scenes at the Auto Supplies Company

In the assembly line (*mindfulness*): The two senior employees at the manufacturing factory shared a workstation but nearly nothing else. Mitch resembled the classic mindless, disconnected worker drone with little sense of his significance or value in the firm. He basically sleepwalked through the day and, as long as there was not a major event like a five-alarm fire, was barely cognizant of what was happening around him. He did not read the company newsletter and only gave a quick scan to the directions for the new shipment of tools. He had little faith in his contribution and frequently asked others to check his work. He was physically present at staff meetings but mentally AWOL and, not surprisingly, never advanced beyond the basic entry-level position in his five-year tenure. Conversely, Troy's mind was definitely tuned in to what he had to do, and he was completely present every day when on the job. Troy was able to grasp the overall logic of his job as well as master the contributing details that drove the production process. He really understood the reasons why the machines did what they did and in the order that they did them in. He executed his assignments well, and this was reflected in his department's smooth production process and consistent profitability. He even had the presence, as well as confidence, to step out of his skin to quickly identify problems whenever they arose and quality control his own work. Even though he had been at the job six months less than Mitch, there was little doubt that Troy's high-level intellectual engagement had him destined for a promotion in the near future.

At the supervisor's office, negotiating with clients about repair estimate (*happiness*): Wendy, the highly capable early-shift manager, approached these types of interactions with all the warmth and joy of an ornery viper slithering across a prickly cactus. She was oblivious to the vibe of her customers' significance and value and utterly detached from their plight. This put everyone in a constant state of stress and antsy unrest. The slightest perceived provocation or pushback would launch her into a rage. There were few happy or empathetic words that escaped her mouth when quoting services and costs. And regardless of the outcome, both parties inevitably walked away battered, bruised, and drained. This is probably why the company's regular customers would wait for her to leave the office until co-manager Ann's late shift began. Ann also knew her stuff but in addition could really relate to her customers, appreciate their concerns, and was really attuned to what they were going through when a part wore down. She remained calm and serene during even the most intense estimates and never lost control of her emotions. She could even maintain this positive, even-keeled demeanor at the end of a hard, long day. Whereas Wendy treated the interaction like a cold, detached cage fight between bitter rivals, Ann saw it as a dance between interdependent, equally important associates. Even when the outcome was not exactly what the customer wanted, the people who dealt with Ann felt heard and cared for, significant and valued partners in the process, and as a result walked away highly satisfied.

On the shop floor (*effectiveness*): At the garage, the two repair shift supervisors Ross and Tam were at the top and bottom of the pay-raise scale . . . and for good reason. Ross ran a true team where each person was built up and positioned as a significant, valuable contributor. Esprit de corps was sky-high. He established a climate, culture, and reward system where everyone put his or her ego aside to contribute and pitch in for whatever was needed whenever it was needed. It was common to hear people say, "I'm on it." Alternatively, Tam ran a group that never really showed much complementarity or teamwork. Aside from the matching uniforms, little else meshed. People in this dysfunctional environment did the minimum required of their individually mandated parts and nothing more. It was common to hear people lament, "No can do" or "Sorry, not my job." More than this, when comparing the two, Ross's team pushed each member to a higher-quality, higher-efficiency level of performance than they could have ever mustered on their own. This translated to a combined output that surpassed company-wide goals and frequently incorporated (and team-taught) new techniques from the monthly trade magazines and best practices sites. This was clearly not the case with Tam's group, which could be better characterized by the words "underachieving," "divisive," and "stagnant." Funny thing is, the skill level of both sets of workers was about even. And Ross and Tam came out of the same graduate school degree program with similar GPAs on their transcripts. You would never know this from their actions and their results.

Can you see how the characters leveraged their self-subjective significant value differently? With different cognitive success? With different affective success? With different conative success? How can you help them achieve better outcomes in and from their Importance?

PERSONALIZE...
The Consequences of Importance

This set of exercises gives you the opportunity to clarify the implications of your significant value. All together, we can say that if you have better cognitive, intellectual outcomes (seeing, or mindfulness), affective, emotional outcomes (feeling, or happiness), and conative, behavioral outcomes (doing, or successfulness), the more positive the results of your Importance. You can use this section to assess the outcomes of your significant value.

General

Come to grips with the outcomes of your Importance.
   At the most basic level, please rate the degree to which the outcomes of your Importance are less (low, say a "1") or more (high, say a "10") developed.

   1. Cognitive: For greater mindfulness?
   2. Affective: For greater happiness?
   3. Conative: For greater effectiveness?

Are you content with your scores? What would you change? How could you change this? Does your ranking suggest a more or less desirable "bottom line" for your Importance? Has the ranking changed as you have grown, experienced things, gone through life changes, or advanced in years? Is there any pattern to be found in these? Is there a sweet spot where everything fell into place? If so then how can you get (back) there?

Specific

Drill down further to isolate specific consequences of Importance and how they impact your outcomes.

Now please note the degree to which you agree with the following ways for completing this sentence, from most to least descriptive of you:

The outcomes of my Importance . . .

- Have positive cognitive consequences and facilitate my mindfulness
  - ○ I think differently/better about my significant value
  - ○ Am more intellectually aware of it
  - ○ Am more intellectually understanding of it
  - ○ Am more intellectually secure in it
  - ○ Am more intellectually in control of it
  - ○ Am more intellectually development oriented from it
  - ○ As a result of all of the above, am more intellectually successful
- Have positive affective consequences and facilitate my happiness
  - ○ I feel differently/better about my significant value
  - ○ Am more emotionally attuned with it
  - ○ Am more emotionally content with it
  - ○ Am more emotionally resilient in it
  - ○ Am more emotionally positive with it
  - ○ Am more emotionally inspired from it
  - ○ As a result of all of the above, am more emotionally successful
- Have positive conative consequences and facilitate my effectiveness
  - ○ I act differently/better about my significant value
  - ○ Behave in a higher-functioning manner
  - ○ Am able to achieve greater synergy by it—pulling things together
  - ○ Am able to achieve greater excellence by it—pushing things forward
  - ○ Am able to achieve greater innovativeness by it—raising things higher
  - ○ As a result of all of the above, am more behaviorally successful

APPLY . . .
The Consequences of Importance

From a personal perspective, the consequences of your Importance are partly determined by the choices that you make about how to leverage its outcomes. From a professional perspective, the consequences of your people's Importance are partly determined by the management strategies that you employ to help them leverage its outcomes.

Please take a moment to apply the material from this chapter to make better choices and craft better strategies about the outcomes of Importance.

Making Personal Choices

Choice 7: You are, to varying degrees, in control of optimizing and evolving the outcomes of your Importance. That is to say, you can influence its short- and long-term effects on mindfulness, happiness, and effectiveness.

Choice 7a. You can choose to monitor, troubleshoot, and improve the cognitive outcomes of your Importance for greater mindfulness.

> In terms of significant value, what is my level of cognitive awareness? Cognitive understanding? Cognitive security? Cognitive control? Cognitive expansion? Does my Importance journey propel or inhibit these in my personal and professional life?

> Looking at the above as if it was a dashboard: How are my intellectual gauges (short term) measuring? Do they look right? How are my intellectual gauges (long term) trending? Are they looking progressively better or worse? Overall, are there any particular areas in need of improvement or correction so that I can become more mindful of my Importance?

Choice 7b. You can choose to monitor, troubleshoot, and improve the affective outcomes of your Importance for greater happiness.

> In terms of significant value, what is my level of affective attentiveness? Affective appreciation? Affective hardiness? Affective affirmation? Affective inspiration? Does my Importance journey propel or inhibit these in my personal and professional life?

> Looking at the above as if it was a dashboard: How are my emotional gauges (short term) measuring? Do they feel right? How are my emotional gauges (long term) trending? Are they feeling progressively better or worse? Overall, are there any particular areas in need of improvement or correction so that I can feel happier in my Importance?

Choice 7c. You can choose to monitor, troubleshoot, and improve the behavioral outcomes of your Importance for greater effectiveness.

> In terms of significant value, what is my level of conative synergy? Conative excellence? Conative innovation? Does my Importance journey propel or inhibit these in my personal and professional life?

> Looking at the above as if it was a dashboard: How are my behavioral gauges (short term) measuring? Do they move right? How are my behavioral gauges (long term) trending? Are they moving progressively better or worse? Overall, are there any particular areas in need of improvement or correction so that I can act more effectively through my Importance?

Crafting Management Strategies

Management Strategy 7: You can, to varying degrees, help others better optimize and evolve the outcomes of their Importance.
This can happen at work, at home, or anywhere.

Strategy 7a. You can help them channel their Importance to optimize and evolve their short- and long-term *mindfulness*. For example:

Show them how to become more cognitively aware, understanding, secure, in control, and developmental of, and through, their Importance. In a nutshell: Help them to intellectually process their significant value to see better!

Strategy 7b. You can help them channel their Importance to optimize and evolve their short- and long-term *happiness*. For example:

Assist them to become more affectively attentive, appreciative, hardy, affirming, and inspired in, and through, their Importance. In a nutshell: Help them to emotionally process their significant value to feel better!

Strategy 7c. You can help them channel their Importance to optimize and evolve their short- and long-term *effectiveness*. For example:

Guide them to become more conatively synergistic (by better pulling things together through inwardly focused action), productive (by better pushing things forward through outwardly focused action), and innovative (by better sustaining and expanding things through upwardly focused action) with and through their Importance. In a nutshell: Help them to behaviorally process their significant value to do better!

Checkpoint

Now that we have concluded this chapter, it is appropriate to pause for a moment at this checkpoint and answer the following questions:

- ○ Do you UNDERSTAND the consequences of Importance? Can you see how Importance might facilitate cognitive outcomes and mindfulness? Affective outcomes and happiness? Conative outcomes and effectiveness?
- ○ Can you IDENTIFY its outcomes in personal and professional settings?
- ○ Have you PERSONALIZED its outcomes by relating it to your own Importance journey?
- ○ Will you APPLY the above to (a) translate/leverage it to make better choices and (b) facilitate others' translation/leverage of it to craft better strategies?

If not, circle back.

If so . . . Bravo!

We have covered the entire Importance model.

Now in our final chapter let's review what we have done so far, extract some of our core points, insights, and themes, and outline some potential next steps . . .

Part III

The Management of Importance

10

Conclusion

Importance is a matter of choice.

Chapter 10 presents the main takeaways of our model of Importance. In this final chapter, we will recap and discuss our (a) primary discussion points, (b) key themes, and (c) main analytical insights. We will then integrate the lessons from our previous chapters to present overall "systems" or guided checklists for making better personal choices (for *your* Importance and being a true VIP) and for crafting better management strategies (for *others'* Importance and helping them be true VIPs). We will conclude with some final thoughts and well wishes.

PRIMARY DISCUSSION POINTS

As per our discussion, Importance has . . .

1. Complex, interrelated *conditions*
2. A multidimensional *nature*
3. Critical bottom-line *consequences*

POINT #1—Importance has complex, interrelated conditions.

As evident in the first part of our theoretical model, self-subjective significant value is (a) created by different drivers, which can range from the internal to the external, (b) filtered through different profiles, which embody a host of individualized factors to make these drivers more or less resonant, and (c) contingent on different external contexts as well as internal criteria, each of which contain numerous dimensions that create better or worse fit.

So do not oversimplify the seeds of Importance. Message: Play chess, not checkers, when managing your and others' significance and value!

POINT #2—Importance has a multidimensional nature.

As evident in the second part of our theoretical model, self-subjective significant value is manifest in different a) forces and (b) forms. It can be of more positive or negative valence as well as of greater or lesser magnitude. It can be more or less personally and collectively anchored as well as more or less stable or variable.

So do not obscure the nature of Importance. Message: Create a balanced and grounded, as well as fused and dynamic, conception of your and others' significance and value!

POINT #3—Importance has critical consequences.

As evident in the final part of our theoretical model, self-subjective significant value is a) employed in different modes and (b) toward different results. It can be used toward better or worse directions, in better or worse functions, and with better or worse expressions. It can facilitate or impede cognitive, affective, and conative outcomes.

So do not misdirect or misappropriate the uses and outcomes of Importance. Message: Strive for a positive, integrated approach toward improving and leveraging the intellectual, emotional, and behavioral effects of your and others' significance and value!

KEY THEMES

Some of the key themes that emerge from the above are that Importance is . . .

1. Perfectly *natural*
2. Largely a matter of *choice*
3. Something that can be well or poorly *managed*

THEME #1—The Importance journey is perfectly *natural*.

That is to say, its reflective consideration and active exploration are commonplace across times, places, peoples, and situations. Its manifest issues relate to a great variety of our daily pursuits and underlie diverse areas of our scholarly inquiries. In addition, there is nothing about Importance that is inherently, inevitably egotistical or necessarily negative. In fact, it is core to our overarching collective quest for significance and for value (that life in general matters) as well as within our individualized personal quests for significance and for value (that our particular lives matter).

So do not feel as though contemplating one's VIP-ness is a waste of time or something to be hidden and shunned. Certainly there are better and worse ways to pursue it. If done prudently, you can clarify and customize your sense of significant value to reconcile Importance within the intimate and the infinite of your experiences, and as such enrich yourself along with those around you. Message: Embrace the Importance journey!

THEME #2—Importance is fundamentally a matter of personal *choice*.

That is to say, to a large extent you can exercise agency[1] and take greater control over your Importance. Insofar as people are "streams of becoming," we can surpass the false masquerades that distract our attention away from the real meaning of Importance and work toward realizing our true significant, valuable selves.[2] Invoking the sentiments of renowned thinker Henry David Thoreau,[3] "There is no value in life except what you choose to place upon it." Applying this to the ideas of leadership gurus Bill George and Warren Bennis,[4] "Your truth is derived from your life story . . . You are the author of your life." Thus you ultimately decide your self-subjective significance. You ultimately decide your self-subjective value.

So be aware of its relationships (good), be reactive and flexible to its contingencies (better), and/or proactively create its dynamics (best). When you accept responsibility and own the process, over your life span[5] you are more likely to enhance your Importance and see, feel, and do better. It is this notion—that being a VIP is a matter of choice—that is, in my view, the number-one takeaway from our book. Message: Get out of the proverbial passive passenger seat[6] and dare to take the wheel!

THEME #3—Importance is something that can be well or poorly *managed*.

Following from the preceding insight, you can also affect others' (family, friends, colleagues, etc.) Importance through carefully or ill-crafted management strategies. That is to say, you can influence for the better or for the worse the resonance of their filtered paths, the appropriateness for their external context and internal criteria, and the impact in their uses and toward their outcomes.

So accept responsibility and master the model. Help others to take the wheel on their journeys. Learn about their key factors and discern their connections. Customize and apply these to facilitate their results. The more you are sensitive to and adept in these exigencies, the better you are able to impact them in desired directions. Message: Invest your time and energy to make a positive difference in people's significant value!

MAIN ANALYTICAL INSIGHTS

As per our *analysis*, we have shown how and why Importance should be . . .

1. *Customized* for the path and person
2. *Fit* for the context and criteria
3. *Optimized* in its nature
4. *Leveraged* in its use and outcomes

INSIGHT #1—Importance should be *customized* for the path and person.

Different drivers can be constructed to a greater or lesser extent, and they can resonate more or less with our particular profiles. Thus Importance is inherently, inexorably a *mediated* function. VIP-ness can mean different things for different people. Message: Tailor your focus and efforts to the particular subject!

INSIGHT #2—Importance should be *fit* for the context and criteria.

Different external and internal factors bear upon its relationships. Thus Importance is also inherently, inexorably a *moderated* function. VIP-ness can mean different things in different places and when measured on different scales. Message: Match your focus and efforts with the particular contingencies!

INSIGHT #3—Importance should be *optimized* in its nature.

It can be more or less balanced and grounded in force as well as fused and dynamic in form. Thus Importance is also inherently, inexorably a *multidimensional* function. VIP-ness can be differentially healthy. Message: Proactively and continuously fine-tune its particular force and form!

INSIGHT #4—Importance should be *leveraged* in its utilization and outcomes.

It can be more or less ably engaged to greater or lesser success. Thus Importance is also inherently, inexorably a *potential*[7] function. The story does not end when Importance is realized and amassed. VIP-ness can be used in better and worse ways to achieve more or less desirable "returns." Message: Employ it wisely for positive results!

All together, capturing and integrating the highlighted messages from each of the prior chapters (chapter numbers are noted below in parentheses), we can in the end say that:

> *(1) Importance is important . . . but despite its complexity can be understood and managed. (2) What we know about Importance is based within and across many different areas of inquiry. Integrating them, we learn that (3) there are many ways to pursue it and that (4) these paths are more or less resonant depending on your profile. Your particular paths to Importance are also impacted by the degree to which they fit (5), the context you are in, and (6) the criteria that you employ for assessing it. Ultimately, your sense of Importance (7) can be more or less healthy, depending on its force and form. Subject to this nature, as well as (8) how your Importance is used (9), it can help or hinder how you think, feel, and act.*

And to be a true *VIP* we can say that:

> From a *personal VIP* perspective: Ideally you should pursue a *path* that resonates with your *profile*, fits with your *context* and *criteria*, creates a healthy force (balanced/grounded) and form (fused/dynamic) within the *nature* of your Importance, and can be *used* in positive ways to facilitate your cognitive (mindfulness), emotional (satisfaction), and behavioral (effectiveness) *success*.

This is captured in Table 10.1 and the subsequent Personal System Guide/ Checklist for Making Better Choices.

> From a *professional VIP* perspective: More than this, to help others (in the workplace, in the home or neighborhood, etc.) become true VIPs, ideally you should embrace a management strategy that empowers them to pursue *paths* that resonate with their profile, fit with their *contexts* and *criteria*, and create a healthy force (balanced/grounded) and form (fused/dynamic) within the *nature* of their Importance that can be *used* in positive ways to facilitate their *success*.

This is captured in Table 10.2 and the subsequent Management System Guide/ Checklist for Crafting Better Strategies.

Now, taking these in turn . . .

PERSONAL VIP SYSTEM:
Choices for You

The following table summarizes the personal choices available to you.

Table 10.1   Personal VIP System—Choices for *You*

PERSONAL VIP SYSTEM	
Choice Category	*Choice Options*
CHOICE 1: You are, to varying degrees, in control of your path(s) to Importance.	**Choice 1a.** Choose to focus on *characteristics*, or not. If so, purposefully select and proactively, appropriately affect your focal characteristic(s).
	Choice 1b. Choose to focus on *actions*, or not. If so, purposefully select and proactively, appropriately affect your focal action(s).
	Choice 1c. Choose to focus on *acceptance*, or not. If so, purposefully select and proactively, appropriately affect your focal acceptance(s).
	Choice 1d. Choose to focus on *roles*, or not. If so, purposefully select and proactively, appropriately affect your focal role(s).
	Choice 1e. Choose to focus on *affiliations*, or not. If so, purposefully select and proactively, appropriately affect your focal affiliation(s).
CHOICE 2: You are, to varying degrees, in control of your Importance's path-profile resonance.	**Choice 2a.** You can choose to align your path with your *values*, or alter your values to suit your chosen path.
	Choice 2b. You can choose to align your path with your *motivations*, or alter your motivations to suit your chosen path.
	Choice 2c. You can choose to align your path with your *aptitudes*, or alter your aptitudes to suit your chosen path.
	Choice 2d. You can choose to align your path with you *personality*, or alter your personality to suit your chosen path.
	Choice 2e. You can choose to align your path with you *archetype*, or alter your archetype to suit your chosen path.
CHOICE 3: You are, to varying degrees, in control of your Importance's external fit.	**Choice 3a.** You can choose to align your filtered path with your *location*—by altering your path to suit the context, or changing your context, or altering the context to suit your chosen path.
	Choice 3b. You can choose to align your filtered path with your *task*—by altering your path to suit the context, or changing your context, or altering the context to suit your chosen path.
	Choice 3c. You can choose to align your filtered path with your *support*—by altering your path to suit the context, or changing your context, or altering the context to suit your chosen path.
	Choice 3d. You can choose to align your filtered path with your *market*—by altering your path to suit the context, or changing your context, or altering the context to suit your chosen path.

(Continued)

Table 10.1 (*Continued*)

PERSONAL VIP SYSTEM	
Choice Category	*Choice Options*
CHOICE 4: You are, to varying degrees, in control of your Importance's internal fit.	**Choice 4a.** You can choose to align your filtered path with your *scope*—the cross-sectional (snapshot) orientation of the lens—by altering your path to suit the criteria or altering the criteria to suit your chosen path.
	Choice 4b. You can choose to align your filtered path with your *time*—the longitudinal (cinema) orientation of the lens—by altering your path to suit the criteria or altering the criteria to suit your chosen path.
	Choice 4c. You can choose to align your filtered path with your *frame*—the amount of "zoom" on the lens—by altering your path to suit the criteria or altering the criteria to suit your chosen path.
	Choice 4d. You can choose to align your filtered path with your *scale*—the comparative benchmarks within the lens—by altering your path to suit the criteria or altering the criteria to suit your chosen path.
	Choice 4e. You can choose to align your filtered path with your *perspective*—the clarity/quality of the lens—by altering your path to suit the criteria or altering the criteria to suit your chosen path.
CHOICE 5: You are, to varying degrees, in control of shaping the nature of your Importance.	**Choice 5a.** You can choose to better balance the force *valence* of your Importance.
	Choice 5b. You can choose to better ground the force *magnitude* of your Importance.
	Choice 5c. You can choose to better fuse the form *level* of your Importance.
	Choice 5d. You can choose to make more dynamic and cumulative the form *stability* of your importance.
CHOICE 6: You are, to varying degrees, in control of using your Importance in better and worse ways.	**Choice 6a.** You can choose to enhance the *direction*—using it more as a means than an end—of your Importance.
	Choice 6b. You can choose to enhance the *function*—using it more genuinely (open) than defensively (closed)—of your Importance.
	Choice 6c. You can choose to enhance the *expression*—using it more implicitly than explicitly—of your Importance.
CHOICE 7: You are, to varying degrees, in control of optimizing and evolving the outcomes of your Importance.	**Choice 7a.** You can choose to monitor, troubleshoot, and improve the cognitive outcomes of your Importance for greater *mindfulness*.
	Choice 7b. You can choose to monitor, troubleshoot, and improve the affective outcomes of your Importance for greater *happiness*.
	Choice 7c. You can choose to monitor, troubleshoot, and improve the behavioral outcomes of your Importance for greater *effectiveness*.

As a result, I would advise:

First (putting on my personal "coach" or advisor hat) . . . You can be a true VIP by constructing a Personal Importance System.

The choices are not exclusive—they are highly independent. As such, they can be mutually reinforcing or mutually destroying.

1. Build solid, vigorous paths to Importance (Chapter 3). Optimize its antecedents. You have choices—How you *pursue* it really matters. The goal here is: Importance = Strong Drivers.
2. While customizing them to gel with your personal profile (Chapter 4). Optimize its filters. You have choices—How you *tailor* it really matters. The goal here is: Importance = Resonant Path-Profile Fits.
3. And creating a match with your external landscape (Chapter 5). Optimize its context. You have choices—How you *locate* it really matters. The goal here is: Importance = Externally Aligned and Enabled.
4. And also fitting them with your internal lens (Chapter 6). Optimize its criteria. You have choices—How you *measure* it really matters. The goal here is: Importance = Internally Aligned and Calibrated.
5. Then shaping its manifest force and form (Chapter 7). Optimize its nature. You have choices—How you *construct* it really matters. The goal here is: Importance = Balanced and Grounded, Fused and Dynamic.
6. To engage it well. Optimize its use (Chapter 8). You have choices—How you *activate* it really matters. The goal here is: Importance = Integrated and Positive.
7. For enhancing its consequences (Chapter 9). Optimize its outcomes. You have choices—How you *leverage* it really matters. The goal here is: Importance = Mindful, Happy, and Effective.

The following Personal Development Guide and Checklist captures and integrates the above. First, *ask* each of the listed questions. Second, *assess* where you are on them. Third, *act* to target particularly relevant area(s) of the model and, drawing from the appropriate chapter, remedy the issue(s).

Table 10.2   Personal Development Guide and Checklist

ASK	ASSESS					ACT	
	NO ---------------------- YES					Target?	Remedy!
CONDITIONS							
Are my paths strong?	1	2	3	4	5	☐	_____
Do they resonate with my profile?	1	2	3	4	5	☐	_____
Are they aligned with, and enabled by, my context?	1	2	3	4	5	☐	_____
Are they aligned with, and enabled by, my criteria?	1	2	3	4	5	☐	_____
NATURE							
Is my Importance:							
Balanced	1	2	3	4	5	☐	_____
Grounded	1	2	3	4	5	☐	_____
Fused	1	2	3	4	5	☐	_____
Dynamic	1	2	3	4	5	☐	_____

(Continued)

Table 10.2   (*Continued*)

ASK		ASSESS				ACT	
	NO --------------------- YES					Target?	Remedy!
CONSEQUENCES							
Do I use my Importance well (in an open, implicit, means-oriented manner)?	1	2	3	4	5	☐	_____
. . . To better achieve:							
Mindfulness	1	2	3	4	5	☐	_____
Happiness	1	2	3	4	5	☐	_____
Effectiveness	1	2	3	4	5	☐	_____

MANAGEMENT VIP SYSTEM:
Strategies for Others

Table 10.3 summarizes the management strategies available for you to help others.

As a result, I would advise:

Second (putting on my professional "mentor" or consultant hat) . . . You can help others become true VIPs by constructing an organizationally based (team, family, friendship, firm, etc.) Professional or Management Importance System.

Again, the choices are not exclusive—they are highly independent. As such, they can be mutually reinforcing or mutually destroying.

1. Help them *build* vigorous, solid drivers to Importance (Chapter 3). You have options. For example, this might be done via better professional and business planning, workplace and job enhancement, and flexible career ladders. The goal here is: Importance "equifinality"—create different paths to significant value.
2. Help them *tailor* their paths to their personal profiles (Chapter 4). You have options. For example, this might be done via improved selection and development procedures as well as personal education or training programs. The goal here is: Importance "customization"—enable a resonant program.
3. Help them *fit* their filtered paths with their external landscape (Chapter 5). You have options. For example, this might be done via better management of organizational dynamics (e.g., leadership) as well as design contingencies and parameters (e.g., structure/culture). The goal here is: Importance "contextualization"—build a better climate to support it.
4. Help them *fit* their filtered paths with their internal lens (Chapter 6). You have options. For example, this might be done via better supported/inclusive decision making and performance evaluation. The goal here is: Importance "validity"—construct better criteria to assess and measure it.

5. Help them *shape* their Importance form and type (Chapter 7). You have options. For example, this might be done via smart organizational development (OD) and change management programs and interventions. The goal here is: Importance "optimization"—construct better quality controls to shape its nature.

Table 10.3   Management VIP System—Strategies for *Others*

MANAGEMENT VIP SYSTEM	
Strategy Category	**Strategy Options**
MANAGEMENT STRATEGY 1: You can, to varying degrees, influence others' path(s) to Importance.	**Strategy 1a.** You can focus them on their particular *characteristic(s)*, or not. If appropriate, and if in need of encouragement, a) purposefully boost and/or b) proactively and positively frame their physical, mental, or spiritual attributes.
	Strategy 1b. You can focus them on their particular *action(s)*, or not. If appropriate, and if in need of encouragement, a) purposefully boost and/or b) proactively and positively frame their levels of achievement, ranking, or involvement.
	Strategy 1c. You can focus them on their particular *acceptance(s)*, or not. If appropriate, and if in need of encouragement, a) purposefully boost and/or b) proactively and positively frame their intimate, private, or public liking.
	Strategy 1d. You can focus them on their particular *role(s)*, or not. If appropriate, and if in need of encouragement, a) purposefully boost and/or b) proactively and positively frame their professional, personal, or fundamental roles.
	Strategy 1e. You can focus them on their particular *affiliation(s)*, or not. If appropriate, and if in need of encouragement, a) purposefully boost and/or b) proactively and positively frame their formal, informal, or vicarious affiliations.
MANAGEMENT STRATEGY 2: You can, to varying degrees, make others' Importance paths-profiles more resonant.	**Strategy 2a.** You can move them on a path that gels with their particular *values*.
	Strategy 2b. You can move them on a path that gels with their particular *motivations*.
	Strategy 2c. You can move them on a path that gels with their particular *aptitudes*.
	Strategy 2d. You can move them on a path that gels with their particular *personalities*.
	Strategy 2e. You can move them on a path that gels with their particular *archetypes*.
MANAGEMENT STRATEGY 3: You can, to varying degrees, influence fit between others' filtered Importance paths and their external context.	**Strategy 3a.** You can create circumstances so their particular paths mesh with prevailing *locational* norms.
	Strategy 3b. You can create circumstances so their particular drivers mesh with prevailing *tasks*.
	Strategy 3c. You can create circumstances so their particular drivers mesh with prevailing *support*.
	Strategy 3d. You can create circumstances so their particular drivers mesh with prevailing *markets*.

(Continued)

Table 10.3   (*Continued*)

MANAGEMENT STRATEGY 4: You can, to varying degrees, influence fit between others' filtered Importance paths and their internal criteria.	**Strategy 4a.** You can create lenses so their particular drivers mesh with prevailing *scopes*.
	Strategy 4b. You can create lenses so their particular drivers mesh with prevailing *times*.
	Strategy 4c. You can create lenses so their particular drivers mesh with prevailing *frames*.
	Strategy 4d. You can create lenses so their particular drivers mesh with prevailing *scales*.
	Strategy 4e. You can create lenses so their particular drivers mesh with prevailing *perspectives*.
MANAGEMENT STRATEGY 5: You can, to varying degrees, help others shape their nature of Importance.	**Strategy 5a.** You can help them achieve a balanced Importance *valence*.
	Strategy 5b. You can help them achieve a grounded Importance *magnitude*.
	Strategy 5c. You can help them achieve a fused Importance *level*.
	Strategy 5d. You can help them achieve a dynamic, cumulative Importance *stability*.
MANAGEMENT STRATEGY 6: You can, to varying degrees, help others use their Importance in better versus worse ways.	**Strategy 6a.** You can help them use their Importance more as a *means*.
	Strategy 6b. You can help them use their Importance more *genuinely*.
	Strategy 6c. You can help them use their Importance more *implicitly*.
MANAGEMENT STRATEGY 7: You can, to varying degrees, help others better optimize and evolve the outcomes of their Importance.	**Strategy 7a.** You can help them channel their Importance to optimize and evolve their short- and long-term *mindfulness*.
	Strategy 7b. You can help them channel their Importance to optimize and evolve their short- and long-term *happiness*.
	Strategy 7c. You can help them channel their Importance to optimize and evolve their short- and long-term *effectiveness*.

6. Help them *use* their Importance well (Chapter 8). You have options. For example, this might be done via an enlightened (public) policy and strategy processes. The goal here is: Importance "engagement"— activate better practices to guide its employment and deployment.

7. Help them *leverage* their Importance outcomes (Chapter 9). You have options. For example, this might be done via broad-based, interactive, and developmentally oriented strategies and institutionalized protocols. The goal here is: Importance "success"—design better synergistic, performance-based, and innovative practices to sustainably grow it.

The following Management Development Guide and Checklist captures and integrates the above. First, *ask* each of the listed questions. Second,

Table 10.4   Management Development Guide and Checklist

ASK	ASSESS					ACT	
	NO ---------------------- YES					Target?	Remedy!
CONDITIONS							
Are my people's paths strong?	1	2	3	4	5	☐	_____
Do they mesh with their profiles?	1	2	3	4	5	☐	_____
Do I create a context that aligns with and enables them?	1	2	3	4	5	☐	_____
Do I create criteria sets that align with and enable them?	1	2	3	4	5	☐	_____
NATURE							
Is their Importance:							
Balanced	1	2	3	4	5	☐	_____
Grounded	1	2	3	4	5	☐	_____
Fused	1	2	3	4	5	☐	_____
Dynamic	1	2	3	4	5	☐	_____
CONSEQUENCES							
Do they use their Importance well (in an open, implicit, means-oriented manner)?	1	2	3	4	5	☐	_____
…To better achieve:							
Mindfulness	1	2	3	4	5	☐	_____
Happiness	1	2	3	4	5	☐	_____
Effectiveness	1	2	3	4	5	☐	_____

assess where your people are on them. Third, *act* to target particularly relevant area(s) of the model and, drawing from the appropriate chapter, remedy the issue(s).

FINALLY:
Well Wishes . . .

Life is just too short, and our best time and energy resources are just too precious for us to invest them in anything less than what we deem most significant and valuable. The very consideration of significance and value in and of themselves, and particularly how they work together to shape our Importance, is therefore vital in helping us to make good personal choices and design sound professional strategies. Thus there should be little remaining doubt that the topic merits our serious attention—*Importance is important!*

I am grateful to the publisher for the opportunity to write this book and to all that assisted me both directly and indirectly in its completion. It has been a wonderful vehicle for my personal and professional reflection and in managing my own Importance journey. I am also grateful to you, the reader, for committing your time and energy to considering it and am hopeful that it served you well—*thank you!*

In the preceding pages we have covered much ground, touched upon many disciplines, outlined many relationships, and put forth several arguments that could be used to guide further contemplation, further consideration, and further action. Please remember, though, that reading about the Importance model, and the potential power that it gives us, is but one step along the journey to becoming a true VIP. In addition to understanding it, we must challenge ourselves to identify, personalize, and apply the model. That is—*use it wisely!*

Some precedent for this exists. For instance, by overlaying the goals of this book on my previous work about approximating wisdom,[8] we might strive to:

- Firstly, understand its elemental *DATA* . . .
  Comprehending the model's components, connections, and mechanisms
- Secondly, identify its composite *INFORMATION* . . .
  Coalescing the model's main insights, themes, and messages
- Thirdly, personalize its essential *KNOWLEDGE* . . .
  Internalizing the above to develop systematic, customizable principles and plans
- Finally, apply its manifest *WISDOM.*
  Actualizing the above to successfully achieve desired real-world results

So, as we literally as well as figuratively turn this page, it is time to bid farewell . . . at least for now. The Importance model has been constructed, the cases have been codified, the exercises have been presented, and the tools have been provided.

I hope that you gain a better appreciation of Importance from our discussion, find some "mirrors" and/or "windows" in the stories, relate the book's lessons to your situation(s), and utilize its derivative tools to help yourself as well as others.

Our VIP story is done. Your VIP story is afoot!

Notes

Chapter 1

1. Hierarchy is defined as "a system in which people or things are placed in a series of levels with different importance or status" (http://www.merriam-webster.com, February 24, 2015). It can also refer to just the upper echelons of a hierarchical system; those in authority.
2. Sartre, J. P. (1957). *Existentialism and Human Emotions*. New York: Philosophical Library.
3. You will notice that throughout the book the term "Importance" is capitalized. This is to distinguish the formally defined and modeled concept from a common, more equivocal and generic use of the word.
4. The idea is widely attributed to philosopher John Dewey.
5. See for example, Qualman, E. (2012). *Socialnomics: How Social Media Transforms the Way We Live and Do Business*. Hoboken, NJ: Wiley.
6. See for example, Kotter, J. P. (2014). *Accelerate: Building Strategic Agility for a Faster-Moving World*. Boston, MA: Harvard Business Review Press.
7. This particular Google search was done on February 24, 2015.
8. This discussion was prompted by a lunch that I had with a Nobel Prize Laureate in the summer of 2014 who pointed out that the nature of Importance is a "good problem" to investigate, but that the term often has negative connotations and might be seen by some people and within some societies in a negative light. It is therefore critical to distinguish a healthy sense of significance and value from an inflated ego. Everyone wants the former; few want, or can tolerate, the latter.
9. This section is based on numerous search results from dictionaries and encyclopedias both in print and online.
10. Value. *Merriam-Webster Dictionary*, http://www.merriam-webster.com, February 24, 2015.
11. See for example, Frankl, V. E. (2006). *Man's Search For Meaning*. Boston: Beacon Books.
12. For example, Clayton Christensen asks a related question in the title of his recent bestselling book *How Will You Measure Your Life* (2012, HarperCollins Publishers). Bill George also uses this as a point of focus to orient readers to their *True North* (2007, John Wiley and Sons).
13. Buffett, W. (2008). From the 2008 Berkshire Hathaway Letter to Shareholders, http://www.berkshirehathaway.com/letters/2008ltr.pdf.
14. Einstein, A. Quoted by William Miller in *Life Magazine*, May 2, 1955. "Conventional" added.
15. Significance. *Merriam-Webster Dictionary*, http://www.merriam-webster.com, February 24, 2015.

16. Kierkegaard, Soren. http://www.brainyquote.com, February 24, 2015.
17. Aristotle. http://www.brainyquote.com, February 24, 2015.
18. Maslow, A. H. (1954). *Motivation and Personality*. New York: Harper and Row.
19. See for example, Rogers, C. (1959). "A Theory of Therapy, Personality and Inter-personal Relationships as Developed in the Client-Centered Framework." In S. Koch (ed.), *Psychology: A Study of a Science. Vol. 3: Formulations of the Person and the Social Context*. New York: McGraw Hill.
20. See Adler, N. J. (2006). "Global Wisdom and the Audacity of Hope." In E. H. Kessler and J. R. Bailey (eds.), *Handbook of Organizational and Managerial Wisdom*. Thousand Oaks, CA: Sage.

Chapter 2

1. See for example, similar, cumulative arguments in Stephen Hawking's recent books: *A Brief History of Time* (1988, Bantam Books), *The Universe in a Nutshell* (2001, Bantam Books), and with L. Mlodinow, *The Grand Design* (2010, Bantam Books).
2. Chemistry and Physics. *Merriam-Webster Dictionary*, http://www.merriam-webster.com, February 24, 2015.
3. Biology. *Merriam-Webster Dictionary*, http://www.merriam-webster.com, February 24, 2015.
4. See for example, Gould, Stephen Jay (2002). *Rocks of Ages: Science and Religion in the Fullness of Life*. New York: Ballantine Books; and Gould, Stephen Jay (2002). *The Structure of Evolutionary Theory*. Cambridge, MA: Belknap Press.
5. Neuroscience. *Merriam-Webster Dictionary*, http://www.merriam-webster.com, February 24, 2015.
6. See for example, Pinker, S. (1997). *How the Mind Works*. New York: W.W. Norton and Company; Pinker, S. (2002). *The Blank Slate: The Modern Denial of Human Nature*. London: Penguin; Ramachandran, V. S. and Blakeslee, S. (1998). *Phantoms in the Brain: Probing the Mysteries of the Human Mind*. New York: HarperCollins.
7. Ecology, Geology, and Meteorology. *Merriam-Webster Dictionary*, http://www.merriam-webster.com, February 24, 2015.
8. See (for Curitiba, Brazil) http://www.ippuc.org.br and (for New York City) http://www.nyc.gov.
9. Whereas I am not employed on a psychology department faculty, my background has a firm foot in its domain. As a student, it was one of my majors (and I completed an advanced research thesis to graduate with honors). I was also inducted into its international honorary—*Psi Chi*. In addition, as a scholar, I have produced numerous papers in the field and, as a professional, have consulted in numerous psychological-related capacities.
10. http://www.apa.org/support/about/apa/psychology.aspx#answer
11. See Jung, Carl. (1955). *Modern Man in Search of a Soul*. Orlando, FL: Harcourt; Allport, Gordon. (1937). *Personality: A Psychological Interpretation*. New York: Holt, Rinehart and Winston; Maslow, Abraham. (1954). *Motivation and Personality*. New York: Harper and Row; Rosenberg, Milton, with C. I. Hovland. (1960). *Attitude Organization and Change: An Analysis of Consistency Among Attitude Components*. New Haven: Yale University Press; and Rogers, Carl. (1961). *On Becoming a Person: A Psychotherapist's View of Psychotherapy*. Boston: Houghton Mifflin.

12. Anderson, M. H. (2013). "Big Five Personality Dimensions." In E. H. Kessler (ed.), *Encyclopedia of Management Theory* (pp. 76–80). Thousand Oaks, CA: Sage Publications; Digman, J. M. (1990). "Personality Structure: Emergence of the Five-Factor Model." *Annual Review of Psychology*, 41: 417–40.

13. See http://www.onetonline.org/find/descriptor/browse/Abilities/1.A.3/

14. Foti, R. J., Allgood, S. F., and Thompson, N. J. (2013). "Trait Theory of Leadership." In E. H. Kessler (ed.), *Encyclopedia of Management Theory* (pp. 882–7). Thousand Oaks, CA: Sage Publications; Boyatzis, R. E. (2013). "Emotional and Social Intelligence." In E. H. Kessler (ed.), *Encyclopedia of Management Theory* (pp. 225–8). Thousand Oaks, CA: Sage Publications; Earley, P. C. (2013). "Cultural Intelligence." In E. H. Kessler (ed.), *Encyclopedia of Management Theory* (pp. 176–9). Thousand Oaks, CA: Sage Publications.

15. Kramer, R. M. (2013). "Self Concept and the Theory of Self." In E. H. Kessler (ed.), *Encyclopedia of Management Theory* (pp. 682–5). Thousand Oaks, CA: Sage Publications; Leary, M. R., and Tangney, J. P. (2003). *Handbook of Self and Identity*. New York: Guilford Press; Gekas, V. (1982). "The Self Concept." *Annual Review of Sociology*, 8: 1–33.

16. See Nicholson, N. (2006). "The Getting of Wisdom: Self-Conduct, Personal Identity, and Wisdom Across the Life Span." In E. H. Kessler & J. R. Bailey (eds.), *Handbook of Organizational and Managerial Wisdom* (377–97). Thousand Oaks, CA: Sage Publications.

17. Showers, C. J., Abramson, L. Y., and Hogan, M. E. (1998). "The Dynamic Self." *Journal of Personality and Social Psychology*, 75 (2): 478–93.

18. Ramburuth, P. (2013). "Individual Values." In E. H. Kessler (ed.), *Encyclopedia of Management Theory* (pp. 364–6). Thousand Oaks, CA: Sage Publications; Rokeach, M. (1973). *The Nature of Human Values*. New York: Free Press; Kohlberg, L. (1981). *Essays in Moral Development*. New York: Harper and Row.

19. Jeffries, F. (2013). "Theory of Reasoned Action." In E. H. Kessler (ed.), *Encyclopedia of Management Theory* (pp. 865–7). Thousand Oaks, CA: Sage Publications; Ajzen, I. and Fishbein, M. (1977). "Attitude-Behavior Relations: A Theoretical Analysis and Review of Empirical Research." *Psychological Bulletin*, 84 (5): 888–918; Ajzen, I. (2001). "Nature and Operation of Attitudes." *Annual Review of Psychology*, 52: 27–58; Greenwald, A. G. (2002). "A Unified Theory of Implicit Attitudes, Stereotypes, Self-Esteem, and Self-Concept." *Psychological Review*, 109 (1): 3–25; Katz, D. (1960). "The Functional Approach to the Study of Attitudes." *Public Opinion Quarterly*, 24: 163–204.

20. Branden, N. (1969). *The Psychology of Self Esteem*. Los Angeles: Nash.

21. Gerhardt, M. W. (2013). "Theory of Self Esteem." In E. H. Kessler (ed.), *Encyclopedia of Management Theory* (pp. 867–70). Thousand Oaks, CA: Sage Publications.

22. Ibid.

23. Brockner, J. (1988). *Self-Esteem at Work: Research, Theory, and Practice*. Lexington, MA: Lexington Books.

24. See for example, Rosenberg, M., Schooler, C., Schoenback, C., and Rosenberg, F. (1995). "Global Self-Esteem and Specific Self-Esteem: Different Concepts, Different Outcomes." *American Sociological Review*, 60 (1): 141–56; Marsh, H. W. (1986). "Global Self-Esteem: Its Relation to Specific Facets of Self-Concept and Their Importance." *Journal of Personality and Social Psychology*, 51 (6): 1224–36.

25. See for example, Leary, M. R. (1999). "Making Sense of Self-Esteem." *Current Directions in Psychological Science*, 8 (1): 32–5.

26. See for example, Brown, J. D. and Marshall, M. A. (2006). "The Three Faces of Self-Esteem." In M. Kernis (ed.), *Self-Esteem: Issues and Answers* (pp. 4–9). New York: Psychology Press.
27. See for example, Kernis, M. H. (2003). "Toward a Conceptualization of Optimal Self-Esteem," *Psychological Inquiry*, 14 (1): 1–26.
28. See for example, Cast, A. and Burke, P. (2002). "A Theory of Self Esteem." *Social Forces*, 80 (3): 1041–98.
29. See Erez, A. and Judge, T. A. (2001). "Relationship of Core Self-Evaluations to Goal Setting, Motivation, and Performance." *Journal of Applied Psychology*, 86 (6): 1270–9. Judge, T. A., Erez, A., Bono, J. E., and Thoresen, C. J. (2003). "The Core Self-Evaluations Scale (CSES): Development of a Measure." *Personnel Psychology*, 56: 303–31.
30. Branden, N. (1995). *The Six Pillars of Self-Esteem*. New York: Bantam Books.
31. See Heatherton, T. F. and Wyland, C. L. (2003). "Assessing Self-Esteem." In Shane J. Lopez and C. R. Snyder (eds.), *Positive Psychological Assessment: A Handbook of Models and Measures* (pp. 219–33). Washington, DC: American Psychological Association.
32. Blascovich, J. and Tomaka, J. (1991). "Measures of Self-Esteem." In J. P. Robinson and P. R. Shaver (eds.), *Measures of Personality and Social Psychological Attitudes*. San Diego, CA: Academic Press.
33. Wylie, R. C. (1974). *The Self-Concept: A Review of Methodological Considerations and Measuring Instruments*. Lincoln: University of Nebraska Press.
34. Jackson, M. R. (1984). *Self-Esteem and Meaning*. Albany: State University of New York Press.
35. See Barrick, M. R. and Mount, M. K. (1996). "Effects of Impression Management and Self-Deception on the Predictive Validity of Personality Constructs." *Journal of Applied Psychology*, 81 (3): 261–72; Leary, M. R. and Kowalski, R. M. (1990). "Impression Management: A Literature Review and Two-Component Model." *Psychological Bulletin*, 107 (1): 34–47.
36. From Gist, M. and Mitchel, T. (1992). "Self-Efficacy: A Theoretical Analysis of Its Determinants and Malleability." *Academy of Management Review*, 17 (2): 183–211.
37. Bandura, A. (2013). "Social Cognitive Theory." In E. H. Kessler (ed.), *Encyclopedia of Management Theory* (pp. 710–15). Thousand Oaks, CA: Sage Publications; Bandura, A. (1986). *Social Foundations of Thought and Action: A Social Cognitive Theory*. Englewood Cliffs, NJ: Prentice-Hall.
38. Crocker, J., Brook, A. T., Niiya, Y., and Villacorta, M. (2006). "The Pursuit of Self-Esteem: Contingencies of Self-Worth and Self-Regulation." *Journal of Personality* 74 (6, December): 1749–71; Crocker, J. and Wolfe, C. T. (2001). "Contingencies of Self-Worth." *Psychological Review*, 108: 593–623.
39. Crocker, J. and Knight, K. M. (2005). "Contingencies of Self-Worth." *Current Directions in Psychological Science*, 14: 200–3.
40. Crocker, J., Luhtanen, R. K., Cooper, M. L., and Bouvrette, S. (2003). "Contingencies of Self-Worth in College Students: Theory and Measurement." *Journal of Personality and Social Psychology*, 85: 894–908.
41. I have studied societies at many levels (e.g., groups, organizations, nations, and cultures), for example as described in my book with Diana Wong-MingJi, *Cultural Mythology and Global Leadership*.
42. Smith, J. R. and Terry, D. J. (2013). "Norms Theory." In E. H. Kessler (ed.), *Encyclopedia of Management Theory* (pp. 508–11). Thousand Oaks, CA: Sage Publications; Cialdini, R. B., Reno, R. R., and Kallgren, C. A. (1990). "A Focus Theory

of Normative Conduct: Recycling the Concept of Norms to Reduce Littering in Public Places." *Journal of Personality and Social Psychology*, 58: 1015–26.

43. Fellows, S. and Kahn, W. A. (2013). "Role Theory." In E. H. Kessler (ed.), *Encyclopedia of Management Theory* (pp. 670–4). Thousand Oaks, CA: Sage Publications; Katz, D. and Kahn, R. L. (1978). *The Social Psychology of Organizations*, 2nd ed. New York: John Wiley and Sons.

44. Randolph, W. A. (2013). "Bases of Social Power." In E. H. Kessler (ed.), *Encyclopedia of Management Theory* (pp. 746–50). Thousand Oaks, CA: Sage Publications; French, J. R. P. and Raven, B. (1959). "The Bases of Social Power." In D. Cartwright (ed.), *Studies in Social Power* (pp. 150–67). Ann Arbor, MI: Institute for Social Research.

45. Hill, C. W. L. (2013). *International Business: Competing in the Global Marketplace*. New York: McGraw Hill.

46. Garibaldi de Hilal, A. V. (2013). "Cultural Values." In E. H. Kessler (ed.), *Encyclopedia of Management Theory* (pp. 179–84). Thousand Oaks, CA: Sage Publications; Kluckhohn, F. R. and Strodtbeck, F. L. (1961). *Variations in Value Orientations*. Westport, CT: Greenwood.

47. Schwartz, S. H. (1994). "Beyond Individualism/Collectivism: New Cultural Dimensions of Values." In U. Kim, C. Kagitcibasi, H. C. Triandis, S. C. Choi, and G. Yoon (eds.), *Individualism and Collectivism: Theory, Method, and Application* (pp. 85–119). Thousand Oaks, CA: Sage Publications.

48. Earley, P. C. (2013). "Cultural Intelligence." In E. H. Kessler (ed.), *Encyclopedia of Management Theory* (pp. 179–84). Thousand Oaks, CA: Sage Publications.

49. Hall, E. T. (1960). "The Silent Language in Overseas Business." *Harvard Business Review*, 38 (3): 87–96.

50. House, R. J., Hanges, P. J., Javidan, M., Dorfman, P. W., and Gupta, V. (2004). *Culture, Leadership, and Organizations. The GLOBE Study of 62 Societies*. Thousand Oaks, CA: Sage Publications; Kessler, E. H. and WongJi, D. M. (2009). *Cultural Mythology and Global Leadership*. Northampton, MA: Edward Elgar Publishers.

51. Hofstede, G. (2001). *Culture's Consequences: Comparing Values, Behaviors, Institutions and Organizations Across Nations*. Thousand Oaks, CA: Sage Publications.

52. I currently hold an endowed senior professorship in management and have produced numerous papers and books in the area, including the seminal *Encyclopedia of Management Theory* as well as the critically acclaimed *Management Theory in Action: Real World Lessons for Walking the Talk*.

53. Becker, G. (1962). "Investment in Human Capital: A Theoretical Analysis." *Journal of Political Economy*, 70: 9–49; Tarique, I. (2014). "Human Capital Theory." In E. H. Kessler (ed.), *Encyclopedia of Management Theory* (pp. 343–6). Thousand Oaks, CA: Sage Publications.

54. Kessler, E. H. (2010). *Management Theory in Action: Real-World Lessons for Walking the Talk*. New York: Palgrave Macmillan.

55. Locke, E. A. and Latham, G. P. (2013). "Goal Setting Theory." In E. H. Kessler (ed.), *Encyclopedia of Management Theory* (pp. 315–18). Thousand Oaks, CA: Sage Publications; Richardson, K. M. (2013). "Reinforcement Theory." In E. H. Kessler (ed.), *Encyclopedia of Management Theory* (pp. 655–9). Thousand Oaks, CA: Sage Publications; Kerr, S. (1975). "On the Folly of Rewarding A, While Hoping for B." *Academy of Management Journal*, 18 (4): 769–83; Gagne, M., Deci, E. L., and Ryan, R. M. (2013). "Self Determination Theory." In E. H. Kessler (ed.), *Encyclopedia of Management Theory* (pp. 686–90). Thousand Oaks, CA: Sage Publications.

56. Brunsson, K. H. (2013). "Principles of Administration and Management Functions." In E. H. Kessler (ed.), *Encyclopedia of Management Theory* (pp. 603–8). Thousand Oaks, CA: Sage Publications; Fayol, Henri. (1916/1949). *General and Industrial Management*, with a foreword by Lyndall Urwick. London: Sir Isaac Pitman and Sons Ltd.

57. Roethlisberger, F. J. and Dickson, W. J. (1939). *Management and the Worker: An Account of a Research Program Conducted by the Western Electric Company, Hawthorne Works, Chicago.* Cambridge, MA: Harvard University Press.

58. Maciarello, J. A. (2013). "Practice of Management." In E. H. Kessler (ed.), *Encyclopedia of Management Theory* (pp. 594–9). Thousand Oaks, CA: Sage Publications; Drucker, P. F. (1954). *The Practice of Management.* New York: Harper and Row Publishers.

59. Tengblad, S. (2013). "Management Roles." In E. H. Kessler (ed.), *Encyclopedia of Management Theory* (pp. 462–7). Thousand Oaks, CA: Sage Publications; Mintzberg, H. (1973). *The Nature of Managerial Work.* New York: Harper and Row Publishers.

60. Ferris, W. P. (2013). "Humanistic Management." In E. H. Kessler (ed.), *Encyclopedia of Management Theory* (pp. 354–9). Thousand Oaks, CA: Sage Publications; Cameron, K. and Spreitzer, G. (2012). *Oxford Handbook of Positive Organizational Scholarship.* New York: Oxford University Press.

61. Fischer, O. and Fischer, L. (2013). "Differentiation and the Division of Labor." In E. H. Kessler (ed.), *Encyclopedia of Management Theory* (pp. 198–203). Thousand Oaks, CA: Sage Publications; Smith, A. (1981/1776). *An Inquiry into the Nature and Causes of the Wealth of Nations*, Volumes I and II. R. H. Campbell and A. S. Skinner (eds.). Indianapolis: Liberty Fund; Donaldson, L. (2013). "Organizational Structure and Design." In E. H. Kessler (ed.), *Encyclopedia of Management Theory* (pp. 569–74). Thousand Oaks, CA: Sage Publications; Spender, J. C. (2013). "Bureaucratic Theory." In E. H. Kessler (ed.), *Encyclopedia of Management Theory* (pp. 87–92). Thousand Oaks, CA: Sage Publications; Weber, M. (1947). "The Theory of Social and Economic Organization." A. M. Henderson and T. Parsons (trans.). Glencoe, IL: The Free Press.

62. Sutcliff, K. M. (2013). "Organizational Culture Model." In E. H. Kessler (ed.), *Encyclopedia of Management Theory* (pp. 530–5). Thousand Oaks, CA: Sage Publications; Schein, E. H. (2010). *Organizational Culture and Leadership*, 4th ed. San Francisco, CA: John Wiley and Sons.

63. Nieminen, L. R. G. and Denison, D. (2013). "Organizational Culture and Effectiveness." In E. H. Kessler (ed.), *Encyclopedia of Management Theory* (pp. 529–30). Thousand Oaks, CA: Sage Publications; Barney, J. B. (1986). "Organizational Culture: Can It Be a Source of Sustained Competitive Advantage?" *Academy of Management Review*, 11: 656–65; Denison, D. (1990). *Corporate Culture and Organizational Effectiveness.* New York: John Wiley and Sons.

64. Choi, Y. and Van de Ven, A. H. (2013). "Stages of Innovation." In E. H. Kessler (ed.), *Encyclopedia of Management Theory* (pp. 758–62). Thousand Oaks, CA: Sage Publications; Greve, H. R. (2013). "Behavioral Theory of the Firm." In E. H. Kessler (ed.), *Encyclopedia of Management Theory* (pp. 72–5). Thousand Oaks, CA: Sage Publications; Cyert, R. M. and March, J. G. (1963). *A Behavioral Theory of the Firm.* Englewood Cliffs, NJ: Prentice-Hall; Liberman, L. (2013). "Garbage Can Model of Decision Making." In E. H. Kessler (ed.), *Encyclopedia of Management Theory* (pp. 307–10). Thousand Oaks, CA: Sage Publications; Cohen, M. D., March, J. G., and Olsen, J. P. (1972). "A Garbage Can Model of Organizational

Choice." *Administrative Science Quarterly*, 17(1): 1–25; Wong-MingJi, D. J. (2013). "Force Field Analysis and Model of Planned Change." In E. H. Kessler (ed.), *Encyclopedia of Management Theory* (pp. 287–91). Thousand Oaks, CA: Sage Publications; Lewin, K. (1951). *Field Theory in Social Science*. D. Cartwright (ed.). New York: Harper and Bros.

65. Newbert, S. L. (2013). "Resource Based View of the Firm." In E. H. Kessler (ed.), *Encyclopedia of Management Theory* (pp. 666–70). Thousand Oaks, CA: Sage Publications; Barney, J. B. (1991). "Firm Resources and Sustained Competitive Advantage." *Journal of Management*, 17: 99–120.

66. Chaganti, R. (2013). "Upper Echelon Theory." In E. H. Kessler (ed.), *Encyclopedia of Management Theory* (pp. 918–21). Thousand Oaks, CA: Sage Publications; Hambrick, Donald C. (2007). "Upper Echelons Theory: An Update." *Academy of Management Review*, 33 (2): 334–43; Schneider, M. (2013). "Agency Theory." In E. H. Kessler (ed.), *Encyclopedia of Management Theory* (pp. 30–34). Thousand Oaks, CA: Sage Publications; Jensen, M. C. and Meckling, M. H. (1976). "Theory of the Firm: Managerial Behavior, Agency Costs and Ownership Structure." *Journal of Political Economy*, 3 (4): 305–60.

67. Furrer, O. (2013). "Business Policy and Corporate Strategy." In E. H. Kessler (ed.), *Encyclopedia of Management Theory* (pp. 94–8). Thousand Oaks, CA: Sage Publications; Andrews, K. A. (1971). *The Concept of Corporate Strategy*. Burr Ridge, IL: Dow-Jones-Irwin.

68. Ang, S. H. (2013). "Modes of Strategy: Planned and Emergent." In E. H. Kessler (ed.), *Encyclopedia of Management Theory* (pp. 487–8). Thousand Oaks, CA: Sage Publications; Mintzberg, H. and Waters, J. A. (1985). "Of Strategies, Deliberate and Emergent." *Strategic Management Journal*, 6: 257–72.

69. Lei, D. (2013). "Core Competence." In E. H. Kessler (ed.), *Encyclopedia of Management Theory* (pp. 156–61). Thousand Oaks, CA: Sage Publications; Prahalad, C. K. and Hamel, G. (1990). "The Core Competence of the Corporation." *Harvard Business Review*, 68 (4): 79–93; Woiceshyn, J. (2013). "Value Chain." In E. H. Kessler (ed.), *Encyclopedia of Management Theory* (pp. 923–7). Thousand Oaks, CA: Sage Publications; Porter, M. E. (1985). *Competitive Advantage*. New York: The Free Press.

70. Manral, L. (2013). "Competitive Advantage." In E. H. Kessler (ed.), *Encyclopedia of Management Theory* (pp. 125–30). Thousand Oaks, CA: Sage Publications; Porter, M. E. (1980). *Competitive Strategy: Techniques for Analyzing Industries and Competitors*. New York: Free Press; Peridis, T. (2013). "Diamond Model of National Competitive Advantage." In E. H. Kessler (ed.), *Encyclopedia of Management Theory* (pp. 193–8), Thousand Oaks, CA: Sage Publications.

71. Vancouver, J. B. (2013). "Systems Theory of Organizations." In E. H. Kessler (ed.), *Encyclopedia of Management Theory* (pp. 815–20). Thousand Oaks, CA: Sage Publications; Scott, W. R. (1998). *Organizations: Rational, Natural, and Open Systems*, 4th ed. Upper Saddle River, NJ: Prentice Hall.

72. Suddaby, R. (2013). "Institutional Theory." In E. H. Kessler (ed.), *Encyclopedia of Management Theory* (pp. 379–84). Thousand Oaks, CA: Sage Publications; Meyer, J. W. and Rowan, B. (1977). "Institutionalized Organizations: Formal Structure as Myth and Ceremony." *American Journal of Sociology*, 83: 440–63; Lorsch, J. W. (2013). "Contingency Theory." In E. H. Kessler (ed.), *Encyclopedia of Management Theory* (pp. 144–8). Thousand Oaks, CA: Sage Publications; Lawrence, R. and Lorsch, J. W. (1967). *Organization and Environment*. Boston: Harvard Business School Press.

73. Zaccour, G. (2013). "Game Theory." In E. H. Kessler (ed.), *Encyclopedia of Management Theory* (pp. 297–304). Thousand Oaks, CA: Sage Publications; Von

Neumann, J. and Morgenstern, O. (1944). *Theory of Games and Economic Behavior*. Princeton, NJ: Princeton University Press.

74. Pfeffer, J. (2013). "Resource Dependence Theory." In E. H. Kessler (ed.), *Encyclopedia of Management Theory* (pp. 659–64). Thousand Oaks, CA: Sage Publications; Klein, P. G. and Mondelli, M. P. (2013). "Transaction Cost Theory." In E. H. Kessler (ed.), *Encyclopedia of Management Theory* (pp. 888–92). Thousand Oaks, CA: Sage Publications; Williamson, O. E. (1975). *Markets and Hierarchies, Analysis and Antitrust Implications: A Study in the Economics of Internal Organization*. New York: Free Press; Gurd, B. (2013). "Balanced Scorecard." In E. H. Kessler (ed.), *Encyclopedia of Management Theory* (pp. 60–3). Thousand Oaks, CA: Sage Publications; Kaplan, R. S. and Norton, D. P. (1992). "The Balanced Scorecard—Measures that Drive Performance." *Harvard Business Review*, 70 (1): 71–9; Harrison, J. S. (2013). "Stakeholder Theory." In E. H. Kessler (ed.), *Encyclopedia of Management Theory* (pp. 763–7). Thousand Oaks, CA: Sage Publications; Freeman, R. E. (1984). *Strategic Management: A Stakeholder Approach*. Boston: Pitman; Elkington, J. (2013). "Triple Bottom Line." In E. H. Kessler (ed.), *Encyclopedia of Management Theory* (pp. 902–4). Thousand Oaks, CA: Sage Publications.

75. I am by no means a professional politician, lawyer, or economist, but I have substantial experience working with them in government agencies (such as the US Departments of State and Defense), think tanks (such as the Citizens for a Sound Economy Foundation), initiatives (such as the National Security Education Program and Fulbright Program), and have exchanged ideas on these and related matters with numerous public officials, leaders, staffers, analysts, and even a few Nobel Laureates.

76. Google definition search, February 24, 2015.

77. Hill, C. W. L. (2013). *International Business: Competing in the Global Marketplace*. New York: McGraw Hill.

78. Google definition search, February 24, 2015.

79. From Farlex Financial Dictionary.

80. Hill, C. W. L. (2013). *International Business: Competing in the Global Marketplace*. New York: McGraw Hill.

81. Google definition search, February 24, 2015.

82. Burton's Legal Thesaurus, February 24, 2015.

83. Law.Cornell, http://www.law.cornell.edu/wex/legal_person.

84. Hill, C. W. L. (2013). *International Business: Competing in the Global Marketplace*. New York: McGraw Hill.

85. Philosophy is not a new thing for me but rather ingrained in my core through an ongoing search for truth and wisdom. In fact, this is what the term *"philo-sophia"* roughly translates to, a "lover of wisdom." As such, it is more a journey than a destination. Along my personal trek, I have published various papers (e.g., Kessler, E. H. [2001]. "The Idols of Organizational Theory: From Francis Bacon to the Dilbert Principle." *Journal of Management Inquiry*, 10 [4]: 285–97) and a book (Kessler, E. H. and Bailey, J. R. [2007]. *Handbook of Organizational and Managerial Wisdom*. Thousand Oaks, CA: Sage Publications) that explored the application of philosophic ideas to practical and professional pursuits.

86. For a general discussion of these issues, the *Stanford Encyclopedia of Philosophy*, Edward N. Zalta (ed.) (http://plato.stanford.edu) is an especially useful source and general reference. The following entries are of particular relevance to the current topic: Gertler, Brie, "Self-Knowledge," Spring 2011 Edition; Olson, Eric T., "Personal Identity," Winter 2010 Edition; Zimmerman, Michael J., "Intrinsic vs. Extrinsic Value," Winter 2010 Edition; and Dillon, Robin S., "Respect," Spring 2014 Edition.

87. Descartes, Rene. (1644/1985). "Principles of Philosophy." In Cottingham, Stoothoff, and Murdoch (trans.), *The Philosophical Writings of Descartes Volume I*. Cambridge: Cambridge University Press.

88. Capra, F. and Luisi, P.L. (2014). *The Systems View of Life: A Unifying Vision*. Delhi, India: Cambridge University Press.

89. Shoemaker, S. and Swinburne, R. (1984). *Personal Identity*. Oxford: Blackwell.

90. Magill, F. N. (1990). *Masterpieces of World Philosophy*. New York: HarperCollins.

91. For example, see Schopenhauer, Arthur. (1818). *The World as Will and Representation*.

92. Kant, Immanuel. (1990 ff). *Collected Writings*, Academy Edition. Berlin: De Gruyter; Wittgenstein, L. (1953). *Philosophical Investigations*, G. E. M. Anscombe (trans.). Oxford: Blackwell.

93. Hume, David. (1739–1740/1978). *A Treatise of Human Nature*. L. A. Selby-Bigge (ed.), revised by P. H. Nidditch. Oxford: Oxford University Press; Locke, John. (1689/1975). *An Essay Concerning Human Understanding*, P. H. Nidditch (ed.). Oxford: Oxford University Press; James, William. (1890/1983). *The Principles of Psychology*. Cambridge, MA: Harvard University Press.

94. Erikson, E. (1958). *Young Man Luther: A Study in Psychoanalysis and History*. New York: W. W. Norton.

95. Gallagher, S. (2000). "Philosophical Conceptions of the Self." *Trends in Cognitive Science*, 4 (1): 14–21.

96. Magill F. N. (1990). *Masterpieces of World Philosophy*. New York: HarperCollins.

97. For example, again see Locke, John. (1689/1975). *An Essay Concerning Human Understanding*, P. H. Nidditch (ed.). Oxford: Oxford University Press.

98. See Bar-On, D. and Long, D. (2003). "Knowing Selves: Expression, Truth, and Knowledge." In B. Gertler (ed.), *Privileged Access: Philosophical Accounts of Self-Knowledge*. Aldershot: Ashgate Publishing; Shoemaker, Sydney. (1994). "Self-Knowledge and 'Inner Sense.'" *Philosophy and Phenomenological Research* 54: 249–314.

99. Russell, B. (1917). "Knowledge by Acquaintance and Knowledge by Description." In *Mysticism and Logic*. London: George Allen and Unwin; Wittgenstein, Ludwig. (1953). *Philosophical Investigations*, G. E. M. Anscombe (trans.). Oxford: Blackwell.

100. Sartre, Jean-Paul. (1957). *Existentialism and Human Emotions*. New York: Philosophical Library; Moran, R. (2001). *Authority and Estrangement: An Essay on Self-Knowledge*. Princeton, NJ: Princeton University Press.

101. Aristotle. (2002). *Nichomachean Ethics*. C. Rowe (trans.). Oxford: Oxford University Press. (Original work published in 350 BCE.)

102. Hägerström, A. (1953). *Inquiries into the Nature of Law and Morals*. Uppsala: Uppsala University Press; Hobbes, Thomas. (1651). *Leviathan*; Hume, David. (1739). *A Treatise of Human Nature*.

103. See Durant, W. (1952). *The Story of Philosophy*. New York: Washington Square Press.

104. Dewey, John. (1907/1975). *Pragmatism: A New Name for Some Old Ways of Thinking*. Cambridge, MA: Harvard University Press.

105. See Dillon, Robin S. (2014). "Respect." Spring 2014 Edition. In Edward N. Zalta (ed.), *Stanford Encyclopedia of Philosophy*, http://plato.stanford.edu, regarding the structure of this analysis.

106. For various typologies of respect see Darwall, S. (2010). "Sentiment, Care, and Respect." *Theory and Research in Education*, 8: 153–62; Feinberg, J. (1975). "Some

Conjectures on the Concept of Respect." *Journal of Social Philosophy*, 4: 1–3; Hudson, S. D. (1980). "The Nature of Respect." *Social Theory and Practice*, 6: 69–90.

107. Kant, Immanuel. (1785/1996). *Grundlegung zur Metaphysik der Sitten*, translated as "Groundwork of the Metaphysics of Morals," in *Immanuel Kant Practical Philosophy*, Mary Gregor (trans. and ed.). New York: Cambridge University Press.

108. Hobbes, T. (1651/1958). *Leviathan*. Indianapolis: Bobbs-Merrill, The Library of Liberal Arts; Smith, A. (1981/1776). *An Inquiry into the Nature and Causes of the Wealth of Nations*, Volumes I and II. R. H. Campbell and A. S. Skinner (eds.). Indianapolis: Liberty Fund.

109. Rawls, John. (1971). *A Theory of Justice*. Cambridge, MA: Harvard University Press.

110. This discussion is based on the following reference source: http://www.bbc.co.uk/religion/religions/. The selected ideas are in no way intended as comprehensive or definitive and represent only a partial interpretation of the BBC amalgamation. The religions are listed alphabetically and not ordered by any hierarchy. Any errors or omissions are unintentional and, if they exist, I sincerely ask the reader for their forgiveness.

Chapter 3

1. See Csikszentmihalyi, M. (1997). *Finding Flow: The Psychology of Engagement with Everyday Life*. New York: Basic Books.

2. http://www.theodore-roosevelt.com/trsorbonnespeech. Theodore Roosevelt, The Man in the Arena (excerpt from the speech "Citizenship in a Republic," delivered at the Sorbonne, in Paris, France on April 23, 1910): "It is not the critic who counts; not the man who points out how the strong man stumbles, or where the doer of deeds could have done them better. The credit belongs to the man who is actually in the arena, whose face is marred by dust and sweat and blood; who strives valiantly; who errs, who comes short again and again, because there is no effort without error and shortcoming; but who does actually strive to do the deeds; who knows great enthusiasms, the great devotions; who spends himself in a worthy cause; who at the best knows in the end the triumph of high achievement, and who at the worst, if he fails, at least fails while daring greatly, so that his place shall never be with those cold and timid souls who neither know victory nor defeat."

3. Leary, M. R., Tambor, E. S., Terdal, S. K., and Downs, D. L. (1995). "Self-Esteem as an Interpersonal Monitor: The Sociometer Hypothesis." *Journal of Personality and Social Psychology*, 68: 518–30.

4. Weber, M. (1947). *The Theory of Social and Economic Organization*. A. M. Henderson and T. Parsons (trans.). Glencoe, IL: The Free Press; March, J. G. and Simon, H. A. (1958). *Organizations*. New York: Wiley.

5. From Plato. (1968). *The Republic*. A. Bloom (trans.). New York: HarperCollins Publishing.

6. See Kant, Immanuel. (1996). *The Metaphysics of Morals*. M. Gregor (trans.). New York: Cambridge University Press; King, M. L. Jr. (1963). "A Letter from Birmingham Jail." *Ebony* (August): 23–32.

Chapter 4

1. Frankl, V. (1969). *The Will to Meaning: Foundations and Applications of Logotherapy.* New York: American Library.
2. Adler, A. (1927). *Understanding Human Nature.* New York: Greenberg.
3. Kessler, E. H. (2010). *Management Theory in Action: Real-World Lessons for Walking the Talk.* New York: Palgrave Macmillan Publishers.
4. Sternberg, R. J. (1986). "A Triangular Theory of Love." *Psychological Review*, 93: 119–35.
5. Ryan, R. M. and Deci, E. L. (2000). "Self-Determination Theory and the Facilitation of Intrinsic Motivation, Social Development, and Well-Being." *American Psychologist*, 55: 68–78; Hackman, J. R. and Oldham, G. R. (1980). *Work Redesign.* Reading, MA: Addison-Wesley.
6. Locke, E. A. and Latham, G. P. (1984). *Goal Setting: A Motivational Technique that Works.* Englewood Cliffs, NJ: Prentice Hall.
7. Vroom, V. H. (1964). *Work and Motivation.* New York: Wiley.
8. Kanter, R. M. (2004). *Confidence: How Winning Streaks and Losing Streaks Begin and End.* New York: Crown Business Press; Bandura, A. (1997). *Self-Efficacy: The Exercise of Control.* New York: Freeman.
9. Kormanik, M. B. and Rocco, T. S. (2013). "Locus of Control." In E. H. Kessler (ed.), *Encyclopedia of Management Theory* (pp. 448–51). Thousand Oaks, CA: Sage Publications; Rotter, J. B. (1975). "Some Problems and Misconceptions Related to the Construct of Internal versus External Control of Reinforcement." *Journal of Consulting and Clinical Psychology*, 43 (1): 56–67.
10. Jung, C. (1968). *The Archetypes and the Collective Unconscious.* Princeton, NJ: Princeton University Press.
11. Pfeffer, J. (2013). "Organizational Demography." In E. H. Kessler (ed.), *Encyclopedia of Management Theory* (pp. 539–42). Thousand Oaks, CA: Sage Publications.
12. Wong-MingJi, D. W. (2013). "Social Identity Theory." In E. H. Kessler (ed.), *Encyclopedia of Management Theory* (pp. 729–33). Thousand Oaks, CA: Sage Publications; Tajfel, H. (1981). *Human Groups and Social Categories.* Cambridge, UK: Cambridge University Press; Ashforth, B. E. and Mael, F. (1989). "Social Identity Theory and the Organization." *Academy of Management Review*, 14 (1): 20–39.

Chapter 5

1. See George Bernard Shaw, *Man and Superman*: "The reasonable man adapts himself to the world: the unreasonable one persists in trying to adapt the world to himself. Therefore all progress depends on the unreasonable man."
2. Garibaldi de Hilal, A.V. (2013). "Cultural Values." In E. H. Kessler (ed.), *Encyclopedia of Management Theory* (pp. 179–84). Thousand Oaks, CA: Sage Publications.
3. See http://geert-hofstede.com/dimensions.html.
4. See http://www.thekingcenter.org/.
5. See Kessler, E. H. and Wong-Ji, D. M. (2009/2010). *Cultural Mythology and Global Leadership.* Northampton, MA: Edward Elgar Publishers.
6. Sutcliff, K. M. (2013). "Organizational Culture Model." In E. H. Kessler (ed.), *Encyclopedia of Management Theory* (pp. 530–5). Thousand Oaks, CA: Sage Publications.

7. Nieminen, L. R. G. and Denison, D. (2013). "Organizational Culture and Effectiveness." In E. H. Kessler (ed.), *Encyclopedia of Management Theory* (pp. 529–30). Thousand Oaks, CA: Sage Publications.

8. Cameron, K. (2013). "Organizational Effectiveness." In E. H. Kessler (ed.), *Encyclopedia of Management Theory* (pp. 533–6). Thousand Oaks, CA: Sage Publications.

9. Smith, J. R. and Terry, T. J. (2013). "Norms Theory." In E. H. Kessler (ed.), *Encyclopedia of Management Theory* (pp. 508–11). Thousand Oaks, CA: Sage Publications.

10. Tarique, I. (2014). "Human Capital Theory." In E. H. Kessler (ed.), *Encyclopedia of Management Theory* (pp. 343–6). Thousand Oaks, CA: Sage Publications.

11. Bassett-Jones, N. (2013). "Two-Factor Theory." In E. H. Kessler (ed.), *Encyclopedia of Management Theory* (pp. 907–10). Thousand Oaks, CA: Sage Publications; Oldham, G. R. (2013). "Job Characteristics Theory." In E. H. Kessler (ed.), *Encyclopedia of Management Theory* (pp. 407–10). Thousand Oaks, CA: Sage Publications.

12. Ferris, W. P. (2013). "Humanistic Management." In E. H. Kessler (ed.), *Encyclopedia of Management Theory* (pp. 354–9). Thousand Oaks, CA: Sage Publications.

13. Kopelman, R. E. and Prottas, D. J. (2013). "Theory X and Y." In E. H. Kessler (ed.), *Encyclopedia of Management Theory* (pp. 874–8). Thousand Oaks, CA: Sage Publications.

14. Eden, D. (2013). "Self-Fulfilling Prophecy." In E. H. Kessler (ed.), *Encyclopedia of Management Theory* (pp. 690–4). Thousand Oaks, CA: Sage Publications.

15. Elkington, J. (2013). "Triple Bottom Line." In E. H. Kessler (ed.), *Encyclopedia of Management Theory* (pp. 902–4). Thousand Oaks, CA: Sage Publications; Ferris, W. P. (2013). "Humanistic Management." In E. H. Kessler (ed.), *Encyclopedia of Management Theory* (pp. 354–9). Thousand Oaks, CA: Sage Publications.

16. Wayne, S. J. (2013). "Leader-Member Exchange Theory." In E. H. Kessler (ed.), *Encyclopedia of Management Theory* (pp. 429–33). Thousand Oaks, CA: Sage Publications.

17. Liden, R. C. (2013). "Servant Leadership." In E. H. Kessler (ed.), *Encyclopedia of Management Theory* (pp. 698–702). Thousand Oaks, CA: Sage Publications.

18. Cropanzano, R. and Mitchell, M. S. (2013). "Social Exchange Theory." In E. H. Kessler (ed.), *Encyclopedia of Management Theory* (pp. 722–7). Thousand Oaks, CA: Sage Publications; Smith, A. (1981 [1776]). *An Inquiry into the Nature and Causes of the Wealth of Nations*, Volumes I and II. R. H. Campbell and A. S. Skinner (eds.). Indianapolis: Liberty Fund.

19. Randolph, W. A. (2013). "Bases of Social Power." In E. H. Kessler (ed.), *Encyclopedia of Management Theory* (pp. 746–50). Thousand Oaks, CA: Sage Publications.

20. Lei, D. (2013). "Core Competence." In E. H. Kessler (ed.), *Encyclopedia of Management Theory* (pp. 156–61). Thousand Oaks, CA: Sage Publications; Manral, L. (2013). "Competitive Advantage." In E. H. Kessler (ed.), *Encyclopedia of Management Theory* (pp. 125–30). Thousand Oaks, CA: Sage Publications; Teece, D. J. (2013). "Dynamic Capabilities." In E. H. Kessler (ed.), *Encyclopedia of Management Theory* (pp. 221–4). Thousand Oaks, CA: Sage Publications.

21. See Weick, K. (1979). *The Social Psychology of Organizing*. New York: McGraw Hill.

Chapter 6

1. See for example, Alpert, S. (1977). "Temporal Comparison Theory." *Psychological Review*, 84: 485–503.

2. Bruce Springsteen, writer and recorder of "Glory Days," recorded in 1982 and released in 1984 on the LP *Born in the USA* by Columbia Records.

3. The Grass Roots, vocal performance of "Live for Today," by Michael Julien, Ivan Mogull, and David Shapiro, recorded in 1967 and released in 1967 on the LP *Lets Live for Today* by Dunhill Records.

4. Carpe Diem. *Merriam-Webster Dictionary*, http://www.merriam-webster.com, February 25, 2015.

5. Timbuk3, vocal performance of "The Future's So Bright, I Gotta Wear Shades." By Pat MacDonald, recorded in 1986 and released in 1986 on the LP *Greetings from Timbuk3* by IRS. Records.

6. *Dead Poet's Society*, directed by Peter Weir (1989; Burbank, CA: Touchstone Home Entertainment, 1998). DVD.

7. Hume, D. (1777; reprinted 1985). *Essays: Moral, Political, and Literary*, Revised edition. Indianapolis: Liberty Fund.

8. Tolstoy, L. (1960). *Last Diaries*. Leon Stilman (ed.). New York: Capricorn Books.

9. Pascal, B. http://www.brainyquote.com, February 24, 2015.

10. Mandela, N. From 90th birthday celebration of Walter Sisulu, Walter Sisulu Hall, Randburg, Johannesburg, South Africa, May 18, 2002. http://www.washington post.com, February 24, 2015.

11. James, W. (1890). *The Principles of Psychology*. New York: Holt.

12. Kahneman D. and Tversky A. (1979). "Prospect Theory: An Analysis of Decision under Risk." *Econometrica*, 47, 263–91; Bromiley, P. and Rau, D. (2013). "Prospect Theory." In E. H. Kessler (ed.), *Encyclopedia of Management Theory* (pp. 628–32). Thousand Oaks, CA: Sage Publications; Cyert, R. M. and March, J. G. (1963). *A Behavioral Theory of the Firm*. Englewood Cliffs, NJ: Prentice-Hall.

13. See, for example, Rogers, C. (1959). "A Theory of Therapy, Personality, and Interpersonal Relationships, as Developed in the Client-Centered Framework." In Sigmund Koch (ed.), *Psychology: A Study of a Science. Study 1, Volume 3: Formulations of the Person and the Social Context* (pp. 184–256). New York: McGraw-Hill.

14. See, for example, Bazerman, M. H. and Moore, D. A. (2008). *Judgment in Managerial Decision Making*, 7th ed. Hoboken, NJ: John Wiley and Sons.

15. See, for example, Kelley, H. H. (1971). *Attributions in Social Interaction*. New York: General Learning Press.

16. *National Lampoon's Christmas Vacation*, directed by Jeremiah Chechik and Written by John Hughes (1989; Burbank, CA: Warner Home Video, 2003). DVD.

Chapter 7

1. Tyson, N. D. (2014). *Death by Black Hole: And Other Cosmic Quandaries*. New York: W. W. Norton & Company; Kernis, M. H. (2003). "Toward a Conceptualization of Optimal Self-Esteem." *Psychological Inquiry*, 14 (1): 1–26.

2. Mayo Clinic. "Self-Esteem Check: Too Low, Too High or Just Right?" http://www .mayoclinic.com/health/self-esteem/MH00128.

3. Some might argue that these estimates may be too pessimistic or too optimistic. Absent aggregated macro data for the worldwide population on the actual distribution of the forces of Importance, for the purposes here, we default to a logical normalized estimation.

4. See Crocker, J. and Knight, K. M. (2005). "Contingencies of Self-Worth." *Current Directions in Psychological Science*, 14: 200–3.

5. Mayo Clinic. "Self-Esteem Check: Too Low, Too High or Just Right?" http://www .mayoclinic.com/health/self-esteem/MH00128.

6. As per endnote 3 (Chapter 7) we adopt a default normalized distribution.

7. Kramer, R. M. (2013). "Self Concept and the Theory of Self." In E. H. Kessler (ed.), *Encyclopedia of Management Theory* (pp. 682–5). Thousand Oaks, CA: Sage Publications.

8. Wong-MingJi, D. W. (2013). "Social Identity Theory." In E. H. Kessler (ed.), *Encyclopedia of Management Theory* (pp. 729–33). Thousand Oaks, CA: Sage Publications.

9. Gerhardt, M. W. (2013). "Theory of Self Esteem." In E. H. Kessler (ed.), *Encyclopedia of Management Theory* (pp. 867–70). Thousand Oaks, CA: Sage Publications.

10. Kernis, M. H. (2003). "Toward a Conceptualization of Optimal Self-Esteem." *Psychological Inquiry*, 14 (1): 1–26.

11. Leary, M. R. (1999). "Making Sense of Self-Esteem." *Current Directions in Psychological Science*, 8 (1): 32–5.

12. Kernis, M. H. (2003). "Toward a Conceptualization of Optimal Self-Esteem." *Psychological Inquiry*, 14 (1): 1–26.

13. Leary, M. R. (1999). "Making Sense of Self-Esteem." *Current Directions in Psychological Science*, 8 (1): 32–5.

14. Deci, E. L. and Ryan, R. M. (1995). "Human Agency: The Basis for True Self-Esteem." In M. H. Kernis (ed.), *Efficacy, Agency, and Self-Esteem* (pp. 31–50). New York: Plenum.

Chapter 8

1. Machiavelli, N. (1532; translated 1983). *The Prince*. In P. Bondanella and M. Musa (eds.), *The Portable Machiavelli*. New York: Penguin Books.

2. Kant, I. (1952). "Grounding of the Metaphysics of Morals." In W. Durant (ed.), *The Story of Philosophy*. New York: Washington Square Press.

3. McClelland, D. C. (1961). *The Achieving Society*. Princeton, NJ: Van Norstrand.

4. Ibid.

5. Festinger, L. (1954). "A Theory of Social Comparison Processes." *Human Relations*, 7: 117–40; Wayment, H. A. and Taylor, S. E. (1995). "Self-Evaluation Processes: Motives, Information Use, and Self-Esteem." *Journal of Personality*, 63: 729–57; Ferris, D. L., Lian, H., Brown, D. J., and Morrison, R. (2015). "Ostracism, Self-Esteem, and Job Performance: When Do We Self-Verify and When Do We Self-Enhance?" *Academy of Management Journal*, 58 (1): 279–97.

6. Mazen, A. (2013). "Double Loop Learning." In E. H. Kessler (ed.), *Encyclopedia of Management Theory* (pp. 210–13). Thousand Oaks, CA: Sage Publications.

7. Wong-MingJi, D. (2013). "Force Field Analysis and Model of Planned Change." In E. H. Kessler (ed.), *Encyclopedia of Management Theory* (pp. 286–91). Thousand Oaks, CA: Sage Publications.

8. Leary, M. R. and Kowalski, R. M. (1990). "Impression Management: A Literature Review and Two-Component Model." *Psychological Bulletin*, 107 (1): 34–47; Farrell, D. and Petersen, J. C. (2013). "Patterns of Political Behavior." In E. H. Kessler (ed.), *Encyclopedia of Management Theory* (pp. 588–9). Thousand Oaks, CA: Sage Publications.

9. Lewin, K. (1951). *Field Theory in Social Science*. D. Cartwright (ed.). New York: Harper and Bros.

10. Crocker, J. and Knight, K. M. (2005). "Contingencies of Self-Worth." *Current Directions in Psychological Science*, 14: 200–3.

Chapter 9

1. Hamalainen, T. J. (2014). "In Search of Coherence: Sketching a Theory of Sustainable Well-Being." In T. J. Hamalainen and J. Michalson (eds.), *Well Being and Beyond*. Cheltenham, UK: Edward Elgar Publishers.
2. Bandura. A. (2013). "Social Cognitive Theory." In E. H. Kessler (ed.), *Encyclopedia of Management Theory* (pp. 710–15). Thousand Oaks, CA: Sage Publications.
3. Brockner, J. (1988). *Self Esteem at Work*. Lexington, MA: Lexington Books.
4. Kanter, R. M. (2006). *Confidence: How Winning Streaks and Losing Streaks Begin and End*. New York: Crown Business.
5. Mindfulness, Google definition, February 24, 2015.
6. "Rewiring Your Brain." (2014). *Time* magazine, February 3.
7. Ibid., p. 46.
8. Neuroplasticity, Medicine.net, February 24, 2015.
9. Boyatzis, R. E. (2013). "Emotional and Social Intelligence." In E. H. Kessler (ed.), *Encyclopedia of Management Theory* (pp. 225–9). Thousand Oaks, CA: Sage Publications.
10. See for example, Rosenberg, M., Schooler, C., Schoenback, C., and Rosenberg, F. (1995). "Global Self Esteem and Specific Self Esteem: Different Concepts, Different Outcomes." *American Sociological Review*, 60 (1): 141–56; Gerhardt, M. W. (2013). "Theory of Self Esteem." In E. H. Kessler (ed.), *Encyclopedia of Management Theory* (pp. 867–70). Thousand Oaks, CA: Sage Publications.
11. Whetten, D. A. and Cameron, K. S. (2011). *Developing Management Skills*, 8th ed. Upper Saddle River, NJ: Prentice Hall.
12. Mayo Clinic.
13. Spreitzer, G. (2013). "Positive Organizational Scholarship." In E. H. Kessler (ed.), *Encyclopedia of Management Theory* (pp. 591–4). Thousand Oaks, CA: Sage Publications.
14. Oldham, G. R. (2013). "Job Characteristics Theory." In E. H. Kessler (ed.), *Encyclopedia of Management Theory* (pp. 407–10). Thousand Oaks, CA: Sage Publications.
15. Gagne, M., Deci, E. L., and Ryan, R. M. (2013). "Self Determination Theory." In E. H. Kessler (ed.), *Encyclopedia of Management Theory* (pp. 686–90). Thousand Oaks, CA: Sage Publications.
16. Seligman, M. E. P. (2002). *Authentic Happiness: Using the New Positive Psychology to Realize Your Potential for Lasting Fulfillment*. New York: Free Press.
17. Kahneman, D. and Krueger, A. B. (2006). "Developments in the Measurement of Subjective Well-Being." *The Journal of Economic Perspectives*, 20: 3–24.
18. Ben-Shar, T. (2007). *Happier: Learn the Secrets to Daily Joy and Lasting Fulfillment*. New York: McGraw Hill.
19. Diener, E. (1990). "Subjective Well-Being: The Science of Happiness and a Proposal for a National Index." *American Psychologist*, 55 (1): 34–43; Diener, E., Suh, E. M., Lucas, R. E., and Smith, H. E. (1999). "Subjective Well-Being: Three Decades of Progress." *Psychological Bulletin*, 125: 276–302.
20. Diener, E., http://internal.psychology.illinois.edu/~ediener/faq.html.
21. Hogenboom, Melissa. (2014). "Equation 'can predict momentary happiness.'" August 4, BBC, http://www.bbc.com/news/science-environment-28592838.
22. Diener, E., Diener, M., and Diener, C. (1995). "Factors Predicting the Subjective Well-Being of Nations." *Journal of Personality and Social Psychology*, 69: 851–64.
23. Sen, A. (2000). "A Decade of Human Development." *Journal of Human Development*, 1: 17–23; United Nations Development Programme, Human Development Reports, http://hdr.undp.org/en/humandev.

24. http://www.happyplanetindex.org/
25. Kessler, E. H. and Bailey, J. R. 2007. *Handbook of Organizational and Managerial Wisdom.* Thousand Oaks, CA: Sage Publications.
26. Mayo Clinic.
27. Kessler, E. H. and Bailey, J. R. 2007. *Handbook of Organizational and Managerial Wisdom.* Thousand Oaks, CA: Sage Publications.
28. See Covey, S. R. (1994). *First Things First.* New York: Simon and Schuster.
29. Mayo Clinic; Rosenberg, M., Schooler, C., Schoenback, C., and Rosenberg, F. (1995). "Global Self Esteem and Specific Self Esteem: Different Concepts, Different Outcomes." *American Sociological Review*, 60 (1): 141–56; Fishbein, M. and Ajzen, I. (1975). *Belief, Attitude, Intention, and Behavior: An Introduction to Theory and Research.* Reading, MA: Addison-Wesley; Bandura, A. (1982). "Self-Efficacy Mechanism in Human Agency." *American Psychologist*, 37: 122–47; Brockner, J. (1988). *Self-Esteem at Work: Research, Theory, and Practice.* Lexington, MA: Lexington Books.

Chapter 10

1. Nicholson, N. (2006). "The Getting of Wisdom: Self-Conduct, Personal Identity, and Wisdom Across the Life Span." In E. H. Kessler & J. R. Bailey (eds.), *Handbook of Organizational and Managerial Wisdom* (377–397). Thousand Oaks, CA: Sage Publications.
2. Rogers, C. (1961). *On Becoming a Person: A Therapist's View.* Boston: Houghton Mifflin.
3. Thoreau, H. http://www.brainyquote.com, February 24, 2015.
4. George, B. (2015). *Discover Your True North.* New York: John Wiley and Sons.
5. Heidemeier, H. and Staudinger, U. M. (2012). "Self-Evaluation Process in Life Satisfaction: Uncovering Measurement Non-Equivalence and Age-Related Differences." *Social Indicators Research*, 105: 39–61.
6. See Barry Schwartz (2004, *The Paradox of Choice: Why More Is Less.* New York: HarperCollins) for an explanation on how choice can cause anxiety and why it is easier to lapse into a more passive traveler or "automatic pilot" mode.
7. This is akin to the concept of potential energy, or the stored ability to act upon and change an object (you or others) in different capacities and directions.
8. Kessler, E. H. (2013). "Organizational and Managerial Wisdom." In E. H. Kessler (ed.), *Encyclopedia of Management Theory* (pp. 521–4). Thousand Oaks, CA: Sage Publications.

Author Biography

Dr. Eric H. Kessler's scholarly, educational, leadership, and professional endeavors integrate around a common theme: giving people the time-tested and cutting-edge tools—used by the most effective individuals and organizations—to achieve their goals and attain greater personal and professional success.

A recognized authority on organization management and global leadership, Dr. Kessler holds the endowed Henry George Professorship of Management at the Lubin School of Business at Pace University in downtown New York City. He is also the founding Director of their Business Honors Program and a winner of the Kenan Teaching Excellence award.

As a management *scholar*, Dr. Kessler has published four previous critically acclaimed books that have been endorsed by an array of luminaries and have sold in over 50 countries: *Handbook of Organizational and Managerial Wisdom*, *Cultural Mythology and Global Leadership*, *Management Theory in Action: Real-World Lessons for Walking the Talk*, and the *Encyclopedia of Management Theory*, the latter a two-volume thousand-plus page field reference source that was named to an annual list of outstanding scholarly book titles. He has also produced more than a hundred academic papers in journals and at conferences, many with distinction, which featured his research in top disciplinary outlets.

As a management *educator*, spanning a more than 20-year teaching career and involving more than 3,500 students, Dr. Kessler has pioneered innovative curriculum development initiatives and received the highest levels of user satisfaction in undergraduate, masters, doctoral, executive, and corporate education. He has also led numerous international field studies, mentored many advanced student theses and service leadership projects, and participated in academic programs spanning six continents.

As a management *leader*, Dr. Kessler has served on a plethora of advisory and editorial boards, was elected President and named a Fellow of the Eastern Academy of Management and received multiple domestic and international society honors in the areas of psychology, economics, business, forensics, and general academics. He has also been recognized as a "public opinion leader" and appointed to several regional and national panels including with the United States National Security Education Program and the United States Fulbright Program.

As a management *professional*, Dr. Kessler has consulted with a broad range of private and public organizations, across a number of industries, from local businesses to Fortune 500 and Global 100 multinational companies. He has also worked with a variety of government agencies (such as the Department of Defense and Department of State) and has been quoted in popular publications such as *Newsweek* and *Bloomberg Business Week.*

Index

Lightning Source UK Ltd.
Milton Keynes UK
UKOW06n1249240316

270816UK00004B/68/P